GROWING UP IN OTTIE'S WORLD

When Self-Forgiveness Seemed Impossible

Mr. Fred Eli Epeley

GROWING UP IN OTTIE'S WORLD

Copyright © 2015 by Fred Eli Epeley
All rights reserved.
ISBN-10: 1508997578
ISBN-13: 978-1508997573

Printed in the United States of America

Library of Congress CIP data applied for.

Front cover design is an actual photo of Ottie's farm looking toward the barn and corn crib. Grassy Knob Mountain is directly behind the barn and Oaky Knob is to the right. The picture was taken in the fall of 1948.

CONTENTS

DEDICATION

♥

To Larry Harold Keagy, my forever friend, who believed passionately in my writing project. When I faltered, he carried me on his shoulders.

♥

ACKNOWLEDGMENTS

I express warm thanks and appreciation to Julia S. Pittman for editing my book. I honor her, too, for thirty-five years of outstanding teaching to college-bound students. She is not only a Teacher of the Year, but also a Teacher for the Ages.

Thanks to Carole Lindstrom for her valuable suggestions of story topics for this book and for lending a critical ear. I enjoyed our morning chats on the phone.

♥

Jim Morgan is my mentor and friend. Without his constant encouragement, I would never have written a book. Thank you, Jim. The gallons of coffee we drank together sparked my imagination.

PROLOGUE

To the People of Ottie's World

Golden Valley is my valley. Its people are my people. This is the story of my life. It is a life lived outside the plenty and freedom enjoyed by most. We people of this valley have made it on our own. We feed ourselves. We clothe ourselves. We educate our own. We break laws when they threaten our way of life. We develop our own codes of honor. We worship God, if we choose.

The people of my valley are good people. Some are heroic. Some are bigger than life. Some are outcasts. Some go to their graves unsung. All face life with courage.

Now I sing these words in tribute to my family, the valley, and all the people of Ottie's world. It is a song whispered on the Appalachian winds telling of a forgotten people. It is my destiny to remember them. Spirit commands that I share my fate with Ottie and the people of her world.

LIGHT

A brilliant light of consciousness moves swiftly across the skeins of Time and Space. It is a point of light connected to all awareness and knowledge through intersecting energy fields. This light is seeking to individualize itself, to take on human form. This energy light cannot be recreated or destroyed, it can only change form. In deciding to be human, it is now searching for an appropriate female vehicle through which to materialize.

Long before the advent of Time, the light became aware of the concepts of love and self-forgiveness and it wanted to experience both. It is only in the human form on planet earth that love and self-forgiveness can be experienced. So the light sped in that direction.

The light felt itself drawn to the blue-green planet earth, to the Blue Ridge Mountains of Appalachia to a forty-year-old woman named Ottie who lived in North Carolina. Ottie was not planning to have another child. She had already birthed six babies without planning the birth of any of them. Ottie did not yet know that she was pregnant and the light that would animate the child and become its soul, had not yet decided to take on its mission.

My light hovered around Ottie for she was my prospective mother. I know that I do not have to take this mission to be a child in Ottie's world. I can enter the fertilized egg if I wish or I can enter the baby's body when it is fully formed at the end of nine months. My light is totally connected to Ottie's energy field, so I know all that she knows and I can feel everything she feels. I'm thinking that my energy light may enter the child at the moment of birth or I may change my mind and scrub this mission altogether.

Ottie is an unhappy woman. She already has six children and the prospect of a seventh does not make her happy. At age forty, she does not think another child will come because her life change is already upon her. Yet, she worries, for she knows there is growth in her womb. Morning nausea makes her wonder. I hear her self-talk and thoughts as she works in the fields:

"Another damn mouth to feed," she thinks to herself. "I've had a baby every two years of the last ten. My husband knows that the last two girls are not his. He is a black-haired man with brown eyes and they have blond hair and blue eyes. He is hostile toward me now and will not do anything for the two girls or me. What will I tell him as my belly begins to grow?"

A feeling of hopelessness washes over her as she sits down on a stump dropping her head into her hands. She is morose. From my vantage point, I see all the events of Ottie's entire life and I feel the emotions she has felt about each and every one of them. I can see her potential life and what I will experience if I choose to become her son.

Ottie had come into a family of eight children. They had survived as dirt farmers in the hills of the Blue Ridge Mountains. It had been a rigid group descended from German settlers. They had been an undemonstrative people who had eschewed any open display of affection. Each had wandered in an emotional wasteland.

The men around her had warped her ideas of love and caring, reducing these two aspects of life to an animalistic level of breeding and reproduction. In her heart, Ottie had known that love was much more, but there had been none to show her how to love.

I looked at the situation lying ahead of me if I chose to become Ottie's child. I would be in a world devoid of love. I would be in a bed wearing wet, soiled diapers while she worked. No one would answer my crying or come to comfort me until the day's work was over. I would often go hungry. If I cried too long or too loudly, Ottie would strike me with her hand.

And so it would go for me if I chose to be this baby. My soul pondered how to learn love and self-forgiveness in these painful circumstances. Some power within urged me onward:

"You can do it. What you will gain eternally in soul growth is well worth any suffering. If you want to know anything of God, you must go to Ottie. She needs you, too. You can show them all a better way or you can choose to hate as they do."

In Ottie's ninth month with the child moving restlessly in her womb, my spirit hovered very near her. In the moments when she wished that she had never gotten pregnant, I felt sad, unwanted, even threatened.

"My life is misery, misery," she said aloud when thinking of how she would care for another child. "Damn all men."

Her anger and negativity shot through my energy field leaving me stunned. At that very moment, birth pains began shooting through Ottie's physical body. She stumbled to the porch of the Little Old House and called for help.

"Run, bring the midwife. My baby's coming."

My last awareness in the energy state was the movement of a baby's body down Ottie's birth canal. I had to make my decision now.

"Do I dare go into this life?" I agonized in my soul.

3

The baby's body sped toward birth. Its head was now crowning. I heard a sweet light speaking to me, a voice from the presence of God:

"Go for love. Go for self-forgiveness. The experience will bring you eternal peace."

My energy light leapt into the baby's body bringing it to life.

The energy light became Fred.

As the baby emerged into life, I screamed in my soul with the greatest of agony,

"Please, Almighty God, don't send me out there to grow up in Ottie's world!"

SHERIFF DAWSON

"Sweet Lord Jesus, won't somebody please come help me! Aaaaaaarh, God, come down from your Heaven and stop my boys from fighting."

Ottie's shrill, plaintive cries broke the silence of the cool, misty October morning. The sounds of a violent, physical struggle shocked me out of a deep sleep. My eyes focused through a foggy brain on three bodies piled in a heap on the floor in the front room of the little white farmhouse. I slept in this room because living quarters were so cramped for Ottie's large brood of children that she set up two beds in the area intended as the living room. It now doubled as a bedroom. Curtis slept by himself in the bed on the left side of the room. Ottie had bought it at the Boneyard and had slushed gobs of green paint on the frames. I slept in a bed with Willard and June Jr. It was made of more ornate ironwork.

I saw Ottie standing between June Jr. and Curtis, trying to pull them apart from the tangled knot their bodies had formed when the fight broke out.

"Stop it! Stoooooop!" Ottie wailed, her voice rising in terror. With super strength born of fear and panic, she physically forced her two sons apart. Curtis was bruised and bloodied from a severe pounding administered by June Jr.'s fists. Because of his small stature, June Jr. had learned to fight skillfully early in life and could now administer a severe beating to older and stronger men.

Curtis rolled on his right side across the wooden pine floor and grabbed his double-barrel shotgun from its rack above the fireplace. He placed a shotgun shell into the chamber, aimed the gun in the direction of June Jr., and pulled the trigger. Hot, blue smoke poured out of the muzzle of the shotgun filling the room with an acrid, burning smell. Buckshot shattered the boards on the wall above where I was asleep. Some pellets dropped on my blanket like winter sleet.

"Oh! Lordy, Lordy! O merciful God!" Ottie lamented in her terror. "They are going to kill each other! Children, run, run get the sheriff! Bring him back to save us all."

Ottie wailed and screamed and pounded her feet on the wooden floor. Her cadence resembled a flamenco dancer as the heels of her shoes caused tiny puffs of dust to rise in spurts from the floor. She flung herself at Curtis, grabbing the barrel of his shotgun, desperately attempting to disarm him. Gertie heard the commotion from the backroom where she was sleeping. She crashed through the bedroom door, flinging it wide open. She pounced on Curtis, twisting his head into a hammerlock in an effort to get the gun.

June Jr., stunned by blows from Curtis' fists, saw an opportunity to break free of the fight and flee. He was seething with rage and hatred. He had already drawn blood; he wanted someone to die! He deftly removed the rifle from its perch in the gun rack above the fireplace and pumped a bullet into the chamber. He aimed the gun in the direction of Ottie, Gertie, and Curtis and pulled the trigger. He did not care whom he hit. A loud "bang" echoed across the room. Ottie collapsed as if she had been shot.

Gertie screamed, "You can't kill my momma, you little son-of-a-bitch!"

She leaped through the air, landing on top of June Jr. and the rifle. With strength beyond rationality, she took his rifle and slammed the butt against his head, drawing blood down from his ear and cheek. June Jr. beat a hasty retreat through the kitchen door and fled to the mountains.

Willard was in the barn milking the cows when he heard two shots fired inside the house. He sprang forward off the milking stool and galloped along the narrow path that led from the barn to the house. The pounding of his shoes on the frozen rime ice made him sound like a wild horse running. He jumped through the kitchen door left open when June Jr. had departed. Seeing Ottie in a dead faint on the floor, Willard took the shotgun from Curtis and slammed his body violently against the living room wall. Curtis crumpled into a heap on the floor.

Ottie revived from her stupor and began to wail like a banshee. "Oh God, my life is misery, misery. These boys will be the death of me." With both hands, she tore at her hair until clumps dislodged in her fingers. "Sheriff Dawson! Sheriff! Somebody go get the goddam sheriff! Kids, run get Sheriff Dawson!"

I was still in bed hiding deeply under the covers hearing the tumult and dodging bullets. I flung the bedcovers on the floor as I put on my pants backwards. I saw Gertie and Justine leap through the front door and disappear into the rainy morning. I ran behind them, half dressed and without shoes.

A gentle mist was falling outside. A cold wind rustled through the gnarled apple trees in the front yard. I jumped from the porch into the raw October morning. My bare feet left deep tracks in the red-clay mud. Rain quickly erased my footprints as if I had never been there, as if I did not exist. At this moment, I wished that I did not exist. Why was I born into this nest of vipers? What was life offering me?

There were little boys in warm, loving homes filled with good things to eat all across America. Here I suffered in the other America in a dysfunctional, redneck, Appalachian family whose members at this moment were trying to kill each other. I resolved then and there to bloom as a wildflower on this pile of manure that was my life. There was a hurting in my physical body, yet worse, there was a hurting in my tiny heart that would never heal.

Rain and mud flew upward around my knees as my bare feet beat a trail along the muddy roadway. My sisters and I ran in silence in the direction of the sheriff's house. We stopped only briefly when our lungs burned from exertion. During one short pause, we cupped our ears listening on the wind for a sign to tell us that all was well where Ottie was. Maybe she would call us back and spare us the shame and embarrassment of having to bring the sheriff to our home. But one of Ottie's screams wafted faintly across the distant breeze. We rushed forward!!

Gertie pulled us onward. We forded the creek the first time. The cold waters rushed over my bare feet leaving me shivering and in pain. At the second fording of the creek near where Gentry and his sawmill crew used to live, Gertie lifted me on her back and portaged me to the other side. We had no more energy left to run. I cried from hunger and exhaustion and from the fear, that if we did not continue to run, we would bring the sheriff back home too late.

The rain grew heavier. Large drops stung my forehead and cheeks leaving them burning a dark red. I whimpered as cold air rushed into my lungs. My body heaved drawing precious oxygen into my aching lungs. Gertie took me by the hand and led me forward.

"I can see it! It's coming into sight! The sheriff's house is just up ahead!" Gertie mumbled through her panting breath. "We've made it."

When we reached the house, the three of us stepped quietly up on the kitchen porch, our clothes and hair soaked in cold rain. None of us had the strength or the desire to knock on the door and share with the world the shame that was our lives this day. What little pride I had managed to build in my six-year old heart lay broken on the wet road we had just trod. We were poor. We were hungry. We were unloved. The wild animals of the fields, forest, and hollows fared better than we. Gertie had awakened a sense of pride and a desire in all of us to rise above our pathetic situation in life. But Ottie's ignorance and bitterness at her own failure in life hung like a millstone around our dreams. The present conflict between Curtis and June Jr. was created long ago when Ottie had left them to run wild and free with no parenting. She had no parenting skills. She was reaping her just reward now for her neglect of the boys. And she was inflicting unbearable pain on the rest us. I resented her driving us into this raw day to bring a stranger to solve the problems that she, herself, had created. I hated this life and I hated living in Ottie's world.

The sheriff's wife heard us weeping and opened the kitchen door.

"Well, I declare, it's Ottie's kids. And they are soaking wet! Come into the kitchen and let me dry you off."

She hurriedly pulled three dry towels from a drawer, warmed them over the steaming hot wood stove, and placed them gently around Gertie, Justine, and me. When I felt the warm towel and her gentle hands hugging me, I began to cry again. Like an island in a storm, this stranger, this kind lady, this sheriff's wife was taking her time to give us what Ottie would not give---her warmth and love.

The warm smell of perking coffee, homemade biscuits browning in the oven, and the pungent odor of bacon frying in an iron skillet spread across the kitchen. It was a haven from our storm.

The sheriff stumbled into the kitchen, pulling his suspenders over a half-buttoned shirt. He was a tall, slender, imposing man with wiry muscles that belied his true strength. A full, fluffy, black moustache rested above his upper lip like the soft down of a gosling. Sleep had not yet left his eyes so his lids drooped lazily over his dark brown pupils which usually looked out on the world with a razor-sharp perception. Our crying had awakened him from a deep sleep. He rubbed his right hand through his black, uncombed hair, yawned, and said sleepily, "Are you kids alright?"

"Curtis and June Jr. are trying to kill each other with guns. Ottie wants you to come quickly and arrest them," Gertie wailed through a wall of tears.

Sensing the urgency of the situation, Sheriff Dawson sprang into action. He buckled his pistol and holster around his flat waist and swiftly threw on a coat, hat, and gloves. As he dressed, Mrs. Dawson pulled a pan of hot biscuits from the oven. She picked out four of them and quickly made a slit with a knife. She filled them with a generous portion of hot butter and fox grape jelly. She wrapped the biscuits in wedges of wax paper and thrust them into our hands. Their warmth washed the cold from my hands and fingers.

"Eat some breakfast, kids," she commanded, her voice filled with pity.

My exhausted body begged for the food, but my emotionally-laden stomach would not co-operate. The intensity of the emotions sweeping over me closed my stomach walls like the fear of my brothers' possible deaths froze my heart. I held the biscuit suspended in mid-air staring at it as if it were a valuable piece of forbidden art hidden somewhere in a museum.

Sheriff Dawson motioned us to his waiting truck where he had already turned on the heater so we could get warm. I sat next to him; Justine sat beside me; Gertie sat against the door to the right. The truck engine coughed and sputtered as he aimed it up the dirt road down which we had just fled in panic. The windshield wipers clicked and clacked across the glass which was foggy from our breath and body heat.

"Eat your biscuits, kids," the sheriff said sweetly.

He stretched his long arm across all our backs, pretending to lock the door on Gertie's side. But he let his big, calloused hand fall on Gertie's shoulder where he pulled all three of us to him in one gigantic hug.

"It will be okay," he whispered.

Sheriff Dawson, sensing our shame and fear, drove in silence. Big tears oozed from his eyes and fell across his cheeks on to the heavy steering wheel. No one felt like eating a biscuit.

Sheriff Dawson parked his truck beneath the gnarled apple trees in our front yard and told us to stay in the truck to keep warm. He cautiously climbed the front steps, crept across the porch, and disappeared through the front door. A hush, a peace, a blessed calm fell over the little farmhouse and edged itself into our hearts.

I sat listening to the rain falling on the metal roof of the truck. I watched the front door of the house intently for some sign from the sheriff that we were safe. The minute hand on the face of a small clock resting on the dashboard of the truck marked the passing minutes with a click, click, and click. I looked over at Gertie hoping that she could give me some assurance, but she had fallen asleep with her head lying twisted against the truck window. Her rhythmical breathing accentuated the clicking of the minute hand on the clock. Justine sat munching her jelly biscuit letting melted butter run down her chin. My sisters could offer no solace, for they were nursing their own pain.

"I've had enough!" I screamed flinging the driver door wide open. I jumped into the cold mud and fled this house of sadness and sorrow. I ran toward the distant mountains. Down the dirt path to the barn I fled, distraught. Fear and rage pushed me in a blind flight across the cow pasture and through the rushing water of the small creek that divided the barn and corncrib from the open fields. The drizzling rain filled my eye sockets, blinding my sight of the path the cows had made up Oaky Knob when they foraged freely. I climbed the mountainside with abandon, through clumps of laurel bushes, digging footholds with my bare feet in the wet, rotting leaves. An occasional twig struck me a stinging blow to the face. I didn't care. I was devoid of feeling. I stumbled across a rocky outcrop which formed a dry shelter on the mountainside. I pushed my small body among the dry leaves which the mountain winds had piled there. My feet were so cold that they hurt. I rubbed them vigorously and stuffed dry leaves on top. I did not care if I died here. If Ottie, Curtis, and June Jr. lay dead, then I wanted to die, too.

As I lay among the dry leaves, warmth reemerged through my body. The dry leaves crackled as I moved my body about seeking comfort. The rain gushed in rivulets from the overhanging rocks and gurgled down the hillside. The wind moaned in the pines. I was a little boy, alone and afraid.

Rage stirred from deep within me. It was a rage born from the hopeless conditions of living in Ottie's world. There was little of value for me in my family circle. I had no real family at all. We were a collection of dysfunctional, redneck Southerners with a single mother who had produced nine children, six of whom were illegitimate. She was legally married to June Sr. who left the family because Ottie continued to lust after Eli. Ottie was my mother in name only. Gertie took care of me and mothered me as best she could. Ottie never hugged me. Eli never claimed me as his child. There was never a father in my home. My brothers and I had no male role models to show us how to be good men. There existed a vast, empty, lonely chasm in my life.

My emotions burst forth in shouts of rage!

"I want a daddy! I want my daddy!" I screamed out at the rocks and hills and sky. I spoke for every child in America who had ever been abandoned by a non-caring father.

"It is my birthright! That is the way life should be! I have been forever cheated! I want a daddy to hug and comfort me!"

My voice rode the wind, striking the distant mountains. My lament came back to me unanswered. In anger, I kicked the leaves, the rocks, and earth on which I rested. The pines and balsams shook their branches vigorously reflecting my anger. The falling rain became my unshed tears. I would weep forever for my absent father.

An acorn fell from a nearby tree and landed in my lap. I looked at it as a promise of hope. The acorn will produce a mighty oak tree. My manure pile could produce a good man. Another acorn flew through the air and thumped me on the top of the head. "Ouch!" I leaned forward searching for the oak tree that was throwing its acorns at me. But it wasn't an oak tree.

I saw the figure of a tall man standing quietly among the laurels. He lifted his hand and threw another acorn my way. I pretended not to see him because I hoped he had not heard my diatribe against my own life.

It was Sheriff Dawson. He stood like a strong oak tree, his arms crossed, rain dripping from his nose and elbows. He fixed his gaze upon me then he glided across the wet forest floor to the rock outcrop.

"Is this seat taken?" he inquired in a calm voice.

I shook my head from side to side to let him know that it was not taken. We sat a while in silence, listening to the distant caw of a crow and the tinkling of a faraway cow bell. Down below us at the little farmhouse, the muffled barking of a dog rode the wind currents up Oaky Knob leaving the sound resounding in our ears. Sheriff Dawson picked up an acorn and flipped it with his thumbnail out into the elements. I copied what he did.

"It's cold up here," Sheriff Dawson finally muttered. "Come sit next to me. You must be freezing." He opened his heavy, wool jacket with its tin badge shaped like a star and pulled me against his powerfully warm body which smelled of tobacco and fresh perspiration. He was a man of power and authority. But today, he was a man of compassion.

"I have a son like you, Fred, but my heart is big enough for two," he said softly pulling me into a bear hug with his left arm. Under the warm coat, I placed both my hands around his waist. He dropped his calloused hands down on top of mine. We said nothing further, for the magic of the moment demanded silence. The moment was pregnant with male bonding and love. I fell asleep to the rhythmical beating of Sheriff Dawson's heart, a heart as big and wide as the blue sky that began to break above us.

Through a sleepy haze, I remembered powerful arms carrying me back down the mountain. He placed me gently on my bed in the little farmhouse and covered me with a blanket. My last memory as I fell asleep was a gentle pat on the shoulder.

All these many years, Sheriff Dawson, I have wanted to tell you that you saved my life that day. You gave me hope. You reached across my deep abyss to show me that all men are not like Eli. You showed me what Eli had missed in never truly knowing his son. You saw the bigger picture of what he had thrown away. It was not just the fight that drew you to our home; it was my need for someone to show me how to love. Your job as sheriff was to keep the peace; but that day you mended a little boy's broken heart. That is why I love you to this very day. I know that you committed suicide later in life. I forgive you that act for no one knows the depths of another's pain. I only wish that I could have found you in your hour of need. I would have opened my coat, placed my arms around you, and loved away all your sorrows.

FREEDOM FROM WANT

Ottie seemed not to recover fully from the emotional effects of the fight between Curtis and June Jr. When I awoke from the peaceful sleep on my bed where Sheriff Dawson had placed me, I saw her sitting in a rocker next to the fire place, her hands covering her face. She was deeply saddened over the event. From time to time, she heaved a deep sigh as she slowly rocked back and forth. Her eyes had a far-away look in them as if she wanted to be somewhere else. She became cold and distant to all of her family. What little warmth that had leaked through her emotional wall before the fight, now disappeared altogether. If any of us children approached her with a problem, a need, a desire to be comforted, she snarled at us uttering harsh expletives while pushing us away physically with her arms.

Ottie fell into a deep depression. She was morose. She let everything in her life go except Eli and her moonshine, for Eli brought her the only joy she wanted and the moonshine brought her money and solace from life's misery. She slept through the late

15

night and most of the day. Gertie took over the responsibility of caring for herself, Callie, Justine, and me.

This deep, dark sorrow consuming our mother robbed us of all support. Gertie awakened us each morning. We dressed in a house with no fire burning to warm us. No one prepared food neither for breakfast nor lunch. There was no cafeteria at the school. Had there been a cafeteria, we would not have had the money to purchase lunch.

When it was time to eat, Gertie, Justine, and I sat staring at the other students in our class munching on ham biscuits, banana sandwiches, peanut butter crackers, and apples. In turn, Miss Lucy eyed us as she chewed her ham and cheese biscuit and drank hot coffee from a thermos. Though she knew we had no food, she made no effort to share with us nor did she approach Ottie and Eli about their responsibility to provide food for their children.

As everyone else ate his lunch, I sat quietly staring at the Norman Rockwell paintings that Miss Lucy had hung above the main blackboard. Rockwell had immortalized the four freedoms that President Roosevelt had said were guaranteed to all Americans in his 1941 speech. These four freedoms----freedom of speech, freedom of religion, freedom from want, and freedom from fear---became part of the United Nations charter.

My eyes glued on the "freedom from want" painting because it depicted a Thanksgiving meal with a grandmother holding a gigantic roasted turkey on a platter. The table presented a bounty of foods that I would not know. Ironic it was that Rockwell painted this picture in the year 1943, the same year I was born.

Roosevelt and Rockwell depicted an America that did not exist for millions of us children. The government had plenty of money to wage war and give gifts to foreign nations trying to buy friendship, but not twenty-five cents to buy lunch for a hungry little boy who was willing to come to school in an effort to better himself.

The gods of karma took note and promised retribution to the braggart politicians who could not care for the nation's children.

One day when Miss Lucy signaled that lunch was over, a kid threw a half-eaten cheese sandwich out the window. My stomach ached as I watched this wanton act of waste. As I walked the path behind the school to the broom sedge field where we played, I happened to pass the half-eaten sandwich lying on the ground I stopped dead in my tracks.

Fear and shame washed over me as my hungry stomach waged war with my reasoning mind. I grabbed the sandwich and gobbled it down. I looked around hoping that no one had seen my act of desperation. I quickly hid myself in the broom sedge field. Hunger had overridden my embarrassment and humiliation. Without my knowing it, eyes had been watching me from the field.

Michael, my class mate, who sat directly across from me at our table, carved a large hole between our two book spaces in the table desk. He wrote a note on a piece of paper and thrust it through the hole on to one of my books. Then he whispered, "Put your hand up to the hole." I hesitated not knowing what he planned to do. With a big smile on his face, he reiterated his request.

"Put your hand through the hole."

I placed my hand in the hole between our desks. Crawford put five peanut butter crackers in my hand. Placing his index finger across his lips, he whispered, "shhhh." Other children observed what he had done and, with compassion felt deeply in their child hearts, they joined in the act of feeding me. They broke their sandwiches in half, passed pieces from child to child down to Michael who handed the food to me secretly through the hole.

A veritable smorgasbord appeared on the desk in front of me. Half a banana sandwich, a piece of homemade ham biscuit, an apple, six potato chips, and a snippet of sweet potato pie were suddenly on my menu. No one looked my way. Even Miss Lucy pretended not to notice.

Children munched their food and stared silently out the windows. I gobbled down the food for I had eaten nothing except corn bread and buttermilk that Gertie had fixed the night before. When Miss Lucy dismissed the class for play time after lunch, many children came to me and patted me on the shoulder or back in an act of compassion.

For the duration of the year, the ritual of sharing food with me continued. Michael brought a small wooden tray from home and placed it on a table next to where I sat. When students arrived at school, they placed gifts of food on the tray. At lunch, Michael proudly set the tray in front of me as if he were serving royalty. Blessed are these children for they were being good from a feeling of compassion.

The fact that Curtis and June Jr. tried to kill each other with guns plus the humiliating visit from the sheriff struck Ottie a severe blow that took away all her caring. She had made moonshine all her life, but I had never seen her drink it until this horrible event befell her. She set a quart of moonshine in every room and imbibed freely as she moved about the house. She left the farm work undone. She did not milk the cows. She cooked food only when she was hungry. She spent her nights at the moonshine still. She slept until noon.

Gertie took charge of the household.

"We must go it on our own or we won't make it," she advised us.

She sent me to gather wood for the cook stove and Justine to pull buckets of water from the well. She milked the cows herself at the barn. Callie was only three years old, so she locked her in the bedroom of the house. Gertie made a roaring fire in the wood stove and baked sweet potatoes and corn bread. We ate corn bread, buttermilk, and green onions for supper.

On Saturdays, Gertie lit a fire under the big, black, iron wash pot at the edge of the front yard in order to wash clothes. Red and yellow flames leapt up around the sides to the wash pot causing the water inside to bubble. White steam hissed upward as she piled dirty overalls and work shirts into the pot. She chipped pieces of home-made lye soap into the frothing water and stirred it with a wooden stick. She washed blouses, shirts, and underclothes in tin tubs placed on a wooden bench Eli had built. I crawled playfully under the wooden bench letting the soapy water dribble into my hair. Gertie's rhythmical scrubbing on the washboard pumped rivulets of water on my world below.

I helped her hang the wet clothes on the clothesline nearby. When we ran out of room, we hung clothes on the plum trees and across the well house. The warm sun sucked up the wetness of the clothes leaving them smelling of lye soap and sunshine.

Gertie abandoned her childhood and assumed the role of our mother at age eleven. We no longer looked to Ottie for anything. She moved along the periphery of our lives like a ghost floating among tombstones. At nightfall she disappeared into the darkness and worked at her moonshine still until dawn. When we arrived home from school, she was not there. Our house was cold and barren. She and Eli travelled often to Forest City to sell their moonshine. Sometimes she sat by the fireside and stared longingly into the hot coals. I wanted to tell her that I began to learn cursive writing today, that I drew a giant orange pumpkin for Miss Lucy, that Michael shared his crackers with me. Under her breath she mumbled, "My life is misery, my life is misery." It did not seem to occur to her that she was inflicting misery on everyone else. I crawled into bed and cried myself to sleep wishing that she would come and hug me.

Spring broke gently across Grassy and Oaky Knobs. Redbuds painted the mountains pink. Sourwood trees pushed their heady fragrance upon the wind. Ottie came alive again when Gentry and his sawmill gang came to cut timber on Old Grassy because she had someone now to talk to besides Eli. Although Ottie made a small effort to pull me back into her life, I refused to return. The void had grown too wide. For the rest of our lives we stared at each other across the void wondering what could have been. There had never been freedom from want in Ottie's world.

GIVE ME SOMETHING
OF VALUE

The room was cold and dark when my sister woke me up. Shadows from the fire in the fireplace danced across the walls of the room giving it an eerie glow. I dragged myself out of the bed putting on my pants as close to the fire as possible. My older sister assumed the role of mother. Ottie assigned her the role of surrogate mother. My sister was twelve and I was eight years old. Ottie stayed in bed most mornings leaving us four children to fend for ourselves as we got ready for school. Maybe she was tired or drunk or just did not care. She often stayed out late with her men or at her moonshine still. I searched to understand her neglect of us but I do not judge her. She stayed in her warm bed as my sister readied all four of us for school. It is my sister who was the driving force that made me go to school. She washed my face with a cold washcloth then combed my hair, parting it on the left side. She rubbed cold water to plaster down the cowlick on my head. My clothes were in tatters and my shoes even worse. The brown sweater I wore was full of holes from wear and washing. My pants had several patches. The tongue of my right shoe was torn and the glue holding the sole to the rest of the shoe had melted long ago, causing the loose piece to make a flapping sound when I walked. My socks were thin. My coat was a light jacket suitable only for summer.

Ottie pretended not to notice my condition. What could she do? Eli did not support his children. Her husband June Sr. had left her. We lived in the other America that did not support its children either. She looked at us in our suffering. She yelled and cursed that she could not "hep" it. She never pronounced the "l" in the word "help." Pulling her hair with both fists, she stamped her feet on the floor just as she did when shouting at Clyde and Jesse Pearl's church.

My mother suffered from a deep depression that left her virtually unable to act or make decisions. Those decisions she did make were bad. She did not care if we went to school. Education meant nothing to her. She did not care if we ate breakfast nor had food to take to school with us. The school had no cafeteria. We stared at the other students eating nice lunches that their parents had fixed for them. We went hungry. Yes, America, we went hungry! The only food we had was on our return home around five o'clock. Ottie cooked pinto beans and potatoes with a pan of cornbread. There was a gallon of milk to drink. Sometimes a baked sweet potato lay on the stove. This day I knew there would be no food. I finished dressing and then sat in front of the fireplace waiting for my sister to give the signal to go.

Flap, flap, flap went my shoe as it struck against the frozen ground, breaking the ground ice pushing up from the path. We doubled our usual walking pace using the path created over the years. In a very few minutes our hands were red and frozen for we had no gloves. Our ears stung from the cold wind. It warmed a bit as we followed the path through the birch trees and mountain laurel to the Ida Place.

"It won't be long now," my sister said encouragingly.

Beulah opened her front door ushering us into her warm living room. Although she did not approve of Ottie, she was good to us children. She had us wait for the bus in her house during the cold. As the warmth from her wood heater drove the cold from my body, I began to cry from the ache in my fingers and face. I covered my eyes with my hands trying to conceal my hurting. I was ashamed. Within the hour we boarded the bus where I sat next to the new girl Phyllis. Noticing my shivering, she wrapped her heavy coat around me until the bus pulled up at the school.

The door to Miss Lucy's classroom was painted green and made of heavy oak. Having eaten nothing since the night before, I did not have the strength to pull the door open. Other children helped me. The smell of chalk dust, floor cleaner, air freshener, and burning coal filled the room. To the left of the entrance door, there was a wall with two large closet doors with a mounted blackboard in between. The wall opposite held another large blackboard with a door leading into the auditorium. The longest wall consisted of huge glass windows reaching to the ceiling. Opposite these windows was another series of blackboards.

Seven huge tables, each seating six students, filled the room. Each seating place had a large opening for storing textbooks. A heavy chair provided seating. This room contained first, second, and third grades. First grade tables sat near the wall with the exit to the auditorium. Second grade tables occupied the middle and third grade tables stood near the closet doors. There was a pot-bellied coal-burning stove on tall metal legs with a stove pipe running up to and through the ceiling in one corner. Eight large electric lamps hung above the room. There was a water fountain outside the door in the hallway.

Even though there was running water in the building, there were no inside toilets. A kid had to walk down the hall past Mr. Rawlins's classroom, go down sixteen steps, and then push open a heavy metal door to an outside wooden toilet. The boys' outhouse was down the hill in a pine grove; the girls outhouse was close to the brooms edge fields. It was an unwritten rule that boys had to stay twenty feet away from the girls' outhouse. Between the two outhouses was an enormous pile of coal which fed the potbellied stove that heated the classrooms. The greatest honor bestowed on a student was for Miss Lucy to ask two of us to bring a bucket of coal for the fire. It did take two children to carry the heavy metal bucket filled with coal. The black soot on our hands was a mark of honor. Miss Lucy provided a large, sweet-smelling soap so we could wash our hands at the water fountain in the hall.

Late one autumn the class was busy with its studies. The only sound was that of pencils moving across large-lined paper. Miss Lucy began calling a boy's name, and then she exited with him through the heavy oak door into the hallway. He's getting a paddling for sure, we thought, but no sound came. Besides, Miss Lucy had no paddle in her hand. We waited, filled with trepidation, not wanting our name to be called. Sure enough, she called my name. My knees were weak as I slowly dragged myself out the door.

"Are those the only shoes you have?" Miss Lucy asked as she looked pitifully down at the flapping sole and torn tongue of my right shoe.

I flushed red in embarrassment as I replied, "yes."

"Are those the only pants and shirt you have?" she inquired.

"I have a few more clothes," I replied.

"Do you have a coat for the winter?"

The line of questioning was so embarrassing that my tongue locked in my throat. I glued my eyes to the floor and refused to answer any more of her questions.

After we returned to the classroom, Miss Lucy announced that a clothing store in Forest City was donating clothes to needy children. She named those of us who would be a recipient of the store's gift. I was selected as one of the "needy" children. She could have used the word "worthy" children but she did not. She should not have named the recipients in front of the other children. Why do adults assume that children have no pride or feelings? The adults who set up this act of giving intended to be benevolent but they botched it from my viewpoint. They could have brought clothes in our sizes and given them discreetly to us, explaining that we deserved them because of our good work at school. They stripped away my dignity.

On the appointed day, Mr. Rawlins took six of us boys in his car to Forest City. It was the largest town in our county. It was only eight blocks long, but to us, it was New York City. There were red lights. The roads were paved. There were beautiful houses, restaurants, and businesses. Our eyes were agog with wonder. Mr. Rawlins parked his car in front of the clothing store. It had a giant glass show window filled with the latest caps, shirts, pants, shoes, and other clothes. On the window, stenciled in big Old English letters, was the name "Tuttle's Clothier, Best Selections in the County". As we entered, we saw rows and rows of coats, pants, shirts, all new, hanging on racks. The store smelled of newness. Rubbing his hands like a motivated undertaker, Mr. Tom T. Tuttle greeted us with the words, "What would you boys like to have?"

We stood in silence.

"What would I like to have? What would I like to have?"

"I want a better life, a real family, food in the house. I want my mother to be kind. I don't want to be poor. I want America to care about me and my family, to use some of the millions it gives away to other countries to help its people in my valley. I want to be respected even though I have nothing with which to bargain. I want opportunity. I want an education. What I want and need in my life far surpasses what you are able to give me on this day, Mr. Tom T. Tuttle."

Mr. Rawlins realized that we were a scared bunch of kids, veritable fish out of water.

"What are you offering them, Mr. Tuttle, a lot or a little?" he asked.

Rubbing his greasy chin with two grubby fingers, Mr. Tuttle challenged his soul to be generous. His whole reason for the give-away was a tax write-off. He wanted to impress his church and community with his generosity, at the expense of a bunch of moonshiners' kids. He allowed a hat, a coat, a shirt, pants, socks, and shoes for each person.

As I stood among all this wealth and plenty, I felt humiliated because of my poverty. I could not abide Mr. Tom T. Tuttle's "holier-than-thou" attitude. Blessed are those who give to satisfy their own need for they shall have their just reward. (You can look that quote up in the "begats.") I couldn't wait to get out of the store.

It took all six of us boys some time to recover from our shock and embarrassment. When we got back to school, Miss Lucy had us stand up one by one and show the other children our loot. How much can a kid endure? The other children were jealous because we got something they did not. More humiliation was piled on me. I was grateful for the shoes, but the price I paid to get them was not worth it. Jealous children struck back. They threw water on my clothes when I wore them. They marked on my pants with crayons. One day I hit Mackie when he stepped on my new shoes. Miss Lucy chose not to punish me. Where were you the day after our visit to your store, Mr. Tom T. Tuttle? Were you there to sooth our broken pride?

When I went to my new school in 1953, for spite, I wore Tom T. Tuttle's new clothes.

I needed the clothes and did appreciate the gift. All the adults involved in this mission of mercy to help me did not realize that, while they warmed my physical body with clothing, they crushed my heart and pride with their callousness. If you take away my heart and pride, give me back something of value, lest I rebuke you in the end. Clothes just didn't do it.

EQUAL TO ALL

S heriff Dawson returned to his family and told them that the experience with my family and the fight between June Jr. and Curtis was the saddest day of his life. He took two days off from his work and went into the forest pretending to hunt. He did not hunt. He sat on moss-covered rocks next to a mountain stream and wept for the conditions of life that he could not change. He had the power to enforce man's laws but no power to enforce the laws of morality. He could not make Ottie love her children, nor take proper care of them. He could not force Curtis and June Jr. to behave. He could not make our lives better. His sadness choked him. His heart felt sick. Sheriff Dawson spent the whole day beside the stream listening to its trickling waters and the caws of a flock of crows that circled above him. He resolved to check on Ottie and the safety of her family weekly.

I heard the drone of its engine as his old truck edged its way up the creek road through the mud holes in the roadway. I strained my eyes to see who was in the truck. Ottie and I walked out on the front porch as a beat-up truck pulled under the apple trees in the front yard. Sheriff Dawson hailed us from the back of the truck where he stood saying, " Good morning you two. How is the family doing?"

Hearing the noise of the truck and the chatter of voices, Eli came from the barn where he was feeding dry corn to the horses. When June Jr. saw the sheriff, he ran out the back door and headed for the hills. Curtis had left earlier in the day to take the Greyhound bus to Forest City. Willard was plowing in the distant north field. Justine and Gertie, who held Callie in her arms, stared out through the windows at the newly-arrived group of men.

Eli came around the side of the house and shook hands with Sheriff Dawson. He greeted Bud the driver of the truck and his friend, Muncie, who sat on the seat beside Bud.

"How are you doing?" the sheriff enquired of my mother.

"Tolerable," she responded.

"How are Curtis and June Jr.?" he wanted to know.

"Curtis is in Forest City and June Jr. ran out the back door to hide when he saw you coming," she retorted.

"I'll get hold of June Jr. one of these days," he told her convincingly.

"Sheriff Dawson, I saved you some sweet potatoes from our crop. Kids, run get the sweet potatoes from the barn. I really appreciate you coming by the other day."

Sheriff Dawson dropped his head and stared at his feet. He pawed the sand with his right foot.

"Miss Ottie," he stumbled over his words. "I'm sorry all of that happened. I came by today to make sure you are okay."

"Much obliged," she said softly as she turned and disappeared into the house.

I remained on the porch staring at the sheriff through the wooden bannister. He bent down to my level peering back at me with a warm smile on his face.

"How's my little buddy?" he asked.

My tongue tied itself to the roof of my mouth. My face flushed red as I stared sheepishly at the floor unable to say a word. Sheriff Dawson reached his hand through the bannister and tousled my blond hair, then patted me on the head and returned to the adult men now gathered in a small group around the pick-up truck. They talked animatedly among themselves occasionally stopping to spit or blow their noses on the white handkerchiefs they carried in the bib of their overalls.

Gertie and Justine came around the house dragging a heavy sack of sweet potatoes. Eli lifted them on to the back of the truck.

Sheriff Dawson walked over to Gertie and Justine and asked, "How are you two fine ladies today? That was a brave thing you did coming to my house the other day. I'm proud of both of you."

Gertie and Justine beamed with pride and shyly ran back around the house to sit on the kitchen steps and enjoy this compliment that they had just received from an adult.

Suddenly all of the men got back in the truck and started to depart. Bud drove the vehicle, Muncie rode shotgun, Eli and Sheriff Dawson rode on the back. As they made their turn, Sheriff Dawson yelled loudly to me, "Hey, Little Buddy, do you want to ride with us? We're going to Stan's Country Store."

I tore across the yard in my bare feet and pulled myself up on the truck bed. I stood next to Sheriff Dawson and held tightly to the truck cab to keep from falling. I did not want to stand next to my dad Eli. The old pick-up popped and growled along the dry ruts in the road. The wind splashed our faces. We shook from side to side as the truck rumbled through mud holes. As we entered the road beside the creek, Bud stopped the truck and pointed upward with his finger. There circled above us an enormous hawk with a wing spread of two feet. Hawks are generally not welcome at our farm for they kill our ducks and chickens. Sheriff Dawson pulled his pistol from its holster and took careful aim, steadying the pistol with his left hand. I stuffed my fingers in my ears. A loud "pop" rang out as blue smoke arched upward toward the tree tops. He missed the hawk. I stared at Sheriff Dawson as he holstered his pistol.

The old pick-up truck groaned forward through the first ford in the creek. The water of the creek washed half the tires of their caked-on mud leaving them a two-tone color. The second fording of the creek cleaned the mud from all the tires. Bud drove us from our side road on to the main graveled road that led across Bolding's Gap. We turned left and sped toward Stan's store. The power of the wind from the speeding truck left us with an exhilarating feeling. We all felt free and alive.

Stan's store was a beehive of activity as we pulled into an empty space near one of his benches. Men loitered in small groups gossiping and drinking some of Ottie's moonshine. Upon seeing the sheriff, they scattered. Some fled into the store; others got in their vehicles and left. Sheriff Dawson just laughed. Inside, Eli ordered me an R.C., a moon pie, and fifteen cents worth of long baloney in a sandwich. I stood proud and tall. I felt important to be among these men. Just then a truck pulled in loaded with a gang of black men. It was Rufus and his work crew. Little did I know that this day Rufus would teach me an eternal lesson about standing proud, equal to all.

I WANT AN RC, A MOON PIE, AND FIFTEEN CENTS WORTH OF THAT LONG BALONEY

Stan's country store stood near the banks of the Broad River, resting in a clearing on the main road through the valley. It was built of plain boards nailed to each other in a vertical step. Two square windows opposite each other on the front entrance let in natural light. Iron bars covered the windows to thwart would-be thieves. The roof was level on top slanting into a v shape on both sides. After many coats of paint over the years, the building showed an off-color red. Two sturdy posts held up a shed covering two gasoline pumps shaped like human bodies. An elongated cylinder held the tank of gasoline. On top sat the head part with colored beads that swirled in a circle when people pumped the gasoline. The handle and hose stood out like arms. The pungent smell of the gasoline penetrated into the store mixing with the smell of fresh coffee, Nehi soft drinks, popcorn, and peppermint candy. This store was an oasis to the valley people who came from far and wide to buy their supplies, food, and lunch sandwiches or just to rest their weary bodies on the benches placed out front.

The store offered three specialties, or at least they were specialties to the valley folk: Royal Crown soft drinks (which people shortened to RC), moon pies, and fresh baloney sandwiches which Stan made himself. He used two slices of thick bread piled high with Duke's mayonnaise (no other would do). Then he cut a thick slice of baloney from a foot long roll placing it inside the bread. No lettuce. No tomato. He put just a generous sprinkling of black pepper on top. He placed a large box of moon pies on the front counter. (A moon pie is a round cookie sandwich with marshmallow in the center, covered with thick, brown chocolate). Most people bought these two items and topped it off with a fizzing R.C. It was this fizzing quality of an RC that people loved. It burned the nose and esophagus when swallowed, generally ending in a loud burp. Around the noon hour a crowd of people gathered at Stan's place, mostly men, chomping baloney sandwiches, savoring moon pies, and guzzling R.Cs. My dad and I joined them on a Tuesday in November. We came to the store with Sheriff Dawson, Bud, and Muncie. I was five years old at the time. I knew very little about anything, just what the limited adults around me could teach. Today would be one of the greatest educational days of my life.

I jumped down from the back of Bud's truck, dodging a large mouth of tobacco spit spurting from a local yokel sitting on one of the front benches and ran toward the store. I loved the smells of the store---leather, chocolate, coffee, sweaty bodies---and savored them as I hesitated just inside the entrance door.

Eli followed me to the counter placing our order for baloney sandwiches and moon pies. I beamed as he handed me an open bottle of R.C., bubbling, fizzing, and so big I had to use both my hands to drink it. My nose burned with the first swig and I belched shortly thereafter. As I enjoyed my treat, there came a life-changing experience. Outside, a farm truck drove up loaded with four white farm laborers and six black men packed on the back.

No black people were ever allowed to live in our valley. There was no tolerance for black people. The valley was only for people of white skin. Black people could work on the farms during the day, but they had to be gone by sundown. Those blacks who did not obey this unwritten law were lynched. We were not yet a hundred years removed from the War of Northern Aggression. Ignorance and hatred ruled here. Everyone told me that black people were bad, that I should fear them. Even the Devil, they said, was black. One had to be carefully taught to hate any people. If the hatred lasts too long, it is almost impossible to retreat from it. I had never seen a black person before.

Eli handed me a baloney sandwich and a chocolate moon pie. We stepped aside to the back of the store. The white boss and crew came into the store, placed their order for baloney sandwiches, and mingled with the other men eating their food. The boss went back to the truck and told the black field hands to enter the store. It was a strange custom that the black people could enter the store to buy their food, but they could not stay inside and eat with the white men. They had to return to the truck and eat lunch among their own kind.

I ducked behind Eli's legs hiding my face, trembling in fear, when the first black person entered the store. I fully expected that he would kill and eat me.

"What would you like to eat today, Rufus?" Stan asked him.

In his thick speech he drawled,

"I want an R.C., a moon pie, and fifteen cents worth of that long baloney."

He was a tall, imposing man. His arms hung low at thigh level. Two bulbous lips protruded in front of pearly, white teeth. He was strong. His skin was so dark from the sun that it took on a purple color. He had round, kind eyes that darted everywhere taking in the activity of the store. Were he anywhere else other than this valley, he would be a king. I trembled in fear remembering all the talk and bad stories about black people told by adults around me. I began to cry and wail out loud, tears running down on my R.C. and moon pie.

Rufus knew I was afraid of him. He had children of his own. He knew how to console them when valley children treated them badly. He was nursing his own broken heart and anger from a lifetime of mistreatment. He had been to depths of despair. Over the years his loving heart had turned to stone.

On this special day, something beautiful moved deep within the soul of Rufus. He paid for his lunch, and then bought five sticks of peppermint candy from a big glass jar on the counter. He slowly walked in my direction. Leaning his face down to my level, a huge smile bursting across his face, he handed me one of the peppermint sticks. I froze. Eli touched my shoulder gently urging me forward to accept the gift. The store fell into a tense silence. The group stared in amazement at the scene unfolding in front of them. I bravely stepped forward and accepted the candy. Then I reached back to touch the kind, Black Hand that had reached out to me. It was soft and warm like mine. Rufus stood back up, paid for his food, and started for the door.

A soft voice came from the back of the store murmuring, "Thank you, Rufus." Then another man said it louder, "Thank you." "Thank you" murmured throughout the crowd. The mouths uttering the "thank you" had heretofore spoken only malicious things about black people. Rufus looked everyone directly in their eyes for a brief moment. He nodded, acknowledging the thanks. He walked with dignity through the door and climbed back on the truck, taking his usual place, where he sat and ate his sandwich in silence among his own kind.

It was the 1960's and I was in college. The war for civil rights was raging in Montgomery. I watched on TV as people were beaten, hosed with water, even killed.

"I have to go," I thought to myself.

Thousands of people marched beside me. I carried a sign reading "God Hath Made of One Blood All Nations of Men." As I walked through a gauntlet of people hurling insults and racial slurs, I began to understand what Rufus had endured every day of his life. I vowed to bring a new birth of love and respect to all peoples of my valley.

"I'm doing this march for you, Rufus," I said to myself out loud. "Thank you for the peppermint candy. And thank you, too, for the love you showed me long ago at Stan's store. I hope my presence here today will help bring you your freedom."

COME BACK TO ME WHEN THE SOURWOOD IS IN BLOOM

E li was born in 1892. Like the year of his birth, he drew little attention in our Appalachian valley. He grew into a man with only one distinguishing characteristic- his ability to procreate. During his life, he traveled about the valley creating babies with any willing female. Eli married three times, each time he lived longer than his wives. I would be his illegitimate son.

My mother, Ottie, was born in the year 1903, when great historical events happened. The year 1903 brought the first heavier than air flight at Kitty Hawk and Ford began production of his Model-T.

Ottie was eleven years younger than Eli. She was much more intelligent than he, yet she foolishly succumbed to his charms.

Ottie's family lived in a log cabin near the CCC road which the government built through the mountains during the Great Depression. They lived so far back in the woods people said that the first piece of sliced bread they ever saw was thrown off the back of a CCC truck. There were no schools, no stores, and nothing

civilized where Ottie lived. She had eight brothers and sisters as
did Eli. An itinerant teacher came to hold school once a year, in
June, July, and August, so the children got a rudimentary education. However, real learning skills for them came through living,
through surviving. Growing corn and tobacco, making liquor,
growing gardens and home canning ensured their survival. Any
learning above and beyond what was practical was superfluous
and actually discouraged. However, Ottie used her intelligence to
survive, to make herself equal to the men she met. The men were
quite dull anyway. They had a dullness brought on by interbreed-
ing and faulty DNA. The gene pool in those hills could have used
a heavy dose of chlorine.

Life brought Ottie and Eli together, but their meeting would
be a cruel fate for her.

He came with the state highway crew to clean and repair the
CCC road. She walked along the CCC road to carry out her moonshine business. On the day of their first meeting, Ottie and her
sister Addie were walking to the Peddler's Stump to sell some of
her liquor. This memorable stump was originally a huge oak tree
killed by a lightning strike. When the road crew cut the tree, they
left a tall, flat stump that became a landmark along the CCC road.
It became the meeting place for people in that part of the valley.
Sweethearts left notes for each other at the stump. People came to
buy moonshine at it. Neighborhood women met there once a week
to gossip, to exchange news, and to lift some boredom from their
lives. People smiled when someone said, "Meet me at the Peddler's
Stump", because they knew something interesting was coming to
their lives.

Ottie and Addie set out their quarts of crystal clear moonshine
along the back of the stump and covered the containers with a
white cloth. In front they placed some apples, pears, and jars of
fox grape jelly to make the operation look legitimate to those who
did not know how they operated. Ottie sat down in the grass and

waited for customers. She was only fourteen years old. It was the year 1917. A war raged in Europe. Young men had gone away to the army leaving only old men available to the women. It was a boring time for these two young women.

Eli finished shoveling out the drainage ditch on his side of the CCC road where he piled mud and sand high on the embankment. He hung the shovel on the side of the truck and resumed his seat on a bench in the back. Thirteen men made up the work gang on this day. Eli was tired. He had worked hard, so he stretched out on the bench and closed his eyes for a moment's respite. He was not in the war. The army deemed him unfit to fight because he had a slight curvature of the spine.

"You will never be able to shoot straight," the recruiter told him.

Eli was twenty-five years old and not exceptionally bright. His education was on the same level as Ottie's, except for one fact. He never learned to count. Numbers were foreign to him. His boss often paid him in one dollar bills. He counted each bill out loud, skipping a number from time to time, thereby cheating Eli in his pay. His boss stuck the extra money in his own pocket.

Formal education was unimportant to Eli's family. Real life consisted of productive work. So the road work fulfilled his needs and the pay made his pockets jingle. He had a real weakness for women though, and he was always on the prowl for new conquests.

Eli was in deep sleep when the truck turned a curve and the work gang saw Ottie and Addie sitting provocatively by the Peddler's Stump. They began to whistle and make cat calls.

The men piled off the truck when it stopped and rushed to the stump to buy apples, pears, and small jars of jelly. Ottie smiled as she eagerly raked in cash. The men gasped when she removed the cloth from the jars filled with moonshine. She opened one of the quarts, pushed her index finger down into the liquid, and then tantalizingly waved it under the men's noses. Their tongues clacked in dry throats as thirst drove their hands deeper into pockets. The boss of the road crew, a no-nonsense burly Scott-Irish type, bellowed that he was not going to deal with a drunken road crew. Lay off the moonshine. Ottie decided that he could not spoil her business venture. Taking a cup of moonshine and an apple in her hand, she went to him. She placed them on the truck engine and leaned low so that her breasts were slightly visible to the foreman. It was Eve all over again with an apple and booze.

"The men can buy their booze now," she suggested to him. "I'll keep it here with me until your return trip home. If the men drink the moonshine then, it won't matter," she purred, rubbing two fingers across her mouth. "There is a free quart for you if you let them buy it now."

She had a mesmerizing quality about her. The boss capitulated. The men formed a loosely joined line, each paying for his quart. Ottie wrote a number on each jar to designate its owner. When Eli's turn came, she paused, studying his physical make-up. He was blond, with medium build and strong arms and legs. She liked his firm shoulders and square-set jaw. She smiled, took his money and wrote his number on the jar.

"What is my number?" he asked her. "I can't count."

"Number nine," she replied noting the fact that he couldn't count in her mind. The moonshine was eight dollars per quart. He laid down a twenty. Grinning, she returned to him ten dollars and kept two more dollars for herself. He never knew the difference.

The men moved on.

While waiting for the men to come back down the road, Ottie tore a piece of paper from an old newspaper tossed carelessly beside the road.

On it she wrote, "Meet me at the Peddler's Stump this Sunday at 2:00 pm. I like you." She signed her name "Ottie."

When the truck stopped again at the stump, her sister Addie distributed the men's purchases to them. Ottie gave Eli his quart of moonshine. As she handed it to him, she placed the note in his hand and winked at him through excited, black eyes.

"Booze is not all I peddle," she laughed.

Eli felt his knees go weak.

Eli did come back on Sunday to see her and they spent the whole afternoon together walking down to a waterfall known as the Pots. They walked back to the local church and through its lines of gravestones in the cemetery. They made love in a grassy spot near the church. For Ottie and Eli, it was the beginning of a life-long relationship which ebbed and flowed like the tides on a beach. He came to visit her every Sunday in the spring. He charmed her young, lonely heart. Ottie fell in love. Eli was just in heat.

He told her one day, "I can't see you again until the sourwood is in bloom."

It was March. What he meant was that he might not come back to see her until the month of June when the sweet-smelling sourwood trees bloomed in the woods. Ottie foolishly believed him. She went to the Peddler's Stump every Sunday and waited patiently for him to return. But he did not come back.

Eli went home and married his childhood sweetheart.

ALIENATION OF AFFECTION

Ottie went to work for Mr. Stoutman as a housekeeper because that is all that she knew how do. Women in the valley either married or hired themselves out to keep house and do farm work for others. Up to this point, she had lived at home caring for her parents, growing tobacco and cotton, plus making moonshine. She had three summers of formal education given by an itinerant teacher. She could barely read, write, or cipher. She had nothing with which to barter other than her body.

One day at the Peddler's Stump, a man named Mr. Stoutman stopped to buy his moonshine. Ottie thought he was handsome. His hair was jet black; he was five feet eleven inches tall with medium build. He wore a nice suit of clothes with a cravat tied in a large bow at his throat. It was evident that he was educated by the way he spoke. Neat and clean, he looked different from the ordinary working men with whom she associated. When he greeted her, she lowered her eyes, afraid to look into his as if he were some sort of royalty.

"What's your name young lady?" he asked.

"Ottie," she stammered, hardly able to find her voice.

"I want a quart of moonshine. How much does it cost?" he enquired.

"Eight dollars a quart," she replied.

"Do you make it yourself?" he wanted to know.

"Are you a revenuer?" She asked.

"No. I'm not the police. Do you know why they call them police?" he joked. "They are the poorest in the county and the least thought of." Ottie laughed and relaxed.

"Where do you live?" he wanted to know.

"In the log cabin around the curve," she admitted.

"Are you married? I am," he told her.

Ottie lost interest in him at that moment for he no longer fit into her search for affection. He was already taken. She would not alienate him from his partner.

"Here's your moonshine," she said handing him his quart. "I wish you and your wife well."

He paid her ten dollars and left.

"What is the extra two dollars for? It only costs eight dollars."

"For love and affection," he smiled as he departed.

This man impressed her, but he was already taken. His journey to affection was accomplished. Or was it?

The threads of karma wove a tapestry catching Ottie in the pattern. She thought often of this man. She had not asked him his name. Maybe he would come by again for moonshine. She described him to her sister Addie, but she did not know who he was.

Weeks passed before Ottie returned to the Peddler's Stump. She had to make more moonshine and lots of work kept her at home. Her brother Grover came to her excitedly saying that there was a good-looking man down at the Peddler's Stump asking to see her. He wanted to buy some moonshine. She hurriedly packed up a case and made haste to the stump. She saw him from a distance sitting on the stump, feet dangling above the ground. Once again he wore a nice suit with a cravat tied in a bow. He smiled at her as she set her jars on the stump.

"I don't know your name," she said out of breath.

"Stoutman," he said eyeing her. "I have a big farm on the road south of here."

"How much shine do you want," she asked.

"The whole case," he replied.

She gasped as he handed her a crisp one hundred dollar bill.

"Keep the rest," he told her.

That money would last her for an entire month.

"There's more where that came from. My farm produces a lot of money. I have a problem, though. My wife has taken to her bed ill with something. We don't know what. I want to hire you to cook and run the household for me. There is some field work as well. I'll pay you well."

Ottie did not think twice about the offer. She accepted.

The following week he came to get her in his new Model-T ford. They drove to his house south of the CCC road.

Mrs. Stoutman lay in her bed, pale and weak from an affliction that was not physical. She suffered from alienation of affection, a disease that strikes when a person no longer loves his life partner. Over the years living with Mr. Stoutman, she grew to dislike him. Her love for him died. He began to seek satisfaction elsewhere. Few options were open for her. She did not want to divorce him because she liked the economic comfort he provided. She feigned physical illness in order to avoid any intimate relationship with him. She grew angry when she suspected that he had been with another woman. She only wanted what he could give her financially. She would not let anyone else have him either.

Ottie walked into this emotional quagmire unaware. Mr. Stoutman brought her into the household to alleviate the burden of work. She could also serve as a buffer between him and his wife. Two women in one house, however, create a power struggle that can explode at any moment. Ottie had no freedom for she had to do everything according to Mrs. Stoutman's dictates. The wife owned the household and lost no time in letting Ottie know it. Mr. Stoutman was less rigid. He gave her some choice in her work in the fields.

Mr. Stoutman was away from the farm on business many days, leaving the two women to run things. Mrs. Stoutman used Ottie as her confidante. Not because of affection for the young girl, but because she shared her inner thoughts about Mr. Stoutman. They were very negative. She admitted that she had taken to bed to be rid of him physically. She stated emphatically that she did not want him and that she would see to it that no else could have him either. She needed his assets and his presence only. She knew that Mr. Stoutman's affections had turned elsewhere but she could not yet identify any woman. Ottie was too simple to understand such intrigue. She did not realize what a monster Mrs. Stoutman would be.

The months of summer blended into a gloriously yellow and red autumn. It was harvest time. Ottie adjusted well to the Stoutman household. He paid and fed her well. Unlike his wife, he treated her with kindness. She was out in a field one day gathering pumpkins and loading them into an empty wagon. Mr. Stoutman intended to sell them at the Boneyard. He came to her in the field with a hot cup of coffee and a piece of apple pie. She was tired. She was lonely. She was vulnerable. Work isolated her on this farm. She had not seen her family in weeks. It pained her to see Mrs. Stoutman throwing this fine man away. She was dying for affection. If someone discards an old piece of furniture, why should another not have it? Ottie was delighted when he asked her to go to the Boneyard with him to sell the pumpkins. He promised her that he would drive back to the farm to check on his wife to make sure she was fine.

Later that week they sat behind a huge pile of pumpkins at the Boneyard and talked. Mr. Stoutman placed his chair close to her so he could put his arms around her shoulders and rub his knee against hers. Ottie leaned into his arm in warm response. Mrs. Stoutman could go to the Devil; she would have this fine man. As they sold pumpkins, he slipped his arms around her waist and kissed her on the cheek. Both were in a high state of emotion. When they returned home, Mrs. Stoutman was quite angry. She had lain there all day, her needs unmet, for he had not driven back to check on her as he had promised. He came to Ottie's bed that night and they made passionate love. Ottie could not look Mrs. Stoutman in the eyes next day. Ottie took over the wifely role for Mr. Stoutman from that day until she learned that she was pregnant.

Mrs. Stoutman noticed that Ottie was with child. She called missionary Bertha to take her to a lawyer's office in Forest City where she promptly charged Ottie with alienation of affection. There still is a North Carolina law that allows it. Ottie stood accused of causing the breach of affection between Mr. and Mrs. Stoutman. The truth is that the break in the relationship occurred long before Ottie came to work for them. Rather than lose his farm and assets completely to his wife, Mr. Stoutman turned on Ottie and testified that she had caused the alienation of affection. It was she who had seduced him. A jury pronounced Ottie guilty. The judge ordered her out of the Stoutman household and placed her on probation for three years.

She returned to her parents' house disgraced. Her actions shamed them. They treated her harshly when she gave birth to her baby girl, Lovada. The entire family heaped coals of emotional fire upon her life. She suffered daily humiliation. Mr. Stoutman got off free. He hired himself another woman to replace Ottie. The fires of Hell burned a little hotter for him.

How could Ottie alienate that which she never had? Mr. Stoutman had no affection for her as he had none for his wife. How could he turn against her so vilely? Ottie's only mistake had been to seek love. She realized too late that she had been looking for affection among monsters. Her probation disallowed her selling moonshine so her sister Addie sold it for her. One Saturday morning Ottie sat quietly beside her at the Peddler's Stump nursing her baby Lovada from her naked breast. Mr. Stoutman drove up for his weekly moonshine. He saw Ottie nursing her baby.

He compounded her feeling of disgust for him when he cruelly and sarcastically called out, "Who is the father of your baby, Ottie?"

"Why do you ask?" she responded with a smirk.

"I just wondered if you had alienated someone else's affection besides mine," he said as an insult.

"It takes affection to help make a baby and you are devoid of that," she chided him. "Besides, you can't possibly be the father of my baby," she mocked back. "Your wife told me you are sterile. You can't have children."

Alienation of affection, indeed!

I'M ON MY WAY BACK HOME

In August Ottie birthed her baby. Lovada came into a world of neglect. Ottie was ill-prepared to care for a child. She did not even know how to care for herself. She had to work the fields and the moonshine still and there was no babysitter. She placed the child on a blanket on the ground or in laurel bushes while she did her work. She fed the baby from her breasts. So weary and tired at night, Ottie had no special time for the child, so she just went to bed. As the child learned to walk, she stayed at home locked in a room alone, left to her own devices.

When she reached the age of six, Lovada behaved like a wild animal. Ottie could not control her then, for she had not disciplined her in early childhood. Ottie's brother, Tom, took her to live with him for a while, but that did not work out either.

So Ottie decided to place her child in an orphanage located in the valley. At the age of six, Lovada left her only home, headed for a life among strangers. Her home had been with Ottie. No matter how bad the situation, her heart still belonged there. That abusive family formed the only world that she had known and she was leaving it reluctantly. They packed her few clothes in a cardboard box.

"I'll find my way back home somehow," she said looking up at her mother.

Ottie did not hear her words, for she had already made the decision to sever Lovada from her heart. She was giving her away to the orphanage, to anyone who would have her. This illegitimate, wayward child, maybe Stoutman's child, born in an alienation of affection was going away and Ottie's heart was not heavy. She was surrendering that part of her that hurt the most, so there was no room for tears or regret.

As the car pulled away from the orphanage, Ottie looked back to see a tiny, frail, scared, hurt little girl weeping, saying over and over, "I want to go home. I want to go home."

Weeks passed and Ottie did not go back to the orphanage to see her child. Her brother Tom did. A deep bond developed between Lovada and her uncle. She saw him as a father figure and he was a link to home. She often imagined a long, steel rail with short crossties supporting them. On the rails was a mighty train speeding through the night with her on it.

"I'm on my way back home," she imagined.

Then day would break with her finding herself, not at home, but among strangers in a strange land.

Six years passed and she turned twelve. The orphanage gave her a cake with twelve candles. She sat that whole day waiting for someone from home to visit her. "I should be on my way back home by now."

Ottie came to visit her only twice in the six years since Lovada had come to the orphanage. Twice, couples wanted to adopt her, but Ottie would not give permission. So, Lovada languished there knowing she could not leave until she turned eighteen and that was six years away. When her uncle came for a visit, she begged him to take her home. He had no legal authority to help her, so she ran away. She stole some money from the headmistress and thumbed a ride from a stranger to Forest City where she boarded a train for Spartanburg.

It was the middle of the Second World War. Thousands of soldiers moved everywhere by train. Some questioned why a twelve-year-old girl traveled by herself on the train. "My mother is waiting for me in Spartanburg," she told them. "I'm on my way back home." The soldiers looked out for her safety. They bought her an R.C. and a moon pie. When she disembarked at the station in Spartanburg, she went to a bench and sat down until night fell. The station was crowded with people and activity. Soldiers scurried to and fro exiting and boarding trains headed for far-away destinations: Atlanta, Augusta, Charleston, and Mobile. A soldier saw her sitting alone and invited her to come to a motel with him. She went. He fed her, gave her a warm bed, and warm, loving arms to hold her through the night.

Time and time again she returned to the train station easily finding a soldier to feed her, to give her money for a room. She became confused about love. Physical activity was the only comfort and warmth available to her. She saved the money the men gave her and rented an apartment a block from the station. Her landlady was very old and appreciated the company of this young girl. In her youth, the landlady had worked as a hairstylist and makeup instructor, so she taught Lovada how to look exceptionally beautiful. Then Lovada no longer accepted donations from the men. She set a high price for her services and became a smart business-woman. But through it all, Lovada's heart longed to go home.

She had not seen her mother now for eight years. Ottie knew that she had run away but did not know where until an official letter came from the Spartanburg Police Department. They informed her that her daughter was in their jail charged with solicitation. She is a minor. You are legally responsible for her. If you do not come and take her home, we will charge you with contributing to the delinquency of a minor. Ottie threw the letter on the ground and walked away.

The next letter brought news that Lovada was in a girls' reformatory school in New Jersey. Ottie wrote her four letters to the address given on the envelope, but they all returned unopened. Lovada was ashamed to write all her information on the envelope, so the prison would not accept the letters.

Eight years elapsed with no further contact. Then one day Ottie got a card from Montana saying that Lovada was living with a family there and doing well. When released in New Jersey, she had gone there by court edict. She informed Ottie that she wanted to come home for a visit. Ottie agreed.

A week later, a second postcard came bearing a photo of the majestic Rocky Mountains and the words, "I'm on my way back home." Tom met her at the train station in Spartanburg and drove her back to my grandparents' house where she had lived most of the first six years of her life.

On the drive homeward, the blooming cotton fields made her cry. The smell of the red-clay earth stirred her brain. The scent of sourwood made her nostalgic. The pine trees lining the highway waved their arms in welcome. The South Mountains came into view and she gasped remembering their beauty. They passed the orphanage, now long gone to another location. She remembered her flight from the place. The stay in New Jersey had been worse than the orphanage.

Ottie stood waiting in the doorway of the little cabin. Lovada saw how she had aged. Her jet-black hair was now streaked with gray. Her strong physical frame carried weight. There were wrinkles in her face, etched from a sad, hurting heart. In turn, Ottie looked at her. No more a six-year old, neglected child, Lovada stood a proud, beautiful lady. She had Ottie's lovely black hair, an hourglass figure and she dressed in stylish, city clothes. The two women were strangers staring at each other. They were different people, for time had changed them both. Each searched for a familiar trait in the other, a long-lost something to connect them to a mother-daughter tie that had broken long ago. Neither knew what to say or do. They stood in heavy silence staring at each other.

Then Lovada spoke: "The long, steel rails brought me home-ward across the Mississippi, across mountains proud and tall, up the hills and hollows to my Appalachian home. My heart never left here. It never left you. It is the dream of being home that sus-tained me all these years."

She walked with hesitation toward Ottie, her arms outstretched. It was a plea, a supplication, a begging to be accepted back home.

However, the bond was so broken in Ottie, the pain so deep, that she could not embrace her own child. Lowering her eyes to the floor, Ottie turned and walked away into the cabin. Lovada was even more heart- broken. She returned to Tom's car and he took her home with him.

Ottie had come from the Great Forever on a journey filled with expectations of love and being loved. It had not happened. She had found herself in a family devoid of love. There was no touch-ing, no hugging, no one walking beside her. Her feelings had fallen on fallow ground and would never be nourished. Hers had been a journey always looking for a lost element denied her. She could not pass to her children that which she had never known. They, too, were cheated.

The two women visited each other from time to time through-out their lives but they remained strangers. They would look at each other from time to time with a deep longing, yet neither had the courage to step across the chasm, the valley of division, the land of broken hearts.

THE LITTLE OLE HOUSE

E li never intended a long relationship with Ottie. He was in heat, she was available. At age twenty-five he held considerable experience over a fourteen year old girl. He did not return to see her when sourwoods were in bloom. He did not return at all. But destiny had a plan for them that would not be thwarted. Their lives went different pathways for a number of years but Eli had not seen the last of her. Nothing worked out in relationships, for Ottie had no luck with men.

Eli lived all his twenty-five years in the farmhouse where he was born. His father, Julius, built the original farmhouse out of wooden logs cut from the surrounding woods. He built a log barn not far from the house. His farmhouse had a living room and one bedroom. That was all. The family cooked over the fire in the fireplace until Julius added a kitchen and dining room on to the house. It is puzzling to consider how ten people lived in two rooms for Julius had a wife and eight children. In later years he built planks over the logs and splashed white paint over them. He added a porch and then dug a well for fresh water. The house looked nice. As the children grew up, they married and built houses near-by or somewhat farther down the valley. When he grew old, Julius went to live with his son Roy, leaving Eli to care for the home place.

Eli decided to get married. He went to Forest City to find another childhood sweetheart, Daisy, who was five years, his elder. Knowing she could not do better for a husband, Daisy married him. He brought her back to the farmhouse to live. In the next six years she gave him three legitimate children. I use the word legitimate because Eli had a number of children with women to whom he was not married. He had two legitimate girls and a boy. I would be the only other son Eli produced. He lost his first son to an early death. He never claimed me as his son. Daisy died of tuberculosis and his son of type I diabetes. His daughters went to live with Eli's sister. He was left alone and lonely in the white farmhouse.

He wanted to remarry. His was an active farm with much work, too much for one person. Besides, Eli needed a woman around. He did not consider marrying Ottie. His guilt for not going back to her was too great. She was such a powerful woman both emotionally and physically that he feared her. This time he courted and married Lily, a spinster who lived in the valley. She came to take Daisy's place on the farm. Eli did not love her. It was a practical arrangement. Together they produced three daughters, all legitimate. Eli had sired six children while married. This second family worked together so the farm flourished. Life was good for him. Life was not good for those whom he had betrayed.

Five hundred feet from his farmhouse, there stood a second house built by one of Eli's brothers. In the valley families subdivided land unto generations. Known as the Little Old House, it was a substantial dwelling containing four rooms and a porch. Wood shingles sealed the roof from the elements. It had a large porch supported by four oak posts and a roof made out of tin. Red-tinted tarpaper wrapped around the four outer walls giving it a stereotypical Appalachian look. The house was vacant. Eli wanted to rent it for extra cash. People wanted to rent it, but Fate kept it open for Ottie.

One day a pudgy, short troll-like figure with dark skin and hair plodded up the road to the farmhouse. He had limited intelligence. His clothes were poor quality and wrinkled all over. Dirt covered the tops of his shoes. He said his name was June Sr. How does a man get the name June? June is a month in summer, not a proper name for a man. His parents had no more intelligence than he, obviously. He had a wife and four children. Three boys belonged to him but the girl was a step-daughter. His wife had had her before they were married. They were down on their luck and needed a place to live. Actually, it wasn't luck at all. June Sr. was too inept in providing for his family. He worked at a saw mill; the work was not steady. Eli agreed to rent him the house in exchange for farm work. He and his wife would be tenant farmers to him like serfs of old. The family moved in the following week.

June Sr. was Ottie's husband. They were moving into Eli's house. The Lords of Karma laughed. As she prepared her new house, Ottie leaned over a cardboard box pulling out some of her meager kitchen utensils. Stacks of clothes, pots and pans, cheap furniture lay strewn about the dwelling. The house was in disarray. There came a knock at the front door followed by a man's voice saying,

"I'm your landlord. I came to meet you."

Ottie opened the screen door and looked directly into Eli's blue eyes. She stepped backward gasping. June Sr. had not told her the name of the person renting them the house. She was shocked to come face to face once again with Eli. All the old emotions swelled within her. She was happy to see him again and angry at his rejection. In anger she wanted to strike him, in joy she wanted to embrace him. She did neither. She remained cold, aloof pretending that she had never before laid eyes on him. But he certainly remembered her. His shock in seeing her again was no less than hers.

"Don't you remember me?" he stammered. "I'm Eli. I met you on the CCC road. I bought some liquor from you."

"Your memory is better than mine," she replied. "There was once a man whom I met on the CCC road who promised to come back to me when the sourwood was in bloom, but he never did," she moaned. "I don't remember his name. You don't look like him at all. That man was handsome and sweet and intelligent." She intended for these words to hurt him, as she was hurt. "Did my husband make successful arrangements for us to live here and work the land?" she asked.

"That man is your husband?" he asked shocked.

"That's the best a jilted girl could do," she retorted. "I met him at the Peddler's Stump, too, when the sourwood was in bloom. He did not lie to me, though. He came back and married me."

These words struck Eli's pride a severe blow as his rejection of her had broken her heart long ago. He now wished he had gone back for her instead of marrying Lily. A deep silence fell over the conversation. Neither knew what to say.

Ottie broke the silence saying, "My four kids will arrive tomorrow."

In his mind he could not imagine her married, much less with four children. That meant that she had not waited for him. She got on with her life, though unhappy it was.

Looking him straight in the eyes she asked,

"Who did you say you are?"

"Eli" he responded.

"I don't know anyone by the name of Eli," she said to him eye to eye, her heart breaking again. "I never did."

THE REUNION

Dust flew as Ottie cleaned out the rental house. She swept dust and dirt out the doorway into the yard, letting some spill on the large granite rock used as a doorstep. She hung curtains made from feed sack cloth over the three windows. There was no privacy in this house because it was one large open square room. There had previously been four distinct rooms divided by walls, but someone had seen fit to knock them down. Kitchen, sleeping areas, dining areas were all one. Ottie strung bailing wire across sections hanging more feed sack cloth to simulate rooms. World War II had just ended and there were few consumer goods available, not even window curtains. Coffee and sugar rationing were still in effect.

June Sr. raked the yard outside and then nailed some loose shingles back on the roof. In the evening he went to get the four children who had been staying with their aunt. The oldest daughter was not his, but he had known that when he married Ottie. No way to deny his paternity of the three boys, however. They were short, had black hair, and were dull-witted just as he was.

A prominent Hapsburg upper lip protruded outward above his mouth, a main mark on his face. The three boys had the lip too. It is a product of family inbreeding. He and his sons reflected a troll-like character, slow and dull. They all settled into their new house as tenant farmers.

They had an immense amount of farm work ahead. It stretched from dawn to sunset every day. Milk cows in the morning and evening. Feed animals twice a day, plant, hoe, harvest. Plough land. Hoe cotton and corn by hand. If the hard labor did not kill a person, the boredom would. Everyone went to church on Sunday- not so much for spiritual direction (none to be found there) - but to break the monotony and boredom of work.

One day in midsummer as all the kids hoed cotton in the lower field, Eli appeared with a bucket of fresh water drawn from the well in one hand and something wrapped in a white cloth in the other. Ottie had not spoken to him since the day she arrived. She let June Sr. deal with Eli. He took the bucket from person to person allowing each to drink from the metal dipper floating on top of the water. He hesitated as he approached Ottie.

He dipped the water himself from the bucket offering the dipper to her in his outstretched hand. She stared intently at the dipper, then back at him. He made a second attempt by gently pushing the dipper close to her mouth. She felt like Judas Iscariot clutching his pouch of thirty pieces of silver as she slowly took the dipper in her hand and lifted it to her lips to drink. Her hand fell limp beside her thigh with the dipper still clutched in it. Eli gently pried it from her fingers. Then he handed her the white cloth. Uncovering it, she found two pieces of cornbread which his wife had intended for him to eat.

As she ate, her mind returned to the Peddler's stump and the unrequited vigil she had kept. "I love this bastard," she mumbled under her breath. "I can't help it." June Sr. watched the scene unfold. Jealousy stirred in him.

Eli met Ottie later in the evening when she drew water from the well. In his conniving way, he told her how much he regretted not coming back to her when the sourwood was in bloom. He was so very sorry. It was Ottie he had wanted to marry when Daisy had died and he had married Lily. His children had pressured him to marry Lily quickly to get a new family started. He really had not loved Lily. The fact that he already had three girls by her belied the fact, for Eli was lying as he always did and always would.

"I want to marry you, Ottie," he wooed her again. "I'm just waiting for Lily to die, she's sick you know. I may divorce her sometime soon. Why should you and I waste any more of our lives apart? We live next door now, so get back together with me again. I'll be at the barn at seven o'clock tonight," he cooed.

When the hour of seven arrived, Ottie rose from her seat at the kitchen table where she was sewing. Laying aside the work, she put on a light sweater and scarf and took the rutted road to the farmhouse.

Lily saw her.

"Working late on the farm tonight?" she asked.

"I'm going to give the cows some fodder," she replied.

"Eli went out a while ago. He'll be out there. No need to be afraid," she answered.

Ottie was more afraid now than at any time in her life. She held a deep mistrust of Eli. He bore a golden tongue, seductive charm, and evil intent. She knew she was sacrificing her life and all in it by going to the barn. For a moment she hesitated, the old wounds of rejection burning in her heart. The pain of the last twenty years made her mind fog. She turned as if to go back home, but a feeling more powerful than hurt consumed her. It was irrational love. She loved Eli from the first meeting at the Peddler's Stump. She missed him and wanted him back again. With resolve, she walked confidently through the barn doors.

She expressed the greatest passion of her life that night with Eli. She was uncontrollable. She hugged and kissed him with passion. Her love grew deeper. She could not save herself. Like an addict she needed a fix and her fix was Eli. When he finished, Eli put on his clothes quickly, exiting the barn without a word to her. His mission for today was accomplished. He satisfied his needs and desires. He did not know how to love. He would never be in love. He would always be in heat. Somewhere deep in her being, poor Ottie knew she would always be a bridesmaid. She sighed deeply, "While I breathe, I hope."

The two hid their relationship as best they could. Since Eli went to work with the state road crew at five a.m., they devised a means to shift their encounters to the morning. Ottie tied a heavy string to her right leg after she went to bed. She draped the long end out the open window so that Eli would pull on it to awaken her. She got up to meet him at the barn.

With the rekindled relationship, Eli felt exonerated. He had one hundred per cent of what he wanted as Ottie fell deeper into his trap. Dull-witted June Sr. had suspicions but could not catch them. Eli's wife Lily didn't care. She was tired of him.

On a hot day in November as the family all picked cotton, Ottie suddenly fell flat on her back in the cotton field, clutching her stomach, moaning in pain. The children carried her under the shade of an oak tree and rubbed her face with cold water. They fanned her. Ottie recovered her composure but then she vomited. June Sr. was at work at the sawmill miles away. Eli was at work with the state highway crew somewhere on the CCC road. Ottie leaned on Gertie's shoulders as she walked her back to the house and her bed. By evening she was up cooking cornbread for supper. She felt much better.

When Eli came home, she pulled him aside, into the apple orchard, her eyes pleading, and told him, "We have a problem. I'm pregnant."

Eli thought to himself a moment, his cold, indifferent eyes cutting across her. Then he said with great hostility, "No, Ottie. You are pregnant. It is your problem. I've got my own damn kids to take care of."

THE SAWMILL

Gentry came with the sawmill gang. He was in his late thirties, thin and muscular with a wiry build. His hair was jet black. His jaw was square with a well-chiseled nose. There was always a hint of a smile around the edges of his well-formed lips. Whether he was married or not, I never knew. I suspected that he was and probably had a child or two. He was leading a white horse when I first saw him walking along the roadway between our farm and Griff's Old House. As the boss of the sawmill crew, he had chosen a location about a quarter of a mile past Griff's Old House where the gang could operate free of wind and weather. Then he and his crew set up living quarters at Grady's Old House about one half mile below our farm. No one had lived in the house for a long time. There were beds as well as a few pots and pans left by the previous tenants. There were ten men in the sawmill gang. They spread their gear and bed rolls on the floor among the three rooms of the old house. It was comfortable enough for their purposes. They washed in a nearby creek.

Every morning Gentry and his crew left the house at seven o'clock and plod the road past the creek, along the edge of our farm, past Griff's Old House to the sawmill. Some of the men led the horses used for logging by their bridles while others rode theirs. Gentry always rode his white horse like a knight of old leading his men into battle. They made this trek twice a day without fail. When they worked, we could hear the hum of the saw as it peeled bark from the logs, sawing them into flat pieces of lumber. The chopping of their axes echoed across the valley. Before long, a large pile of sawdust formed nearby. The dust came along a chain that cut through the logs. It deposited small grains of wood dust until a huge pile formed. Work ceased at five o'clock. Manmade sounds abruptly stopped and the woods returned to silence. The men, smelling of sawdust and pine, gathered their tools and horses, and began the weary journey homeward.

My sister and I built a playhouse on a hill in the woods near the road. We could hear the clip-clop of horse hooves as Gentry and his men slowly approached our playhouse. He stopped his horse to talk to us. One day he took two fifty cent pieces from his pocket and flipped them toward my sister and me. Mine fell into a small bucket of water we used in our playhouse. Being shy, I did not say much to him. I really liked Gentry. He was a kind man. I even fancied him as my father, since my real father never showed up in my life. I wish now that I would have gotten to know him better. When they left us, we watched intently from our perch on the hillside as the group of men turned a curve and disappeared toward Grady's Old House.

Our fortunes changed the day my mother met Gentry. One evening as the sawmill men returned home from work, my mother went to the side of the road and waited. Under her arm she carried a glass jar of moonshine that she had made herself in her own moonshine still up on Devil's Creek Fork. At this time my dad, Eli, was in prison in Chillicothe, Ohio, so my mother mastered the art of making liquor on her own. She was smart. She never got caught. As the sawmill group approached her, she lifted the jar of moonshine into the air. Gentry signaled the men to stop by raising his right hand into the air like a cavalry officer on patrol.

"Thought you might be thirsty," said my mother pushing the open top of her sack cloth dress across her breasts. Gentry stared at her intently.

"Are those your two kids up on the curve?" he asked.

"Two of my eight," she replied. "I have four by my husband and four by Eli."

"Well, which one of them is your man?" he asked, puzzled.

"Both of them are. One is for Sunday and the other is for the rest of the six days of the week."

"Where are your men right now?" he inquired.

"Eli's in the Federal penitentiary," she mumbled barely audibly. "The other son-of-a-bitch is shacked up with Caldonia over on Cane Creek." Ottie was forthright in her answers for she was not a complicated person.

He held up the quart of crystal-clear moonshine Ottie had given him.

"Boys, you want a drink?" Gentry asked them.

"No," protested my mother. "This drink is for you, not them."

Gentry lifted the jar to his mouth and took a long, deep drink. Moisture dripped along the sides of his mouth as he handed the jar back to her.

"Much obliged," he said as he pushed his horse forward.

My mother took a backward step watching intently as he disappeared down the road. The other men eyed her suspiciously longing for a taste of her moonshine. Not to worry. My mother would deliver moonshine and more.

A few days later Ottie gathered up her jar of liquor and a cake of cornbread she had baked earlier and set out down the river road to the camp. It was dusk. Dark shadows of evening were falling across the valley. Farm animals were gathering into their stables for the night. Having finished her daily work, my mother was now intent on some personal recreation. It did not bother her to leave her and Eli's four children alone in the dark. It was assumed my older sister Gertie would take care of us. She slammed the front door shut and we heard her footsteps glide across the porch and disappear in the distance. I overheard my mother telling Aunt Lela years later what happened when she went to visit Gentry.

Gentry sat drying his socks in front of the fireplace when a soft knock struck the outside door. All the men in the room looked toward him with worry in their eyes. Who would be at their door after dark? Was it the owner of the house come to evict them as squatters? Gentry quietly reached for his rifle, holding it down his left side as he moved toward the door.

"Who's there?" he cried out.

"Ottie," he heard the reply.

He opened the door and stared down into my mother's eyes.

"I brought you some moonshine," she whispered to him.

He swung the door open for her to come in as the other men scampered to pick up clothes and trash strewn across the room, hiding them in diverse places pretending that they were adequate housekeepers. She sat down on the edge of a wooden crate, thrusting out her arms as if to warm them by the fire.

"You can all drink if you want," she said to him.

He opened the jar and gulped some of the liquid. Then he passed it to another of the men who took his turn and passed it on. She stared directly into the fire.

The room was filled with tension.

Without any embarrassment, Ottie stood and said,

"My man is in prison these last few years. I have been lonely for a long time. I want you, Gentry."

She walked slowly toward one of the bedroom doors and disappeared into the darkness of the room. Gentry looked around with confusion at the other men. Their eyes passed judgment on the decision he had to make. Each of them knew exactly what he would do in this situation, but since they were not presently included, they intended to make Gentry's decision difficult. It did not matter that all of them had wives at home. The nature of the male of the species is to make sexual conquest when he can. Gentry followed her into the room unbuckling his pants as he walked. The other men sat in silence as they passed the moonshine jar from person to person. His sawmill gang now could hold Gentry hostage. When morning light came, Ottie rose silently, donned her clothing, and disappeared into the mists.

That evening she met the caravan of woodcutters at the same place in the road. This time she handed Gentry a dried apple pie she had baked, averting his look as she stared at the ruts in the road. He acknowledged her with a nod and rode on. Another time she brought him a jar of fox grape jelly from grapes we kids picked up on Oaky Knob.

As days turned into weeks, the sawmill crew stalled in their work. Autumn rains swelled the streams while the logging roads turned to mush. No work was possible and their timetable turned on its ears. They were stuck inside makeshift quarters.

Ottie went to keep them company and do some cooking until the weather turned better. This time the other men were not going to be left out of Gentry's fun. They cut nine long straws and one short one from broom sedge. Whoever drew the short straw got his turn with Ottie. They repeated the ritual until every man had his turn.

"I'm making up for lost time," Ottie smirked rolling her eyes in circles.

She plopped a fresh glob of snuff in her lower lip and trumpeted, "Next short straw!"

Christmas Eve was cold when December finally came. Our little pretended family went to the church play and returned with our expected gifts of a comb, socks, and chocolate covered cherries. We laid them under our tree, a cedar cut from a nearby field. It was a nice tree decorated with red and silver cords, ceramic balls, and tinsel. We had no electricity, so there were no electric Christmas lights. We lived so far back in the hills that Santa always ran out of everything nice when he got to our house. That is why we got a comb, socks, or chocolate covered cherries or nothing at all.

My mother stoked the wood in the fireplace sending sparks flying over the hearth. As the room warmed, she looked at all of us and said, "Go to bed."

Her voice sounded distant, far away, preoccupied. So we went to bed. Lying there not wanting to go to sleep, we heard her open and close the front door. Her footsteps cracked across the frozen dirt in the front yard. A deep silence fell around the house. Ottie was on a Santa errand of her own. She intended for her children to have a bountiful Christmas like everyone else who had both a mommy and daddy to look after them.

Christmas morning dawned clear and cold. I awakened with no excitement in my heart. How can a person be excited over a box of chocolate covered cherries at Christmas? Gertie built a fire in the kitchen stove. She baked brown biscuits for us and smeared them with wild fox grape jelly. Ottie was nowhere to be seen. The two of us moped around the kitchen until Gertie let out a squeal as she ran to the window that faced the front porch. Justine, Callie, and I ran to join her. Through the hoarfrost of the windowpane, I saw piled high on the porch swing boxes of oranges, apples, tangerines, stick candy and other treats we had never had before for Christmas. There was a doll for each of my sisters and a dump truck for me. Was it possible that Santa stopped at our house first, this time, and that some other unlucky kid got the box of chocolate covered cherries?

The day Gentry and his crew went back to work after Christmas, my mother stood at her usual place by the roadside. As the sawmill crew approached, she lifted her head upward with tears flowing from her eyes.

"The Christmas food and toys you left for my children," she stammered losing her voice.

"Shhh," Gentry whispered placing his index finger across his lips. "The children of these mountains and valleys are all our children. We honor all their mothers, too. It is not our place to judge what life has handed anyone. God bless you and your children, Ottie."

These precious, kind words, so rare in Ottie's life and experience, brought a wellspring of tears to her eyes. Her knees weak, she slid gently like a carved, marble Madonna to a seated position on the ground.

Gentry doffed his hat to her respectfully and then rode slowly onward. Each man of the sawmill crew, in turn, saluted her, respectfully. They all understood what she had to do to survive in Ottie's world.

THE REVENUERS

The old jalopy Modal-T bumped and sputtered along the gravel road toward Toney's country store at Bostic. Ottie sat next to Eli on the front seat of the car, her swollen belly protruding uncomfortably toward the dashboard. It was an uncomfortable ride for her for the unleveled highway bumps jarred her seat and belly. Eli was an untrained driver. He never bothered to get a driver's license at any time in his life, but he drove wherever and whenever he wished. He did not have driving skills good enough to make the car go smoothly for her, neither did he care. The fact that she was pregnant with his child did not concern him one bit. In his mind, if a woman got pregnant, it was her fault. The man was just enjoying himself. Besides, he had no intention to care for this out-of-wedlock child. Ottie sat proudly in her seat as if the two of them were married. Life for her was present time. She did not care about the past or future. That is probably why she never learned from her mistakes. It is only the "now time" that mattered. At this present moment Eli belonged to her and they were on a mutual business adventure.

They wanted to buy sugar to make moonshine. Toney's store sold sugar. He would sell them sugar, all they wanted. Stan's Store carried only small amounts at a time in the valley. The amount they wanted to buy would raise suspicion, for everyone there knew the both of them. Toney's store was a large building which was divided by partitions so that feed sacks, sugar, and larger items were separated from groceries. He carried a wide variety of merchandise. Besides, he did not know Ottie and Eli very well. They felt safer buying what they needed from him.

Ottie squeezed out of her seat easing her heavily pregnant belly down toward the ground. She smoothed out the wrinkles in her sackcloth dress as best she could, then she waddled into the store. There were lines and racks of goods, saddles, farming implements, parts for model-t cars, in addition to groceries. Ottie paused for a moment to smell the aroma of cinnamon, cloves, fresh leather, soft drinks, and moon pies that wafted across the air inside the store. She fixed her eyes on the shelves that carried round, chocolate, cream-filled moon pies. It had been a long time since she had eaten a moon pie. But Eli carried the wad of money rolled up in the pocket of his bib overalls. She knew he would not buy her a moon pie. She would think on it.

Eli worked with Toney stacking bags of sugar and cases of mason jars into the back seat of the model-T while Ottie enjoyed the variety of the store. Unknown to her, her neighbor Beulah was also in the store watching her every move from behind one of the partitions. Beulah did not want Ottie to see her. Wherever Ottie moved in the store, Beulah walked parallel to her hidden from her view. Ottie never knew that her nosey neighbor was there.

When Eli finished with the sugar, he came back into the store and called for Ottie to come count out money in payment for their purchases. Eli never learned to count so Ottie saw her chance to get a moon pie. She took the roll of cash from him and began to count out loud. As she counted, she skipped several numbers and said others out of order. She deftly removed a twenty dollar bill from the bottom of the stack for herself. When Eli went to the car, she paused as if in deep thought. She walked to the shelf and picked out, not one moon pie, but two, and an R.C. soft drink. She paid for them from the money just scalped from Eli.

Beulah came out of her hiding place and walked to the door of the store so she could watch Eli and Ottie leave. They headed back east to the valley as Beulah headed west toward Bostic and the sheriff's office in Forest City. She reported to the sheriff that she suspected Eli and Ottie were making illegal moonshine. She told the law about the day she had gone to Devil's Creek Fork and smelled the burning wood and cooking mash. She told them about Ottie's many trips up and down the road on foot and in different cars. She was a class- A snitch.

On April 17th Ottie gave birth to a six pound, two ounce baby girl, her first child with Eli. He barely looked at the baby. She named her Gertie.

The fire roared under the cooker as the mash bubbled inside and steam rose up through the laurels. Ottie placed a coon pecker in the worm so the fresh moonshine would flow properly into the mason jars under the copper spout. Then she capped each quart jar with a metal lid and stacked them into a cardboard box. She had two cases finished, twenty-four quarts in all. Eli gathered large pieces of wood to place under the cooker. It was just a premonition, but Ottie had brought along her trusty shotgun. She laid it within the work area near the still. Each time she brought an extra box of shotgun shells in the event she had to use her gun. Ottie was an expert shot. All was going well. It was noontime.

A sheriff's car pulled into the yard at Beulah's house. Two fat-bellied deputies got out and knocked at the door. They told her they had come in response to her complaint given at the office in Forest City but could not figure out where the liquor makers lived. Could she ride with them and show the way? Beulah responded with glee. The patrol car rumbled over the heavy ruts past the Ida Place, around two switchbacks, in front of the Wright Old House and down to Eli's farmhouse. Lily saw them coming. She sent her son Pet to warn Ottie and Eli. He ran up the Fork, picked up a piece of wood, knocked it against a tree three times. Ottie heard the warning knocks and went to talk to him.

"Revenuers," he shouted at the top of his lungs.

She sprang into action. Grabbing a bucket, she dipped water from the stream and threw it on the fire. It spewed throwing steam high into the air. She carried the two finished cases of moonshine into the laurel and covered them securely with heavy leaves. Grabbing her gun, she ran down the hill where she could see clearly down Devil's Creek Fork. Eli was too far away to hear her warning cries. He lingered at the moonshine still when he returned and did not see her there. He figured she had stepped away for a moment. The two deputies slipped up the path to the Fork trusting their noses and Beulah's vague directions to lead them to the still.

Ottie decided to fight for what was hers. Lawmen or not, they were trespassers. She opened fire with her shotgun above the heads of the deputies. Had she wished, she could have blown off their heads. The pellets struck high in the sourwood trees, knocking light yellow blossoms down on the deputies' heads. They drew their pistols and returned fire in her direction. Ducking behind some large boulders in the creek, Ottie let fly a second barrage. It struck the ground in front of the lawmen pushing up dust on their shoes. She had the advantage of knowing the terrain. The deputies and Beulah would not take away her livelihood. She placed fresh shotgun shells into the chamber of the gun, cocked it shut, and took careful aim. Squeezing her right eye shut, she looked down the gun barrel carefully setting its sight on a handkerchief hanging out of the back pocket of one of the rotund deputies. When she pulled the trigger, the handkerchief exploded in the air like a skeet target. Some of the buckshot lodged in the fat folds of the deputy's back. "I've been shot in the ass," he lamented to his partner who snickered from behind a buckeye tree where he had taken refuge. Like a wild-west outlaw, Ottie ran down the middle of Devil's Creek so she would leave no footprints. They could not track her. Having made her point that she would fight for what was hers, she made her way across the meadow to her house. The deputies never saw her.

Hearing the firing of guns, poor Eli ran the wrong way and landed squarely in the arms of the two deputies. Thinking Eli was the culprit who had just shot him; the rotund deputy dunked him in the cold water of Devil's Creek. They cuffed his arms behind him and led him back toward their patrol car where Beulah sat watching the fireworks with glee.

"If you make any move to escape," the deputy informed Eli, "I'm going to shoot the hair right off your ass."

Eli calmed down.

From her location on the front porch of her house, Ottie saw that they had arrested Eli. She was not going to jail to save him. It was his land she lived on. It was his house she lived in. It was his still and his liquor. The son-of-a-bitch had gotten her pregnant and would not even buy her a moon pie. Nothing tied her to any of this. She decided to let Eli take the rap for making illegal moonshine and for shooting at the deputies.

Then she saw Beulah sitting smugly in the patrol car enjoying their plight. One deputy kept yelling gleefully that they had caught the moonshiner. As they cranked the patrol car and turned it around, Ottie grabbed her shotgun once more and ran into the woods next to the road the deputies had to use to go back to Beulah's house. As the car inched by, she blew out both back tires with two blasts from her gun.

"Damn you, Beulah, you can walk back home," she snarled to herself. They never caught Ottie. But Eli could not get out of this one.

The last Ottie saw of poor Eli the two deputies held him hand-cuffed between the two of them. He was looking back at her, staring blankly, as the deputies and Beulah dragged him toward the main road. Two months later Ottie heard that a jury had found Eli guilty of making moonshine and shooting at a law enforcement officer. A judge had sentenced him to five years hard labor at a federal penitentiary in Chillicothe, Ohio.

"Good," Ottie thought. "You can wait for me to come see you in prison like I waited for you at the Peddler's Stump!"

SOWING BAD SEED

B reathing deeply from the exertion of working in the early spring garden, Ottie set her hoe against the kitchen door. She took off her straw hat and hung it on a wooden peg beside the door. Strands of wispy hair fell down the sides of her face blowing listlessly in the breeze. All spring long her efforts at growing beets had failed. The seeds did not germinate. She replanted them. She soaked the seeds overnight in warm water in order to break the hard coverings on the outside, to no avail. The seeds would not come up. This very morning she labored again in the narrow rows. There would be no beets this year.

Ottie stared at the brown paper bag she held in her left hand. Some few beet seeds remained there.

"Bad seeds," she murmured throwing the near empty bag on the ground. "You can't make good seeds out of bad ones."

At that moment our dog Bruno came howling around the side of the house. Close on its heels came June Jr., beating the mutt across the head and shoulders with a very large stick. The poor dog barked and screamed in pain all the while trying to escape the blows by squeezing behind some low lying bushes. June Jr. was relentless in his beating. When his fit of violence abated, he let the poor dog limp away from him licking its wounds.

Ottie and June Jr. stood staring at each other. She made no attempt to stop his assault on the poor animal nor did she try to discover the why of his actions. They stood in silence sizing each other up. Ottie had never bonded with him when he was a baby. She rarely hugged or cuddled him. He came along at a time in her life when she could not care for another child. She cared very little for his father June Sr. June Jr. never felt that he was a member of the family, so at the age of nine, he set himself free. He quit school in the third grade. Wild and free, he rambled through field and forest, mountain and stream learning to survive on his own and being a general nuisance to all he encountered. He became like the wild animals. Whatever he found was his. He took whatever he wanted unless someone stronger than he came along. June Jr. seemed to have no soul. The fires of love and caring had passed him by long ago resulting in a cold and ruthless being. He lifted his gaze from Ottie and then broke the dog stick across his knee, mumbling curses defiantly as he disappeared around the corner of the house. Ottie simply shrugged her shoulders and entered through the screen door into the kitchen.

June Jr. sulked as he sauntered up the road to Griff's Old House. Today was one of the rare times that someone actually lived in the house. Dahlaree and her mother had moved in a month earlier. They said they were Cherokee Indians. I believed them because they had very black hair and dark skin. She and her mother made mud pigs from clay that they dug out of the creek. I thought Indians would probably do something like that.

On this day she and her mother were not at home. Ever the opportunist, June Jr. went to the back of the kitchen window, raised it, and climbed inside. He found some peanut butter and crackers which he promptly ate. He went from room to room looking for something to steal but he found nothing of value to satisfy his third grade mind. He shuffled out the front door without closing it behind him. He turned left as if he were going up Devil's Creek Fork. Thinking better of it, he crossed the creek to the barn shed on the other side. Just inside the barn, he saw a flock of chickens pinned up. These were Dahlaree's prized fowl, her pride and joy. He reached inside and grabbed one of the roosters. He swung the fowl round and round by the neck until it broke. Blood and feathers flew all over the barnyard. June Jr. held his prize tightly in his hand as he walked across the horse pasture with the dead rooster dangling from his side.

He took the chicken to Ottie who was busy baking biscuits in the wood stove in her kitchen. He plopped the rooster on the table saying not a word. She looked first at him, then at the rooster. Well, it meant food for her table.

Seeking no explanation, she merely uttered "I'll boil some water."

Steam rose from the gurgling hot iron pot and fogged the kitchen windows. Ottie plopped the chicken into the water, swirling it around several times, then she pulled it out and began plucking feathers. Wet feathers stuck to her hands and some even got on her face. She looked tarred and feathered. As she busied herself plucking the bird, there came a sudden, forceful knock on the kitchen door. Ottie and June Jr. looked at each other attempting to ascertain who might be on the other side. Swiftly my mother began an effort to hide the stolen chicken. But there were pots and feathers all over the place. June Jr. opened the door. There stood Dahlaree and her mother with puzzled looks on their faces. Having returned home, they had discovered that someone had been in their house. They had gone immediately to the barn to check on their prized chickens. They had followed the blood and feathers across the horse pasture directly to our kitchen door. Did we know anything about their chickens?

"Well, I declare," said my mother wiping wet chicken feathers off her hands and face. "I can't imagine who would bother your rooster."

"Who said it was a rooster," Dahlaree said accusingly.

"That's usually what people kill and eat," Ottie reasoned sheepishly.

The aroma of hot steam with boiling chicken feathers wafted across the room. The odor was unmistakable. It was pungent. It was useless to try to hide the smell of chicken from those who claimed to be First Nation people. It would have been easier to slip dawn by the dead rooster than to fool Dahlaree and her mother.

"Are you fixing chicken for supper?" Dahlaree's mother asked her.

"No, no," replied my mother. "You smell dumplings that Griff"s wife Lela brought us yesterday. I'm rewarming them for our supper."

Dahlaree and her mother shook their heads mumbling something about people being "bad seed." They remained unconvinced. As they went back up the road to their house, they stole an axe and hoe from our blacksmith shop. That would be about equal to their loss. They never spoke to us again.

In his corner chair in the kitchen, June Jr. saw the humor in the situation. He howled with laughter, for he intended to go back and steal the rest of her chickens. When my sisters asked where we got the chicken and dumplings that they ate for supper, my mother said that Lela had brought them for us. June Jr. simply grinned and asked for a second helping.

One day I was at school in Miss Lucy's classroom reading a story when the classroom door burst open. In came Mr. Elam, the school truant officer, with June Jr. in tow, his big hand around the nape of June Jr.'s neck.

"Here's your truant. You can't quit school in the third grade, sonny," roared Mr. Elam. "We have laws in this state." He shoved

June Jr. into the nearest chair then left the room, his face flushed red.

My face flushed red in embarrassment at my brother. I hid my face deeper in my book hoping no one was looking at me.

Miss Lucy settled June Jr. into a book. Everyone got back to work. Within minutes June Jr. began making farting sounds through his pursed lips. We children howled with laughter. Chaos reigned. Miss Lucy got her paddle from the closet and proceeded to administer two enormous whacks to June Jr.'s rear end. The sound echoed down the hallway accompanied by June Jr.'s yelling.

"You've learned how to make those farting sounds with your lips, Mister, now let's see what you can do with the real thing." Miss Lucy was really angry. She whacked June Jr. again with her doomsday paddle right across the gluteal cleft. And sure enough, he popped a real one.

That settled the classroom for a while. Trying to push Miss Lucy's limits, June Jr. attached a stretched bobby pin to his desk seat. It produced a high pitched twanging when he flipped his finger across the edge. After the third twang, Miss Lucy grabbed him by his shoulders and pushed him into the hallway up to Mr. Rawlin's classroom. Good riddance to him. Mr. Rawlins punished him by leaving him in the classroom while all of us went outside to have lunch and enjoy some play time.

Who would leave June Jr. alone in a classroom unsupervised? Who would leave June Jr. alone anywhere? While the children yelled and played outside, he prowled through Mr. Rawlin's classroom looking for some booty. Finding nothing of interest there, he went to Miss Lucy's classroom. He searched the two big closets first. Nothing. He went to her big desk and pulled open each drawer. Bingo. He found her large handbag with a wallet containing fifty dollars in various denominations of bills. He took the money and wallet and went back to the other room.

Outside the windows of Mr. Rawlin's room there stood a platform which supported a large, heavy, metal bell that he rang to regulate the school schedule. June Jr. reached through the window and rang the bell several times. The clang-clang went out across the playground telling all children to come back into the building. A massive group of children descended on the front door at the same time creating disorder and confusion. June Jr. slipped out of the building to the broom sedge field to a copse of pine trees where he had hidden the money. He slipped silently to the girls' outhouse where he tossed the wallet down the hole on top of a pile of manure. He moved deftly back into the mass of kids and returned to his seat unnoticed. He sat there with a smug look on his face.

Miss Lucy and Mr. Rawlins whispered animatedly in the hallway. There was anger in Miss Lucy's eyes. She gesticulated with her hands as if she were expounding on something very important. Mr. Rawlins announced for all children to assemble in the auditorium.

"Someone has stolen Miss Lucy's wallet containing fifty dollars in cash. The guilty person must confess or tell us if you know who did it."

Several students fingered June Jr. as the culprit even though they had no evidence. June Jr. said that Harold Cody, the new kid from Florida, took the money. He saw him do it. Mr. Rawlins strip searched June Jr. in the bookroom but found nothing. They ordered everyone outside to search the premises. Kids searched the playground, the building, and the broom sedge field. They found nothing. Two girls ran back from the outhouse yelling that the wallet was in there. Mr. Rawlins fished it out with a pole and washed it off in a bucket of water. Shoving the wet wallet under June Jr.'s nose, he accused him of stealing the money. June Jr. just smirked and said, "That thing smells like shit. Get it out from under my nose." Mr. Rawlins sent the delinquent home immediately.

June Jr. did not go home. He prowled around the valley to find something else to steal.

Next Saturday morning June Jr. woke up early, got dressed, and set out down the road toward the schoolhouse. The incident of the stolen wallet was past but not forgotten. He made his way carefully so nosy neighbors' eyes could not see him. He cut through the pines at the school, crossed the broom sedge field, and went directly to a large pine tree standing alone in the field. Digging with his bare hands, he uncovered a wad of paper money which he quickly stuck in the bib of his overalls. He emerged from the woods taking the road toward Bostic.

June Jr. intended to buy a bicycle. Upon arriving in Bostic, he changed his mind. He would steal a bicycle and keep the money to spend at a later date. It did not take him long to find a bicycle lying in front of a house. June Jr. grabbed it and rode eastward out of town. He pedaled furiously to put distance between him and the owner.

When Ottie saw his new bike, she merely uttered "nice bike."

In the summer of 1952, June Jr. turned sixteen. Nothing in his life changed. He added one more year to his life. He made a decision, however, that changed the lives of the whole family profoundly. He stole a car. He had not intended to steal a car. The car presented itself in his world. He was opportunistic. Like the animals of the wild, he took whatever he wanted from the weak and weak of mind. The owner left his car parked outside, keys in the ignition and title in the glove compartment. He obviously had not heard of June Jr. Though he could not really drive, June Jr. cranked the car and headed it for the open road. He cared not a whit about being able to drive properly. He instinctively steered the vehicle toward home. He veered into a side ditch when another car approached. He sped up the dirt highway leaving a trail of dust behind him.

Beulah heard the roar of a car engine as it approached her house. A car in her part of the valley was a rarity so she ran from her house to a hillock for a good view of it. Car watching was a popular pastime in this isolated part of the valley. Beulah squeezed her eyes into tiny slits, pursing her lips as she recognized June Jr. in the car that sped by. It was not normal in her world that he have a car much less be driving one. He couldn't drive. She sat down to write out a letter of all that she had seen to the county sheriff, implying that June Jr. was guilty of something. She put the letter in the mail the next day.

In the meantime, June Jr. drove the car up the road toward our house. He found a thick copse of trees letting the '52 ford coast into it. He broke pieces of thick pine boughs to cover his prize. Ottie sauntered over to the hiding spot to take a look at his new acquisition. She touched the car with her hand leaving a slight print on the metal.

"You're going to prison for sure this time," she spoke out loud.

He paid no attention to what she had to say. He cleaned the steering wheel with a wet cloth.

Ottie walked away toward home. She was troubled. She found a large boulder where she sat in deep thought. Night fell. She rose from her pensive state and went to talk to Gentry, then returned home around midnight, promptly going to bed.

Early next morning, I heard the droning of a truck engine as it slowly wound toward our farm. My mother roused us all out of bed yelling for us to tear down the beds and pack whatever we could into the truck. Bring clothes, bedding, pots and pans, whatever we will need to survive. Leave behind the farm animals, the tools, and the wagon. We have to get out of here right now.

We complied with her orders as best we could. The truck pulled away, packed to the top of its sideboards with our meager belongings. We children walked barefoot to the main road. It was Feb. 2nd, 1953. It was cold. My family looked like Oakies from the dust bowl heading to California. As we were crossing the county line, the sheriff arrived with the owner of the stolen car to search our farm and arrest June Jr.

My family disappeared into a new place to start a new life. We were strangers to all we met. We created new identities for ourselves. I can now see how my life changed for the better because June Jr. stole the car. I had a new school, new friends, and new life. Well, June Jr. sold the car to an unscrupulous dealer and promptly bought a new one.

Late one night June Jr. sped down the road in his new car. He missed a curve at the main bridge over Silver Creek because he had been drinking. The car smashed the lower section, taking out all of the wooden planks on the south side. It landed in the dark water twenty feet below. The horrible crash awakened Ottie from a deep sleep. She knew it was him. He had already tried her patience beyond the breaking point. She had no more caring to give to this evil little delinquent. Her heart had turned to stone. She uttered, "He's hopeless." Then she pulled the covers over her head in the warm bed and went back to sleep. June Jr. lay drowning in the murky water of the creek.

THE EXONERATION OF
HAROLD CODY

Grandma Cody lay on her sickbed, her emaciated body wrapped in white sheets. She struggled to breathe, sucking air deeply into her lungs with a rasp. Medicine bottles lay around, some empty, some filled, a testament to her struggle to get well. Sickness was melting her body away, squeezing the life out of her. The time to die had come and she was determined to do it with dignity. No longer able to care for herself, she sent for her son, Roy Cody, to come from Florida back home to the valley to see her through her transition. He came with grateful heart to return the love she had given him all his life. She got an extra gift in the form of her grandson, Harold Cody, who came with Roy and would live at her house. Roy had grown up in the valley but it was a new place to his son, Harold, who visited infrequently. What a new adventure it was for him.

Other children misunderstood Harold's kind nature for he was not like them. They made him an object of their bullying, their jokes and sometimes their physical violence. He was more sophis-ticated than they. He carried deep scars on his face from unfortu-nate encounters with pugilistic kids in Florida. At times they beat him across his back with a baseball bat, accusing him of being a "queer," a real sissy. Once they played a game called "army" where the leader forced him to disrobe and march naked in front of the other children. They stole his books, his hat, and his watch. But they could not steal his spirit or his goodness. In coming to the valley with his father, he had a new beginning or so he thought.

Bullies are everywhere in the world. Nationality does not matter. Family background does not matter. Religion does not matter. Such individuals are weak inside. They think they make themselves look strong by demeaning others whom they perceive as weaker. They are pathetic representatives of the human species. The valley had its share of them.

Harold was too old for Miss Lucy's class, thus Mr. Cody enrolled him with Mr. Rawlins in the sixth grade. Children do not like new kids coming into their world as evidenced with their reaction to Phyllis and her family. Their resentment grew quickly toward Cody because he was more sophisticated. Resentment turned into physical attacks. Harold took refuge with Phyllis and me who were already outcasts. Other outcasts and exiles in the school joined our group. There is safety in numbers. Soon we presented a formi-dable presence. There was strength our determination not to be mistreated. We decided one day to strike back against our tormen-tors, not individually, but as a group. We chose Harold as leader of our group. It was a life-altering day when he met June Jr.

Mr. Rawlins wanted to expel June Jr. from school but he couldn't. June Jr. swore that he had quit school in the third grade anyway, but the authorities would not allow it. So he sat in the classroom like many children, bored, angry, unable to do the class work, a genetic gift from his troll father, June Sr. He was a genuine juvenile delinquent. He relished creating problems, rebelling, and doing harm to others. He pounced on the opportunity to get the new kid. At recess he went right to work.

June Jr. went straight to Harold telling him,

"I am king here. I run things. You do what I tell you to do. Now, give me a nickel."

Harold told him he did not have a nickel and if he had one, he wouldn't give it to a moronic hillbilly. June Jr. clenched his fists and struck Harold a hard blow across the right eye. Harold crumpled upon the floor as June Jr. gave him a kick in the stomach. Phyllis, Rex, Percy, Dogtooth, and Pansy, members of our outcasts ran to him lifting his aching body into a chair. They soothed his wounds. Rex and Percy began a chant of, "Revenge, revenge, revenge." Little Eva reminded them that the Bible taught, "Revenge is mine saith the Lord, I will repay." When? Where? How? In their hurt, the two boys told Little Eva to shove her Bible up her ass. If you want to assist, help us beat up June Jr.

Harold came to school the following day wearing a black eye as if it were a trophy. It was the opening salvo in a child feud that would last the rest of the school year and into the summer. At recess we outcasts plotted retaliation against June Jr. During lunch, we set the plan in motion. Phyllis, Percy, Dogtooth, Pansy, Rex, Harold and I went to the broom sedge field looking for June Jr. who was playing with his cronies.

"June Jr., you are a prick," Phyllis yelled into the broom sedge. "We intend to yank your kinky hair out by their roots."

"You won't live to tell about it," June Jr. snorted back.

"Come on out, I'm a girl. You are too much of a pussy to whip a girl," she retorted.

At that moment kids from all over the yard converged to watch the impending conflict. June Jr. had to save face as all bullies do in front of their cronies. He went for Phyllis with fists clenched, swinging wildly at her face. She stepped out of the way of the first blow. At that time all nine of the outcasts grabbed June Jr. holding his hands behind his back. Phyllis proceeded to beat his face with her fists, aiming especially for his eyes where he had pummeled Harold. June Jr. slumped to the ground, out cold. Leaving him dizzy and stunned, Harold flipped a nickel on to his heaving chest with his thumb and index finger.

"Here's a nickel for the king who is now deposed from his throne," he mocked. When June Jr. came back to class, his eye was already swollen and turning black.

June Jr. and his trolls struck back. At recess, Phyllis went to use the outhouse. As she climbed the sixteen steps leading to the upper level of the school, June Jr. dumped a small pail of molasses down on her head. The sweet, viscous liquid soaked into her hair and scalp clinging like glue. We poured water on her hair trying to dilute the molasses, but to no avail. Our gang wiped her head with towels, but the molasses stuck. Pansy got a pair of scissors and started whacking off her hair. She did not stop until Phyllis' head was bald. She tied a head scarf around her head. It took several weeks for the hair to grow back.

June Jr. pranced around the school yard mocking her with, "Who got snatched bald? The bitch, the bitch, the bitch."

Then someone stole Miss Lucy's purse. June Jr. rang the bell early when Mr. Rawlins mistakenly left him in the classroom as punishment. All students came back early from lunch because of him. June Jr. made up a blatant lie that he had seen Harold Cody come into the building and take the purse. His criminal buddies substantiated his claim. The truant officer took Harold to the sheriff in Forest City where he spent a month incarcerated in juvenile jail. Grandma Cody died while he was in jail. He did not get to say goodbye. Harold returned to school tainted; he was a thief. His hatred of June Jr. grew astronomically. He intended to kill the little troglodyte if he got a chance.

In late April, the school became a beehive of activity as students prepared for the May Day picnic at Lake McCall. This annual outing signaled the end of the school year, a reward to all students. Two orange school buses carried kids the two miles to the lake. Everyone poured off the buses running to enjoy the playground, the diving boards, the hiking trails, and the lake.

Harold was an expert swimmer. He had belonged to a swim club in Florida where he had developed skills swimming in the waves of the Atlantic. The placid nature of the lake presented no challenge for him. It was like his bathtub. He dove into the cool water, swam the length of the lake, rolled over on his back and swam back using a back stroke.

As he swam, he saw June Jr. and two of his bully friends jumping up and down on the highest diving board, a place they had no reason to be. None of them could even dive or swim. Losing his balance, June Jr. fell sixteen feet into the water. The impact knocked him unconscious. He could not swim a lick. The weight of his clothes dragged him under the water, leaving concentric circles on the top. Giant bubbles flowed to the top of the water where he had gone under. June Jr. was drowning. Kids screamed from the banks of the lake for somebody to do something. Miss Lucy and Mr. Rawlins ran to the edge of the water with long poles in a feeble attempt to save him. The bullied outcasts stood on the shore of the lake staring coldly at the unfolding drama hoping the little bastard would drown.

June Jr.'s life finally caught up with him. In the midst of the fear and horror, all the students spotted a lone figure swimming with powerful strokes and great speed across the lake toward the bubbles and concentric circles marking the spot of the drowning. It was Harold. He dove downward, his feet and ankles disappearing under the murky water. In an instant he reemerged holding June Jr. under his left arm. He flipped June Jr.'s body on his back placing his arm around his neck. With powerful kicks, he swam June Jr. to safety on the shore. Plopping him face down on the sandy shore, Harold pushed both hands on his lungs expelling water from his mouth onto the ground. June Jr. coughed, snorted and finally groaned, pulling air into his lungs. His bully friends stared in amazement.

Adults and children alike felt a great sense of shame about the way they had treated this Florida kid since his arrival. Miss Lucy lowered her head knowing he had not taken her money. Yet, he had spent a month in jail and endured the reputation of a thief. Phyllis came up to hug him. The other outcasts carried him on their shoulders to the bus where they dried him off with a towel, each person caressing his head.

Some days later, Mr. Rawlins's students were working quietly on math. A deep silence reigned as everyone worked in deep concentration. June Jr. was restless. He fidgeted and squirmed in his seat making those around him quite uncomfortable. Breaking the silence, he spoke coldly,

"He didn't do it."

All work stopped. Pencils stopped in midair.

Again the voice said, "He didn't do it. I did. I stole Miss Lucy's purse."

Mr. Rawlins spoke up, "What did you just say, June Jr.?"

"I said I lied. I stole the purse. Harold is innocent."

Mr. Rawlins immediately sent for the sheriff who arrested June Jr. The school expelled him permanently.

Toward the end of May, Mr. Rawlins called the entire school to assemble in the auditorium. The time had come to exonerate Harold Cody. The sheriff came from Forest City and presented Harold with a paper that stated he was innocent of the theft. A Forest City judge expunged his record. As an apology, the sheriff raised money to buy Harold a brand new bicycle. He presented it to him to thunderous applause from the student body.

In his mind Harold was thinking, "This is all fine and dandy, but where do I go to get back my dignity. And if by chance I can retrieve it, do I parade it around the valley on the back of this brand new bicycle? Can they exhume my grandmother's body so I can tell her goodbye?"

Now that Grandma Cody was dead, Harold's father sold her house and farm. He informed his son Harold that they were returning to live in Florida. Phyllis and his friends came to say goodbye to him. He gave her the bicycle because he wanted no reminder of his unfortunate experience here.

"I'm sorry they tromped all over you and stripped away your dignity," said Phyllis. "It's hard to get that back."

"You can't get it back," Harold mumbled through clenched teeth.

Harold leaned over and kissed her on the cheek. He hugged all the outcasts.

Then he proudly announced to them, "I lost no dignity in this place. Anything that I know of dignity, love, and acceptance, I learned from all of you. You are the love and beauty and hope of this troubled valley."

JUST BEYOND THE COUNTY LINE

M y mother rushed us to load the truck with our meager belongings that Saturday morning on February 2, 1952, when
we hurried to escape the sheriff when June Jr. stole the car and we
had to flee to safety. June Jr. drove the car ahead of the loaded
truck up the curving hills above Lake McCall. Our stove pipe,
which was tied across the roof of his car, broke loose and fell into
the middle of the road forming a barrier that blocked our forward
progress. Curtis and Willard jumped from the front seat of the car
on to the gravel road to retrieve the stovepipe. It took them several
minutes to tie it back across the roof. They ran the rope through
the open windows and tied it securely to the front seat of the car.
We were all in a state of panic.

My three sisters and I rode on the back of the loaded moving
truck. Since we stood on pieces of furniture, we had an elevated
view of the roadway looking forward and backward. The driver of

the truck could not see behind him because the pieces of furniture blocked his view. The pipe secured once again, June Jr. rushed the stolen car forward toward the waterspout that Eli and his crew had built on Bolding's Gap long ago. Both vehicles stopped and the group all piled out for some fresh water and a short rest.

One quarter mile ahead of us there stood a sign erected by the North Carolina Department of Transportation which read, "You are leaving Rutherford County. Welcome to Burke County." On the other side of the road stood a sign reading, "Welcome to McDowell County." Three counties came together in this unusual spot in the road. My older brother Curtis had pointed this spot out to me long ago each time we passed it on our way to ride the Greyhound bus to Forest City. A person could stand with one foot in Burke County and the other foot in Rutherford County or one could stretch his body out on the ground and be in three counties simultaneously.

Our group spread out, some got water, and some of us went to relieve ourselves in the woods. Curtis walked a long way down the road back toward Lake McCall from where we had come. All at once Curtis began to wave his hands and yell. At first no one could understand what he was saying. Then we saw the sheriff's car with its red lights and siren blaring bearing down on our little group. Curtis slowed them down by rolling a fallen log into the path of the onrushing patrol car. There was no time for everyone to get back into the vehicles. June Jr. jumped into the stolen car and sped toward the county line. The loaded moving truck filled with our possessions followed close behind him. Ottie yelled for us all to get out of Rutherford County. Kids scattered to the wind trying to outrun the sheriff and his deputies.

The sheriff stopped his car at the Rutherford County line and he and the deputies pursued us on foot. Curtis and Willard, along with June Jr. and the moving truck made it safely into Burke County. My sisters and I ran up the bank into the thick woods making our way into McDowell County. The sheriff and his crew stood in Rutherford County staring at us with fire in their eyes.

Being fat and slow, Ottie got left behind in the furor of the chase. She crawled down out of the thick bushes directly in front of the sheriff and his deputies. Unfortunately she was still in Rutherford County with them. Gertie reached across the Rutherford County line and pulled Ottie's arms and one leg into Burke County where we were now standing. She straddled the line now, caught between two groups that would not let go. She yelled that her arms hurt but no one yielded. Willard rolled out of Burke County into Rutherford County and shoved Ottie into McDowell County. In the final melee, June Jr. cranked the stolen car and drove deeper into Burke County, disappearing down a curve in the road. The sheriff informed Ottie that he had reciprocity with Burke County. Hearing that, all of us jumped across the line into McDowell County. The sheriff had no jurisdiction in this county. He could neither arrest nor detain us.

"Where are you moving to, Ottie?" he shouted.

"To Hell and back," she yelled back.

"We have an arrest warrant here for June Jr. for theft of that car," he said.

"Shove it up your ass," Ottie retorted. "I know your butt is big enough to hold the warrant for I've seen it often enough naked. You want me to tell your wife about our roll in the hay?" she taunted him.

The sheriff quickly reconsidered, "We'll send the warrant to Burke County and they will arrest him there," he said.

"Can you prove that car is stolen and doesn't belong to June Jr.?"

"This man here in the patrol car with us is the owner and he says it is stolen," the sheriff told her.

"Does he have the registration and title to the car in his possession," Ottie challenged the sheriff.

"Well, no, they are in the car," the sheriff responded.

"You have no proof, then," Ottie finalized.

Enough said. Our group climbed on the truck and sped toward highway 64. The sheriff did not follow us into Burke County. He did, however, ponder the words Ottie had said about seeing his ass. Vaingloriously, he looked at his butt in the outside car window to ascertain if it were actually fat.

Meanwhile, June Jr. turned on to highway 64 but did not stay there. He took the first state road on his left in order to ditch any police who might be following on his tail. He wound through gravel roads passing ploughed fields already turned for spring planting. On the hillsides there stood large farmhouses with dog-trots through the middle. Most were in the shape of a T with rock chimneys standing on all three sections. He continued to turn left on unfamiliar roads knowing that he would eventually come to a familiar road.

The little group of fugitives crossed Silver Creek three times and saw different signs pointing the direction to Glen Alpine. June Jr. was smart enough not to take this stolen car to the house where we were moving. Instead, he went to Morganton to talk with an unscrupulous car dealer named Pipes, who made deals with everyone. He forged titles, registrations, and signatures. He paid off the police so they rarely bothered him. Just during election years, politicians had the law hassle Mr. Pipes just to please the religious voters. The police loved their graft, so they would not bring Mr. Pipes down. He took June Jr.'s car promising him a new one. He erased the serial number on June Jr.'s stolen car and replaced it with one stolen from another vehicle. When the Burke County sheriff finally caught up with June Jr., there was nothing they could do to him. He owned a new car with all papers in order. He was not driving nor did he own the car described in the Rutherford County warrant. "We'll keep an eye on you anyway," the Burke County sheriff told him. "Rat's ass," June Jr. shot back. He didn't care. As the Burke County sheriff drove off, June Jr. held up one of the hubcaps of his patrol car. He had stolen it right under the sheriff's nose. June Jr. had been driving this new car when he wrecked on the Silver Creek Bridge nearly killing himself.

June Jr. was safe, but those of us on the moving truck were lost. Only Curtis knew the directions to our new house, but he was riding with June Jr. In an effort to find our way, we stopped at several farmhouses inquiring if they knew of any farmhouses for rent. "Damn hillbillies," the people inside murmured as they slammed the door in our faces. "We don't want any poor white trash around here." June Jr. borrowed a truck from Mr. Pipes and came back in search of us. We connected a bit west of Glen Alpine. I was excited as the truck pulled up in front of our new house because it had an upstairs section. Built in 1903, the house had outlived its usefulness and barely managed to stand on its well-used foundation. Ottie did not care. We were so tired that we were willing to sleep in a teepee. I ran up and down the steps a few times until Ottie ordered me to help unload the truck. Unknown to us, strange people, our new neighbors, lurked unseen among the huge oak trees on a small hill above our house. Several pairs of eyes mentally listed what property we owned. The new location was about to introduce the despised Piggott family to Ottie and her band of gypsy moonshiners.

IF THE SHOE FITS, STEAL IT

June Jr. decided he needed a new pair of shoes. It was not in his nature to pay for a pair of shoes because he had no money. He survived by his wits and by his wits he would get new shoes. The shoes he now wore were threadbare with holes underneath that allowed the bottoms of his feet to make contact with grass, asphalt, or just plain dirt. Ottie allowed each of her children one pair of shoes per year. She paid for them out of the money from the sale of the cotton crop. If a shoe tore up before November, one had to tough it out until the cotton crop came in. If shoes had holes, one's feet got wet. If the laces wore out or broke, one made some out of strips of cloth. If the tongue broke off, one sewed a piece of leather in its place. The ruts and mud holes in the roads were rough on a pair of shoes so her children often carried their shoes in their hands until they walked past the mud and dirt. Then they washed their feet in a branch of water and put their shoes back on. Walking in red clay aged shoes more than anything.

Curtis, Willard, June Jr. and Bud headed for town and the nearest shoe store. An elderly Jewish family named Geldfarb owned the only shoe store in our small town near where we had relocated. The Geldfarbs were an institution in the area for they had sold shoes there for fifty years to several generations of families. They had come south from New York during the early years of the Great Depression because they had lost their fortune when the stock market had crashed in 1929. Mr. Geldfarb had rented a small, narrow building and stocked it with twenty pairs of shoes. He had called his business The Eagle Shoe Store. The Geldfarbs had suffered from hunger and discomfort in their early years. It had not been their real intention to settle here, but their money had run out and they could get no closer to Florida which had been their original destination.

Their building was only thirty feet wide but it extended back for almost a city block. Mrs. Geldfarb had set up living quarters in the far back part of the store. They had strung bed sheets as dividers across the interior to form a semblance of rooms and privacy. They had a bed, a table, two chairs, a mirror, and hooks on which to hang their clothes. They built the original public restroom into a comfortable bathroom where they could bathe and clean up. Mrs. Geldfarb washed their clothes by hand in the bathtub. They cooked on a double-burner hotplate that plugged into an electric socket in the wall. The whole building smelled of cooking odors, cabbage, matzo balls, latkes, and garlic-imported dishes from the North.

They allowed no one into their private quarters because it was a question of pride. From wealth in a Northern city, they had come to hard times among the locals in a southern town. They opened their store, The Eagle Shoe Store, at nine o'clock and sat patiently for customers like spiders who spin their webs and lie in wait for their prey. It was a long-held belief among their people that a merchant must sell something to the first customer or he would have bad luck all day.

No one came to buy shoes, but that fact did not deter the Geldfarbs from their mission to succeed with their store. When the money ran completely out, Mr. Geldfarb went to the local soup kitchen and brought back two bowls of soup and two chunks of bread. His wife heated the soup on the hotplate and poured it into her two china bowls with red roses painted on them. They were suffering, but they would conduct themselves as civilized human beings.

Mr. Geldfarb took a position washing dishes in the diner next to his store. Mrs. Geldfarb took care of the store from nine to five o'clock each day. There were three things wrong with their situation which they failed to grasp immediately. They were Jewish. They came from New York. They talked funny. No one cared what a Jew was. Their funny accents in English formed from a mixture of Yiddish and New York brogue fell harshly on Southern ears. Their negative attitude toward the people of the town did not bring buyers into their store.

The town was not impoverished. People were clannish and very slow to accept outsiders or people who looked and acted differently from them. On a cold winter day in January, their lives changed when they met Mrs. Pearl Haverstick.

Mrs. Haverstick had considerable wealth which her husband had left her when he died. She was not ostentatious with her money, but she was generous. A warm, kind heart beat beneath the mink furs wrapped around her shoulders. During her thirty-five years of living in down south, she never revealed to anyone that her background was Jewish. She wanted no more suffering for herself or her people. She learned to speak with a Southern accent that showed no trace of outside influence in her speech. She acted more redneck than the local yokels. Everyone in town loved and respected her because she chose to be one of them.

On this cold January day, Mrs. Haverstick sat in Roden's café, drinking hot coffee and eating a sweet roll. Everyone entering and leaving the cafe greeted her, wishing her well. Steam from her coffee cup fogged the window where she sat. With a napkin, she wiped away the fog so she could watch people on the street go about their business. From the soup kitchen there emerged the figure of Mr. Geldfarb with two steaming bowls of soup and bread in his hands. He waited for the street to clear of traffic and he shuffled across it making sure not to spill the precious soup. Something familiar about him struck Mrs. Haverstick. His walk, his looks, his manners took her memory back to her childhood.

"Jude." She did not realize that her lips spoke the word out loud. She quickly rose from her table spilling coffee from her cup. "Mr. Roder, I'll be back to finish my coffee," she yelled to the cafe owner. She stepped outside and turned left down the street. She met Mr. Geldfarb as he stepped on the curb of the street. Without hesitation she addressed him in German, "Bist du Jude?"

"Jude bin ich," he responded with tears forming in his eyes. He had not spoken German in a very long time. "Meine Frau sitzt im Shuhgeschaft und wartet auf Suppe. Wir haben Hunger, einen Barenhunger."

He told her his wife was waiting in the shoe store and they were very hungry.

Mrs. Haverstick peeped in the door and saw a frail, graying, sick woman sitting on a stool at an open, empty cash register. She wore a thick, hand-knitted shawl over her shoulders to keep warm. Her husband placed the soup and bread in the bowl in front of her. She ate hastily as hungry people do.

Mrs. Haverstick saw only a few pairs of shoes offered for sale in their store. "I want to buy all these pairs of shoes," she blurted out.

Mrs. Geldfarb held her soup spoon suspended between bowl and lip as she stared at her husband, then at Mrs. Haverstick.

"How much for all of them?" asked Mrs. Haverstick.

Mr. Geldfarb was speechless. Mrs. Haverstick stepped inside the store to look at the price marked on one of the shoe boxes. The sticker showed eight dollars per pair. There were twenty pairs of shoes in all. That would be one hundred sixty dollars for all of them. She opened her purse and counted out one hundred dollar bills and three twenties and laid them in the empty cash drawer. "I'll send someone to pick up the shoes," she said departing as quickly as she had come.

Mr. and Mrs. Geldfarb hugged each other and wept at their good fortune. "She asked me in German if I were Jewish," he excitedly told his wife. "Yes, I am, I told her. Who is she? She gave us no name. Bless her and blessed be this day."

Mrs. Haverstick packed up the shoes and placed them in her basement. She got in touch with a shoe company in Charlotte where she ordered five hundred pairs of shoes to stock Mr. Geldfarb's store. She put the twenty pairs of shoes stored in her basement back in the stock so they could sell them again. Mrs. Haverstick brought her neighbors and friends to help stock the shoe store. Mr. and Mrs. Geldfarb watched these people help salvage their lives. They had misjudged these simple people. If they had reached out sooner, life would have been infinitely easier. They arranged a formal opening for The Eagle Shoe Store and most of the people in the town came. The rest is history. The Geldfarbs became wealthy, for people came from far and wide to patronize their store. The thieves and rogues came too.

June Jr. and company chose a Saturday morning for their antics. Bud drove his beat-up truck with all four packed into the cab. He drove directly on the yellow line dividing the highway lanes. No one had taught him how to drive so he held his own ideas about the matter. He flew exceedingly fast, swerving around curves and running stop signs. June Jr. admired his driving. He parked the truck in a lot behind the shoe store. The four loitered on the street out front of the Eagle. They waited until several customers went inside to spring their plan.

Inside there burned one large electric bulb hanging from a long wire suspended from the ceiling. Mr. Geldfarb chose not to expand the lighting because he feared a rise in his electric bill. The store was dingy. It smelled of new leather and shoe polish. Figures moved like ghosts in the dim light of the store. They opened and closed shoe boxes as they sat on short stools trying on new pairs of shoes. There were white and black saddle oxfords, work boots with reinforced, steel toes, as well as loafers in various shades of browns and blacks. Mr. Goldfarb scurried around helping customers as Mrs. Geldfarb guarded the cash register and took payments.

The four boys entered the store and sauntered around two at a time. They paused at the front of the store until their eyes adjusted to the dim light. Each sauntered toward the new pair of shoes that he intended to steal. June Jr. spotted a pair of brown saddle oxfords but the size was wrong. He wore size nine and one-half and these were elevens. He asked Mr. Geldfarb if he carried his size. The aged proprietor told June Jr. he would have to get them from storage in the back. That was a mistake. June Jr. grinned because he knew Mr. Geldfarb had fallen for his trick. He had already spotted a pair of nine and one-half pair of penny loafers sitting temptingly on the second shelf. He quickly removed the shoes from their perch placing them on the floor next to one of the fitting stools. Mr. Geldfarb shuffled back with the brown saddle oxfords and placed the box in June Jr.'s hands. "Try them on back there," he said.

Willard, Bud, and Curtis wandered around the store eyeing the rows of new shoes. Each looked for a specific shoe and size. They continually looked at the Geldfarbs to determine if they were being watched. The Geldfarbs paid no attention because they were busy taking in money. June Jr. slipped the new shoes on his feet and placed his worn out shoes back in the new box. Curtis and Willard did the same. Bud was greedy. He laid several pairs of shoes at his stool, trying on separate pairs at the same time. When the signal came to leave the store, Bud was caught with a saddle oxford on his left foot and a penny loafer on his right one. They sauntered to the door still pretending to look at shoes on their way out.

Without looking up from his busy work, Mr. Geldfarb said, "If you didn't find what you want, come back next week. We have a new shipment of shoes coming in."

Mrs. Geldfarb noticed that all four boys were wearing new shoes. "Come back, thieves," she yelled. They broke into a run for Bud's truck parked behind the store. Some of the men customers ran after the four boys and dragged them back to Mr. Geldfarb's store to face judgment and justice. They hung their heads, embarrassed at being caught.

Mr. Geldfarb looked them over carefully. He could see that they were poor. Their second-hand clothes were dirty. One of his customers brought the box where June Jr. had left his dilapidated shoes. Mr. Geldfarb thought about the situation. When he turned the shoes over and saw the holes, he began to cry. He remembered his struggle when he had first come to America. He remembered his parents in Europe during the war when they had gone barefoot and hungry. He wept unabashedly that in this great land of plenty there were children with no shoes.

"We'll get the police," one of his customers shouted.

"No, no," Mr. Geldfarb said. "I remember a time not so far away when I was barefoot and lonely. Boys, I give these shoes to you as a present. You don't look like anyone has given you any shoes in your lives."

He let them go. As the customers in his store paid for their own shoes and left, each laid an extra five dollar bill on Mr. Geldfarb's counter to help pay for the shoes the boys had stolen. Love and goodness were very much alive.

June Jr. promptly crossed the street, went into another shoe store, and shoplifted two more pairs of penny loafers.

THIS DO IN
REMEMBRANCE OF ME

Ottie decided that June Jr. would go to church. She did not consult him as to his wishes on the subject; rather, she gave him an ultimatum, a directive. You will be in church come Sunday. Ottie did not believe in nor practice democracy. She was the penultimate dictator, sometimes benevolent, more often not. When she spoke a command in the life of one of her children, it stood in stone where God himself would have difficulty in removing it.

Well, June Jr. protested her edict, but to no avail. He was sixteen and considered himself an adult and had done so since he had quit school in the third grade. He was not interested in hearing church people spout their "thou shalt nots" and the interminable "begats" Sunday after Sunday. (If you can't find a verse in the Bible, it is probably in the "begats.") His associations with the Devil up to this point in his life had paid dividends; thus, he saw no reason to antagonize his best friend, the Devil. June Jr. did not view God as good and the Devil as evil. Whoever gave him what he wanted was the good guy. So far the Devil had given him money from Miss Lucy, a bicycle, and a car. When was God going to deliver? Maybe he, God, and the Devil could work as a team.

Ottie told him to walk proud and erect with us to church or she would drag him there by his collar. He decided to go, but like the proverbial horse, she could lead him to gospel water, but she could not make him a believer. But Ottie could drown him.

June Jr. dressed in his clean overalls and blue cap. In anticipation of a boring two hours sitting in a pew, he sought out a small tin box which he filled with thumb tacks, paper clips, bobby pins, a pen knife as well as wax, a black marking pen, and rubber bands. He could amuse himself with these items or he could torment others for his own amusement. He placed the tin box in the pocket of his bib. As we walked the gravel road to the church, June Jr. kept ten paces behind my mother, my sisters, and me, in an effort to declare independence from this prison sentence.

The church spire beckoned to us pointing above the treetops toward Heaven as a reminder that it was somewhere up among the clouds and Hell was in the opposite direction. As our family climbed farther up the hill, we could see the entire church building. It was built of brick and had six faux stained glass windows that appeared black from the outside, but took on a heavenly air when viewed from the interior with light shining through.

Along the walls inside there hung twelve pictures illustrating the life of Christ: Christ Entering the Garden, Christ Praying in the Garden, the Resurrection, the Ascension, and the Crucifixion. Fifteen rows of pews lined the sides of an aisle covered with a brown, plastic rug. An offering and communion table sat at the end of the aisle. Carved on the front of the table were the words, "This Do in Remembrance of Me."

A cloth with an embroidered cross hung across the pulpit rising elegantly above the table. Two large armchairs sat on each side of the pulpit. Seats for a small choir lined the walls to the right. Six large globed electric lights hung down from the ceiling suspended on wires. The ambience was nothing special, the decor not especially inviting. There was nothing there to attract a person like June Jr. In his philosophy, if you could not milk it, it was no good. If you could not eat it, it was no good. If you could not steal and sell it, it was no good. This place was slim pickings for June Jr.

Ottie's group joined the others who filed into the sanctuary. The aspiring Saints of God filled the pews, broke out the hymnals, and began the service with song. Miss Prue played the piano. She was a paragon of virtue and church going. She was unmarried, lived within walking distance of the church, and had given herself to no man. She was saving herself for God. But God had a better taste in women. She poured her love into the playing of hymns, gyrating on the piano stool as she did so.

June Jr. took out one of his bobby pins, pulled it opened, and stuck it into the wooden pew. He plucked his finger across it producing a high-pitched twanging. Miss Prue struck the piano key of A in the key of C to let the congregation hear the pitch for the song. She had no sooner struck the note for the first stanza than June Jr. hit his tuning fork with his finger. Being the last sound they heard, the congregation sang with the note produced by June Jr. and not by Miss Prue. It was a cacophony of off-tune singing that rang through the sanctuary. Each time Miss Prue hit a note, June Jr. echoed with his twang. Miss Prue ran out of the sanctuary weeping, vowing never to play the piano again. Even when the choir tried to sing a capella, the twang threw them off key. As Miss Prue raced up the aisle, June Jr. whipped out another bobby pin, broke it in half, and thus produced a second pitch. Plucking two in quick succession for the second stanza, some of the congregation heard one pitch and others heard the other pitch, resulting in more confusion. At the end of the disastrous verse, the congregation could hear Miss Prue screaming as she sped into the woods.

Some of the ladies of her circle exited to find and comfort her, although none of them quite understood what was going on with the music.

June Jr. snickered and smiled like a cherub. The preacher passed over the singing of the final stanza and went directly to a Bible reading. Afterward, the ushers brought collection plates for offerings. They passed the plates down one pew and collected them at the end of the next one. When the collection plate reached June Jr., he placed his hand inside, took out a crisp, new five dollar bill for himself and stuck it in his pocket, then sent the plate to the next person. Kids along the row saw what he had done and they imitated him. At the end of the collection phase for the church, there was very little money left. Praying to God brought June Jr. nothing that he wanted, so he just took it. Let God and the Devil sort it out. He intended to make everyone at the church pay for Ottie forcing him to come there.

The preacher signaled for everyone to retire to the Sunday school classrooms for their hour of theology study. The women's circle, having located Miss Prue and calmed her somewhat, led June Jr., Miss Prue, and her group (aged six to sixteen) to the Sunday School classroom. Upon entering the room, June Jr. took out one of his thumbtacks, placed it in a chair, and sat down to watch the fun. As luck would have it, Little Eddie Piggott came in and sat down on the tack. He and June Jr. had already tangled with each other at the fight at Silver Creek Bridge. Grabbing his buttocks with both hands, rubbing furiously, Little Eddie let fly with an oath, "Who put this damn tack in my chair?" Miss Prue, caught off guard by an eight-year old using curse words, attempted to insert a moral lesson into the fray.

"Now, now, boys," she said, "what would Jesus do in a situation like this?"

"He would kick somebody's little ass," June Jr. told her.

"No, no," she said, "Jesus did not use violence."

"The heck he didn't," June Jr. told her. "What about the bull-whip and running the moneychangers out of temple? Cast the demons into the swine. He cursed the fig tree. Now Miss Prue, Do you think he said, 'Damn this fig tree, or this damn fig tree?'"

The poor lady was overwhelmed. Frustrated, she gasped, "Let's not use vulgar language in the Lord's house. June Jr. did you put the tack in his seat?" she asked him directly.

"Heck no, Jesus put it there." he answered her. "Take it up with Him."

Little Eddie glared at him hissing; "You'll wish you knew Jesus when I stomp you after church."

"The Devil is on my side," said June Jr., "you are outclassed. The last time you tangled with me and the Devil, we left you bleeding and whining on Silver Creek Bridge. We'll gladly do it over again."

Miss Prue wept at the sheer bravado of these two little hea-thens, knowing that God might strike them dead at any moment. Then, again, He might have the best laugh of the century at these two precious boys. In order to distract the two boys from their confrontation, Miss Prue opened her purse and took out a long row of multi-flavored suckers to give to each person for attending church that day.

"Good," smirked June Jr. "it is payoff time."

She put the left-over suckers back in her purse leaving the ends dangling. When she turned her back, June Jr. shoplifted the whole lot and put them in his pocket. In view of all that had just happened, Miss Prue had herself a good cry before returning to the sanctuary to play the piano. She complained to the preacher about June Jr.'s behavior, so the preacher threw him out of the church building.

What weak-minded adult could possibly think that the world was safer with June Jr. wandering freely outside? Left to his own devices, was he supposed to find salvation among the unlocked vehicles in the church parking lot? The evil little jerk looked for a way to get even with the preacher.

The proud juvenile delinquent went directly to the cars in the parking lot and began to riffle through all their glove compartments. He stole cologne, candy, gloves, pencils, and writing paper. When he pried open the glove compartment to the preacher's car, he hit pay dirt. There in plain view lay a condom wrapped in a green wrapper. Thinking it was a balloon, June Jr. decided to blow it up and have some fun. During intermission, he slipped back into the church, crept up to the pulpit where the preacher would speak, opened the condom, blew it up, and laid it under the preacher's Bible. He secured the end with a thumb tack. He gently pulled the Bible over the condom, covering it securely.

"Open your Bibles to Second Peter," the preacher announced to the congregation. As the preacher opened his Bible, he accidentally flipped the condom over, leaving it hanging suspended between the embroidered cross and the table with the inscription "This Do in Remembrance of me."

Without thinking, the preacher blurted out,

"Damn! Who hung that rubber up on the pulpit?"

All the blue-haired ladies in the congregation let out a collective gasp. Goody Gavin passed out. The blue hairs made a dash for the exit. They hobbled, stumbled, waddled on their walkers, and skipped down the aisle as if the Devil himself were after them.

June Jr. began to snicker; then he broke into full-fledged laughter. The men in the church roared with laughter too. Even the preacher saw the humor in the situation and began to play the comedy.

"I don't remember praying for that," he said. Everyone roared.

"I love your bookmark, Preacher" one of the men howled with laughter.

"Is that why you took your lesson from Second Peter today?" someone added.

"Tell us, Reverend, did God send you the right size?" one man in the congregation joked.

"Blow it up and pop it," they begged.

"Pop!" He actually did it.

Even the blue-haired ladies began coming back into the church giggling and snorting. Waves of laughter poured across the little church. The more they looked at the condom, the harder they laughed. A wonderful, mirthful, spirit of love, laughter, and appreciation of God took hold of the little group and they felt for the first time what it is like to be in the presence of a loving God. For years thereafter, everyone spoke of that day as being the best church service they had ever had. Everyone suspected that June Jr. had set up the prank, but they forgave him anyway because they gave him the balloon as a souvenir.

When the group returned to the church for services the following Sunday, they found a strange, hand- written note attached to the church door. It read:

THIS DO IN REMEMBRANCE OF ME.

I've been by your church many times looking for people to worship me with fun, laughter, and love. I couldn't get any fun or laughter out of any of you until I left you the condom. Be sure to use it. I don't want any more sour-faced, sad, straight-laced people reproduced to sit sullenly in my house of worship. My house must be filled with joy and laughter. Don't screw yourselves with that judgmental attitude you tend to have, either. I work in mysterious ways. Don't get your nose out of joint over Fred's writing this story. Remember, I love him too---and, I told him every blessed word to write!

God

THE SLINGSHOT

It was autumn and the fields around Frog Level were filled with orange and yellow pumpkins. Farmers grew them for the making of lush pies at Thanksgiving and Christmas as well as to carve toothy jack-o-lanterns at Halloween. The baking pies sent out a smell of nutmeg and molasses on the air. Some people bought the pumpkins to use as Jack-o-lanterns. They carved them into snarling faces with toothy grins and lit the insides with a candle. The sinister smiles glowed in the darkness with an eerie countenance for All-Hallows-Eve. Other people considered the pumpkins worthless, leaving them in the fields to rot. Naughty teenagers threw them out car windows, spiking them against the pavement with a pop. The more insane people used them in a sport known as "pumpkin chunking." For this sport one needed a catapult, the simplest being a long string of rubber tube strung between two trees. Using it like a slingshot, one could send a pumpkin flying through the air like a cannon ball. It was safer to chunk pumpkins in an isolated field where no one lived or worked, because this sport could be lethal.

June Jr. sat leaning against a haystack in one of these richly-laden pumpkin fields. The drying hay smelled good. He leaned his arms above his head and stared out at the orange and yellow pumpkins as far as the eye could see. "What a waste," he said out loud. "I could have some fun with those suckers." It had been quite a while since June Jr. had any excitement in his life. He was rusting from boredom. He picked up one of the smaller pumpkins tossing it from one hand to the other guessing its weight. He stood up with the pumpkin in his right hand and assumed the position of an ancient Olympic discus thrower from Greece. With his knees slightly bent, he spun twice and released the pumpkin. Whirring, it flew through the air, landing some distance in the field. It broke open, strewing dozens of seeds across the sandy soil. June Jr. was pleased with his efforts. He picked up another pumpkin and rolled it this time as far across the field as it would go. It did not cover the same distance as the discus throw. He wiped crushed pumpkin from his hands and sat back down against the haystack. His eyes glinted and his lips curled as he invented the sport of pumpkin chunking in his mind. As it is said, an idle mind is the Devil's workshop. Now, we all know June Jr. had a special relationship with Old Scratch. He took a slingshot from his back pocket that he made himself. It consisted of a small Y-shaped twig with rubber thong attached to each prong. A small piece of leather was attached to the back of the thong to hold a small pebble. "If I have a larger sized slingshot," he thought, "I could shoot pumpkins at buildings and people." He was such an ELF (Evil Little Fuck). He made up his mind then and there to make himself a giant, pumpkin-chunking slingshot.

June Jr. came to me, saying he wanted me to go with him to the local junkyard. We made our way down an asphalt highway to the south end of Frog Level. The houses here were in need of paint and repair. Public housing units stretched along several blocks. Litter covered lawns and sidewalks, and clotheslines lined every back yard. Drying clothes flapped in the breeze. Untended babies crawled along front porches. People called this section of Frog Level "The Hatchery," because most frogs came here to lay their eggs and hatch tadpoles. Diabolical schemes, robberies, crimes and other plans came oozing out of the Hatchery. June Jr. felt at home here.

It held a junkyard called "Total Wrecks" named after all the wrecked cars stored in it. June Jr. figured he could find his makings for a slingshot at Total Wrecks.

Flapjack ran the junkyard. He was so dedicated to his work that he knew not only what junk was there, but also its location on the lot. Flapjack had received his name from an accident when he was seventeen. He had built his own car from spare parts in a junkyard and had propped it on four jacks out in front of his mobile home. It had fallen on him one day as he worked underneath on the muffler. It had smashed him flat as a pancake. Poor fellow had recovered partially, but the accident had left him with brain damage and a heavy limp. Friends affectionately had named him Flapjack.

He was middle aged now with a fat, pot belly that pushed out the front of his work overalls. He turned up the ends of the overalls, forming a cuff above the top of his shoes as cowboys do. He arranged all wrecked cars in neat rows as if they were for sale on a car lot. He categorized every piece of the junk. The junkyard was his library, he was head librarian, and his memory of things was the card catalogue.

June Jr. told him that he wanted some old rubber inner tubes to cut apart to make a giant slingshot. Flapjack had them stacked in neat piles at the back of the yard. June Jr. studied the make-up of the yard for he did not intend to pay for the merchandise. There was a fence running the length of the front and, since it faced the frog marshes on the back, management had not seen fit to fence it there. "How much would five tubes cost me?" June Jr. asked him

"I can let you have five for eight dollars, fifty cents," Flapjack told him.

June Jr. scratched his head and pounded the dirt with his heel on the hard ground, giving the proposal consideration.

"I don't have but three fifty in my pocket now," June Jr. lied. This was idle talk for he intended to steal them anyway.

"If you will save them for me, I will bring the money by first thing in the morning."

Flapjack agreed.

As we walked back down the main street of The Hatchery, I looked at June Jr. and said, "Where are you going to get eight fifty?"

"I'll use my West Virginia credit card." June Jr. laughed. He used that expression when he intended to steal something.

That night June Jr. made me go back with him to steal the tubes. I convinced myself that I was not stealing. I was going to carry what June Jr. stole. That way God would only give me a slap on the wrist.

We entered the marsh at the edge of The Hatchery. We walked gently through rancid water causing little sound. The water was waist deep when we reached the Total Wrecks. June Jr. hoped there was no guard dog.

"I'll help you carry the tubes, but I'm not going in there," I informed him.

"OK, OK," he said in an irritated voice.

The water in the marsh lapped around my feet and strange creature noises broke the silence from time to time. June Jr. moved as silently as a tiger through the rows of junked cars, until he found his prize. He took five tubes winding them around his shoulders for easy carrying. He eased his way back to where I was waiting at the edge of the marsh within eight feet of him. His foot caught in a discarded car bumper, throwing him head first into the row of abandoned cars making a terrible crashing that awakened the night. Lights came on suddenly in several houses in The Hatchery.

At the front of Total Wrecks, the deep voice of a probably huge dog barked furiously and raced closer and closer.

"Someone is coming with a flashlight," I whispered.

June Jr. had miscalculated. Flapjack not only slept at the junk-yard, but he had a guard dog. Holding tightly to the tubes with one hand, June Jr. pulled me with the other into deeper water. "Hold your breath and duck," he ordered. I did.

Flapjack and his dog, Radiator, came to the edge of the marsh where he shone the light over the water. He saw some concentric circles where we had ducked.

"They are growing some mighty damn big frogs down here now," he muttered aloud to his dog Radiator.

I popped out of the water gasping for air. June Jr. and I dog paddled across the water. Big frogs jumped from tree roots into the marsh. 'If we see a snake, I'm going to walk on top of this wa-ter like Jesus did," I told June Jr. I arrived back home unimpressed with June Jr.'s ability to be a thief.

With the greatest of bravado, the next day June Jr. went to Total Wrecks and asked Flapjack for his tubes.

"I don't have them anymore," Flapjack said sorrowfully.

"Well, I'm sorry about your theft," June Jr. said out of the blue.

Flapjack looked at him in a funny way, because he had not shared with anyone the events of the previous night. How did June Jr. know it had been theft?

With his loot in hand, June Jr. cut strips of rubber and tied them together in long strands. He found two trees near the pump-kin fields. They were several feet apart. He tied one end of the tube strings to each tree forming a giant slingshot. He chose a small pumpkin from the patch and sent it spinning through the air. It crossed Silver Creek and knocked out one of Burley's cows in the far pasture.

June Jr. jumped for joy! It was working! He had new entertain-ment. He sent a second pumpkin hurling toward the pack of cows huddled in the pasture. It struck one and sent the rest reeling like bowling pins. June Jr. cackled with diabolical laughter. He now had a way to really annoy people, and he intended to eat his fill. The ELF was on the prowl.

June Jr. had a traveling slingshot. He went back to Total Wrecks and stole two large wagon wheels while a customer distracted Flapjack. He built a small cart with the wheels so that he could carry pumpkins along with him. His operation was now completely mobile. He told me that I would pull the pumpkin cart for him while he chunked them wherever he pleased. A slingshot in his hands was like nuclear bombs in the hands of apes.

"Not me," I protested.

He picked up one of the rotten pumpkins and smashed it over my head. I saw stars. Smelly pumpkin juice ran down my face and seeds stuck to my hair. "You want more of that?" he challenged me. My life of crime with June Jr. was inevitable.

He informed me that our first pumpkin-chunking attack would be Tuesday night at the Piggott house. We still had some scores to settle with our neighbors for stealing our furniture and fighting us at the Silver Creek Bridge. June Jr. walked ahead of me, the slingshot draped around his shoulders. I followed behind lugging the cart. We filled the cart at one of the pumpkin fields; then he helped me pull it. We worked our way through pine tree thickets close enough to the Piggott house to make the shots effective. When darkness hid our forms in the trees, June Jr. tied his slingshot to two trees. He chose a plump, over- ripe pumpkin and placed it in the leather part of the sling. We both pulled it back as long and far as it would go. The force of the heaving pumpkin knocked us both backward to the ground. The pumpkin sailed over the roof missing the house and landing in the chicken enclosure. It knocked over a couple of chicken coops sending the hens running and cackling.

Someone's dark silhouette appeared in the lighted window. It stared for a moment, then disappeared.

"We put too much elbow grease on that sucker," June Jr. laughed. Picking up an orange pumpkin, June Jr. placed it in the sling. We pulled less hard. This pumpkin hit the top of the chimney with a splat. Juice and pulp ran down the stones on the roof.

"Damn," said June Jr., "we've got to improve our aim."

The third pumpkin hit the side of the house and splattered deliciously all over it.

The Piggotts came out of their house scratching their heads and behinds, puzzled at what was happening. We aimed the next pumpkin directly at them. It crashed right in their midst throwing pumpkin pieces all over each one. I heard someone say, "Oh, shit, rotten pumpkin." As they ran back into the house, we unhooked the slingshot and fled deeper into the woods. Gunshots rang in the trees above our heads. We sat down on a bed of moss dying with laughter. I sort of liked June Jr. and his Devil's friendship.

At Wednesday night service, we targeted Soul's Salvation church. At midday the two of us set up the huge slingshot and left the cart of pumpkins with it. The church janitor always opened the windows a couple of hours prior to the service, so the room could air out. Since people would be present, we chose soft, rotten pumpkins because we did not want to hurt anyone. We slipped into our places when we heard the choir begin its first number. We divided the pumpkin into smaller chunks. Brother, did they smell. With smaller pieces, we could be more accurate. We aimed our first salvo through the window not knowing what it would hit.

The choir sang, "Jesus, Lover of my Soul," as a huge chunk of pumpkin flew through the window and stuck on the piano right above Miss Prue's nose. A gossamer orange mist settled over her. The second chunk ripped across the sanctuary and plastered a picture of "Jesus Praying in the Garden of Gethsemane" on the opposite wall. The third one knocked a collection plate off the table with the slogan, "This Do in Remembrance of Me." It rolled down the aisle and came to a rest against one of the pews. Our assault continued. The church bell hung from a brick wall outside, where the deacons rang it by hand. June Jr. took deadeye aim for it, let fly and sent it tolling. We packed three separate pumpkin pieces together in the leather holder and let fly like a MERV warhead. One chunk hit Goody Gavin's beehive hairdo and knocked it flat. The second struck Mr. Morrison's hearing aid startling him awake. The third one zapped the preacher's wife landing directly in her lap with all its goo. Bedlam broke loose in the church. We quickly packed our slingshot and rolled rapidly into the woods. Miss Prue looked dejected wiping chunked pumpkin off her piano. Someone retrieved the collection plate.

But the preacher's wife, Prunella, was furious. "It has to be that little ELF June Jr. doing this," she railed. "Just let me get my hands on that little bastard."

"Oh, let's not be angry in the Lord's house," Miss Prue urged calmly. "What would Jesus do?"

"I don't care what Jesus would do. I'm telling you what I intend to do. I'm going to kick his little ass," she said in her best church way.

"Let's pray for him," Miss Prue suggested. "Help him Lord," Prunella prayed, for if you don't, he's dead meat.

Prunella went into a psychotic rage. She screamed,

"I'll trade my seat in Hell for a cracker box to get my hands on him."

"Bring all the plagues of Egypt down upon his head."

"May the fleas of a thousand camels nestle in his little armpits."

"Fourscore and seven years ago..."

"Now I lay me down to sleep..."

"Into the jaws of death rode the six hundred."

"Ay cuh zimba, zimba zaya, ay cuh zimba, zimba zee."

"lalalalalalalalalalalalalalalalal," she screamed.

She was so angry she went into glossolalia. Amen.

Prunella stormed out of the church with three pieces of pumpkin still stuck behind her ears. The rest of the congregants picked pieces of pumpkin off the floor and themselves, trying to regain their sense of composure.

"God won't miss these people for one week," June Jr. laughed derisively. "You chunked me when I was in your church, now I've chunked you. God bless punkins!"

I never realized how much fun June Jr. could be. He was a bonafide ELF (Evil Little Fuck). I understood why people wanted to kill him on sight. Yet, he had a great sense of humor. Were it possible to turn him into a positive force, he might be productive. I couldn't be sure he was corrupting me. Maybe I corrupted myself. I knew I was having a great time at the expense of foolish people. June Jr. got very bold, suicidal even. He planned to attack Mrs. Whitrock's fifth grade class during play time on the ball field.

"I don't want to die," I begged him. That woman is lethal."

June Jr. was cocky, arrogant even. He counted on his friend the Devil for support, and not even Mrs. Whitrock was a match for him, (a relative maybe), but no match. "We can do it," he assured me. "There are trees and bushes covering all around the field."

"I'm wearing a mask," I said. "I don't want that woman knowing my identity." Against better judgment, I agreed to walk into the jaws of Hell.

The day of the suicide attack arrived. I wrote out a will on a brown paper bag, leaving my pocket knife to Melvin and my collection of Red Ryder comic books to Larry. We arrived an hour early at the playground to set up the slingshot and pumpkins. We waited.

A group of goose-stepping kids rounded the gymnasium, walking in perfect military order that would put a marine drill sergeant in tears. They marched in unison down the steps and came to military parade rest at the bottom. Drill sergeant Whitrock gave an "at ease" order and kids dispersed to play. This time of day

Mrs. Whitrock allowed herself some down time. She sat down on a bench and poured herself a hot cup of coffee from her thermos. Its delightful aroma and taste rejuvenated her. Children played various games and baseball.

Looking at her with keen interest, June Jr. wagered, "I'm going to knock that coffee cup right out of her hand."

"No, no," I cried, "what if you miss."

"What if I hit?" he replied. "Either way, we're dead." With all his former chunking, June Jr. now had a razor-sharp aim. He could send a pumpkin through the eye of a needle. He took aim. I closed my eyes and prayed to the Devil. "Old Scratch," I prayed, "make him miss the cup." I thought I heard a giggle in my head. I heard the whiz of the chunk as it left the slingshot. I prayed harder.

The pumpkin chunk knocked the cup right out of Mrs. Whitrock's hand. "Damn," she muttered under her breath looking up to see if anyone had heard her. She thought a pinecone had fallen from a tree and struck her.

June Jr. snickered.

I opened one eye to see if I were still alive. "Ha, ha, ha," June Jr. laughed sardonically. He got braver. He waited until one of the fifth graders was at bat. He timed his shot with the pitcher's throw. It worked. The kid missed the ball but chucked the piece of pumpkin for a base hit.

"Let's not press our luck, June Jr. Come on, out of here," I begged.

Like a tree planted by the water, June Jr. could not be moved. His success was muddling his thinking. He was aiming a gigantic pumpkin for the school building, when Mrs. Whitrock's head appeared above the bushes. I messed my pants. Thank the Devil I had on a mask. June Jr. tried to run, but the gigantic claw of death descended on his neck. He was caught. Mrs. Whitrock ejaculated the words, "No one destroys my cup of coffee." She hooked the slingshot around June Jr.'s waist, pulled it back as far as she could, and let it fly. June Jr. rocketed out of the bushes, arms and legs gyrating in all directions, and landed in the school sewer located down the hill from the playground. Kids ran over to see what just flew across the baseball field. Then there came a big pumpkin over the bushes landing with a splat in the middle of the playground. Mrs. Whitrock was having her fun. She chunked a pumpkin over the elementary building right into a Home Economics class where they just happened to be making pies. Thinking some boys were teasing them, they threw a pie back over the bushes.

Walking with decorum out of the bushes, Mrs. Whitrock deftly retrieved her cup and poured herself some more coffee. Kids ran over excitedly telling Mrs. Whitrock that a UFO flew across the field. "It was a bird," screamed one. "No, it was a plane," cried another.

To herself Mrs. Whitrock smirked, "No children, not a bird, not a plane, not a UFO. It is just a piece of shit that I just chunked into a pile of shit."

Little ELF that he was, June Jr. just couldn't stop chunking. He decided to change his genre. He would go to the watermelon patch and chunk Mr. Ingle's watermelons. Of course, I had to play sidekick. We slipped in at night and set up operations. The watermelons were heavy and hard to manage. Besides watermelon rind could do some damage. June Jr. didn't care. We aimed the first practice shot at the Mill Shoals. It struck the rocks with a "thwack" throwing seeds, pulp, and rind all over the water. We sent the second watermelon in the opposite direction across the main road into a lover's lane parking area. We heard squeals and saw two people run from their cars into the woods half naked. June Jr. could not control his mirth. The one he aimed at Mr. Ingle's house veered to the left and struck the outhouse. We fled when Mr. Ingle opened the door and emerged with trousers down and corncob in hand.

The community was up in arms, especially Prunella, the preacher's wife. She put out a bounty on June Jr. They described his partner, me, as a masked man. The Piggotts, Mr. Ingle, Prunella, Mrs. Whitrock and Flapjack had been chunked and they wanted remuneration, actually revenge. Prunella summoned me into the church Sunday school room for interrogation. She knew she would never break June Jr. if she found him. Looking directly into my eyes she asked, "Did you know you can go to Hell for chunking pumpkins? I just looked at her. "God doesn't like you destroying his pumpkins. There are hungry people in the world and you are destroying food," she chastised me.

I imagined some hungry kid in Ethiopia sitting on a rock chomping on pumpkin sandwich thinking, "What is this shit? I wanted a hamburger."

"Who eats pumpkin?" I challenged her. "There are hundreds rotting in the fields over by Silver Creek. I don't see your missionary ladies collecting them to send to Ethiopia," I said.

"Did you chunk pumpkin through the windows of Soul's Salvation church and knock the roses off my hat?" There it was. A direct question. Now I had to lie.

"Well, no," I said, "My aim is not that good. But June Jr. could shoot the notes out of a hymnbook." Oops! There, I had told on him.

Hell hath no fury like pumpkin-chunked, God-fearing, church people scorned.

I heard yelling outside the room. Mr. Ingle came in, dragging June Jr. by the scruff of his neck. The two of us sat alone for an hour in the room, each pondering his fate. The verdict came back. Mr. Ingle required us to shovel out his cow stalls and transport the manure on our pumpkin cart to his watermelon patch and spread it all over the field. Flapjack made us build the rest of a fence around the back of his junkyard. The Piggotts made us wear a sign around our necks reading, "Piggotts are great, Piggotts are grand, I love all the Piggotts in our land." We had to chant those words all day. Mrs. Whitrock made us collect the hundreds of pumpkins left in the fields, pack them in to-go boxes in refrigerators, and mail them to hungry children in Ethiopia. We were thoroughly chunked.

The two of us sat crying for a while. "Screw them all," June Jr. said as he retrieved the slingshot, found a pumpkin, and proceeded to chunk it straight into the local Police Department. Police ran out like a bomb had gone off in a doughnut shop. What more could happen? We had already walked through the jaws of Hell.

Postscript: On my cell they placed a card with the words: "Inmate # 477311. Anyone out there have a cake with a file in it?"

Underneath the card someone had written with sarcasm, "No, but I have some pumpkin pie you can have."

UNREPENTANT BRIDGE

June Jr. lay drowning in the murky waters of Silver Creek. He had drunk a case of beer earlier in the evening at the pool room, then foolishly had driven home drunk. He had sped up the road to where our family now lived. By the time he had reached the curve at the bridge, his senses had been deadened and his muscles were unable to steer the car. The car had broken the lower side of the bridge going into the creek. June Jr.'s head had gone under the cold water where he could not breathe.

Avery's house was located several hundred feet from the bridge. The sounds of breaking glass and splintering wood awakened him from his deep sleep. The horn of June Jr.'s car stuck wailing like a siren across the quiet night. Avery quickly dressed and ran down to the stream. The car was upside down but from the side he saw a body pinned in the front seat, its head submerged in the water. Avery climbed down the dirt bank, waded through the cold water to the car, and grabbed the person's head lifting it above the rushing water. He recognized June Jr. The little heathen was still breathing. Above the stream banks, car lights appeared. They threw an eerie glow over the wreck. Arthur, Edwin, and Nate, nearby neighbors, had heard the noise from the wreck and rushed to help. All the men worked in unison, lifting June Jr.'s battered body back on to the bridge. Arthur and Nate wrapped his body in a warm blanket and sped him in their car toward the hospital in town.

After hearing the noise of the wreck, Ottie did not go back to sleep. She tossed and turned in her bed, hearing from time to time voices and shouts from the men at the creek trying to save her son's life. Their voices came across the night muffled, words barely audible. Ottie woke Curtis up and asked him to go to the bridge to see what had happened. He put on a light jacket, went down the path on the hill, and ran around the curve to the bridge. The night was cool. Millions of stars blinked in the dark sky above him. He breathed heavily from the physical strain of his running. In the distance he saw car lights and the silhouetted shadows of men running urgently back and forth across the bridge.

Curtis recognized Avery among the men. Going to him he asked, "What happened, Avery?"

"It's your brother June Jr. He's hurt bad. Arthur is on the way to the hospital with him," he explained.

Curtis understood the situation right away. He had no driver's license. He had been driving drunk. He had no title to the car. He had damaged state property. June Jr. was headed for jail unless they acted promptly.

He pulled Avery aside and begged him, "Please help me and my family. It will kill Ottie if her son goes to prison."

Curtis remembered when Eli had been caught twice for moonshining and had gone off to prison for five years in Chillicothe, Ohio. He recalled the pain and suffering his mother had endured. He did not condone the stupid choices his brother had made. He hated what June Jr. had become. But he cared for his mother and did not want to see her suffer again.

"We've got to move the car into hiding," Curtis explained.

All the men gathered around to talk.

Edwin said, "We have to call the police. It is a destroyed car, a damaged state property, and a personal injury. We can go to jail if we change anything about this situation."

"They don't have to know," Curtis countered his reasoning.

Nate asked why they should risk themselves and their families for the sake of a juvenile delinquent who would probably never change. Glenn reminded them that the happiness and well-being of June Jr.'s family was also at stake.

They could not absorb the legal and financial burdens of this wreck.

Mark interjected that as a community, "We bear responsibility for our own neighbors. What have the police ever done to help us? They ignore us or sit behind a billboard to catch someone speeding down the highway. "

"Men," Avery addressed them, "there is no higher calling than to love your neighbor. Ottie and her children deserve our compassion and love without judgment. They are our neighbors. God commands us to reach out to them in their time of need. Given this choice between what the police may say and what God will say, I choose to go with God."

The men pondered his words in silence.

Edwin agreed that he would say nothing to the police if the entire community agreed to confront June Jr. and Ottie on his behavior and make an effort to change it.

"Men, get your tractors and cables; we'll tow the car to a hiding place. The police might see the bridge but they will not know who wrecked. No one must admit to what they saw here tonight," Melvin said.

Everyone agreed to remain silent. A moral dilemma presented itself here. These men seriously broke some laws for which they could be punished. They lied, they cheated, they misrepresented, and they conspired to break human and religious laws. Why did they do it? They did it for the benefit of a juvenile delinquent in the hopes that he would become a decent citizen and adult in their community. Like God, these men would give June Jr. a second chance. How could they correct what Ottie had not done for him since birth?

The carpenters among them hurriedly rebuilt the broken railing on the bridge. Curious neighbors, who did not come to help, surveyed the bridge thinking the state had decided to build new railings at night. These people acted on a higher commandment to "love thy neighbor as thyself." Many disliked what June Jr. had done, but they could love the lost, wayward child he was.

And their compassion for his mother rose to the level of Mother Mary at the cross. If by their actions they sinned, they left it to a higher assessment. This night they refused to judge.

The men towed the crushed car up the dirt road to hide it among bags of trash discarded in a makeshift dump. They cleaned up all debris from the creek and bridge. They returned to their homes hoping that they could bring June Jr. into the fold of decency away from his criminal way. These community men then went to Ottie and told her that it was time to bring June Jr. under control.

Her response as usual was, "I can't hep it; I can't do anything with him."

The men of the neighborhood intended to bring him under control. They set up a meeting at Avery's house for the next Saturday. Ten men, Ottie, and June Jr. attended. It was time, they said, that June Jr. curbs his behavior and act like an adult.

Ottie had never given him any guidance or exercised any control over him. She had let him do as he wished. She had set no limits on his behavior. He had beaten the dog; she had not reprimanded him. He had stolen Dahlaree's chickens; she had cooked and eaten them without a word of censure. He had stolen a bike;

"Nice bike," is all she had said. She had not taught him right from wrong. When he had stolen the car, he should have gone to prison. Ottie had fled, uprooting the whole family to save him. He had just transferred his criminal behavior to a new community. It was partly her fault that he was a juvenile delinquent. Her actions and choices had deprived him of a father when he needed him most. Alone, she could not care adequately for her many children.

Ottie was very much like him. None in her life had ever set limits or helped her to make good choices. The men assembled to alter both their lives.

The new community rules were:

They would not tolerate criminal behavior of any kind in their community, especially theft.

June Jr. would have a curfew. He must be home by eight o'clock each night.

They assigned him one week to work with each of the men in the group. They would pay him for any work and would give him male guidance.

The men's wives agreed to teach him to read and write.

If he broke any rule, they had the right to punish him.

He must obey and respect Ottie.

He went to live the first week at Avery's house. They fed him breakfast and put him to work in the cornfield. Avery did not let him slack in his work and rewarded him with an R.C and a moon pie when he did well.

The second week with Arthur, June Jr. showed up late for work and did not go home at curfew time. When Arthur confronted him, he smarted off. Arthur grabbed his shoulders, shaking him strongly, pushing him into a chair.

"Apologize to me or I intend to inflict pain on you." He apologized.

"Now call me sir. "

"Sir," he muttered.

They planted cotton the rest of the week.

Nate served June Jr. notice the following week that he was to close his mouth, do his work, and adopt new attitudes toward adults. They went to chop wood but got little done because June Jr. would not work. Nate refused to feed him supper and sent him back home.

At Edwin's house, June Jr. returned to his old ways. He stole jewelry from Edwin's wife and sold it at the Boneyard. Irate, Edwin beat him badly and ordered him off his property, threatening to kill him.

These good men failed in their efforts to reform June Jr. They did not fail in their desire to keep their homes and families safe. June Jr. bought himself another car, but he could not buy back their good will. They stopped his car on the road as he came home one day and told him he was now persona non grata. He was no longer welcome in the community. They told him and Ottie to go live somewhere else. They intended to shoot him on sight if he returned.

Edwin made good on the promise when June Jr. did not listen. He shot at June Jr.'s car one night as he drove home. These good people would not suffer scum to live among them. All members of our family were attacked, at school, at church, along the roadway. June Jr. could not be reformed from the outside and all spirit had died within him. No one cared about his fate anymore. They just wanted rid of him. He disappeared for three years without a word. Ottie fled with her family back to the valley. She wanted to be with Eli again anyway. The community named the bridge where the accident occurred, "Unrepentant Bridge." In June Jr. they had met their greatest failure. They wished that he had died there.

SHOO-FLY PIE AND COFFEE

B urt was the youngest worker on Gentry's saw mill crew. He was eighteen and full of life. World War II had come to an end before he had been of age for the draft, so he had never been a soldier. He had come to Gentry because the boy's father and Gentry had been long-time friends. This was Burt's first official job so he wanted to do well for himself and his father. He was good with his hands. He could carve, saw and build at a level far beyond his eighteen years. He had a keen mind that quickly analyzed situations and saw solutions that older men could not match. He was very smart.

However, Bert had a flaw. He loved to have a good time, all the time. And he loved women passionately--- all women, any woman, any time. Never in a bad mood, he laughed often and generously. He saw fun and joy in everyone he met. Women returned his friendship gladly. Burt flirted with all of them but had never been intimate with any woman, yet. His big secret was that he was still a virgin. No one knew the secret except Burt himself. He thought a lot about what an intimate encounter might be like. He imagined a beautiful, blond girl, curvy hourglass figure, shapely legs, firm, adequate breasts, and a passionate demeanor. He imagined that she would seduce him, make all the correct advances, and teach him what he did not know. He loved women but he was dreadfully ignorant about them.

The men with whom he worked on the sawmill crew teased him because he had no real girlfriend and they noticed he spoke of women in idealistic terms. They were vulgar. They had all already experienced women, some rather low class. They joked about Gumtooth and Hustlebutt even offering to set him up with one of them. Burt politely declined and they laughed in vulgar derision describing what an encounter with Gumtooth might be like. When the group of men rode on the back of Gentry's truck down the valley, if they saw a woman, they yelled at Burt, "Is that the one for you?" He took the teasing in good stride. They all thought highly of Burt.

Mrs. Lindendahl, the missionary from Pennsylvania, (the one no one liked,) the foul-tempered Yankee who disdained the valley folk, placed an order with Gentry for a load of lumber to build herself a pig pen. Her pigs, living under the cabin since her arrival, made a mess. It was time to move them to a new location. Because Burt was so lively and good-natured, Gentry chose him to deliver the lumber and build Mrs. Lindendahl her pig pens. He figured Burt would tolerate her loud mouth and rudeness better than the older, married men whose wives already kept them on edge with their nagging and caustic remarks.

The sawmill crew laughed fully when Gentry named Burt to deliver the lumber and build the pens. They decided to play a joke on Burt. None would volunteer to deal with Mrs. Lindendahl. Those who had dealt with her told of her penchant for making passes at any man who happened by her house no matter what the reason.

She was not married, but they would pretend that her husband was seldom at home for he was a long-haul truck driver. Despite

130

the fact that she came to the valley as a missionary, she was still a woman not able to deny her human side and its needs. Religion took a back row seat to passion. Gomer was the only man in the valley rumored to have been intimate with Mrs. Lindendahl. It was said that she had seduced him with shoofly pie and coffee. Gomer could not resist food. He had thrown up the pie and coffee after the encounter and had remained celibate for the next six months. Gomer had become the laughingstock of the valley. Even Gumtooth and Hustlebutt had removed Gomer from their list of customers.

Burt whistled happily through his two front teeth as the heavily-loaded truck droned up the road toward the Lindendahl cabin. His mind imagined beautiful women in all shapes, their faces smiling at him, their lips kissing him on his brow. He could feel their warmth, their scent of sweet perfume. One day he would have his way with one of them, he was certain of that. But for today, he contented himself to live out his fantasies in his mind.

He pulled the truck into the yard of the cabin. Mrs. Lindendahl appeared in the cabin doorway and gestured with her hand to unload the wood at the back of the cabin. Burt busied himself unloading the planks. As he worked, he felt eyes staring at his back. He turned to see Mrs. Lindendahl undressing him with her eyes. She liked his buttocks made firm from bending and lifting. She liked his slender physique. Burt was superior to Gomer in all aspects.

"I'll pay for the wood when you are finished unloading. Come to the cabin." she purred in a sexy voice.

The hair rose on Burt's back. Why hadn't Gentry sent one of his older men to do this job? He did not yet realize that Gentry and the crew had set this situation up. They were playing a joke on him. He didn't feel like whistling any more.

He walked up the steps of the cabin and knocked on the door. "I've finished," he said.

"Come in," she invited.

He had to go inside to get the payment for the wood. He saw arranged on the kitchen table two plates and two coffee cups resting on a white, lace tablecloth. Mrs. Lindendahl opened a glass cover over a brown shoofly pie just baked in her wood stove. She cut two generous servings, placed them on the plates, then poured two cups of steaming hot coffee.

"Eat," she enticed.

Burt remembered tales about Gomer. Was he, like Gomer, to succumb to the temptation of Pennsylvania shoofly pie and coffee? Was he to be a second laughing stock of the valley? His heart sank.

"I gotta go," he blurted. "Gentry wants me to bring the truck back."

"I won't pay you for the wood unless you eat the pie," she informed him.

Burt was trapped and he knew it. He grabbed up the fork and gobbled down the pie. It was quite good.

"You men do not know that I am married," she said out of the blue. "My husband drives a truck and is seldom home. I ride with him when I can. You have all seen his truck thinking it is a local delivery truck. No one in the valley has much to do with me, so they know very little of my affairs." She was a good liar.

"People would be friends with you if you would stop acting like you still live up North," Burt interjected. "Be a part of the valley and people will accept you. Where is your husband?" he asked.

"He could be most anywhere. He shows up when he shows up," she replied.

Burt continued eating the pie and sipping the coffee. Mrs. Lindendahl turned her knees in his direction, crossing her legs in a most provocative manner.

"I want to get in bed with you," she said to him. "You know that people in Pennsylvania also call what I'm offering you "Shoofly pie?"

He froze in fear and consternation. The piece of pie he was eating got stuck in his throat. He flushed red as his heart beat out of his chest. Yet a strange feeling of desire crept over him. He had waited all his life for a moment like this, but he always assumed it would be a stunningly-beautiful girl of his dreams. Here before him sat a frumpy, middle-aged graying missionary woman offering an invitation for him to become a man. At age eighteen one rarely thinks with his brain. In a half trance, Burt rose from the table and walked into her bedroom.

"Oh God, he thought," I am a Gomer."

Even a blind hog finds an acorn occasionally. Led now by his hormones, Burt yanked down his pants and jumped on to the bed.

Mrs. Lindendahl waddled in behind him. Suddenly she stopped dead in her tracks, turning her head sideways, listening intently to the sound of a large truck engine pulling into the front yard.

"It's my husband," she warned, "get under the bed."

Grabbing his pants and shoes in hand, Burt rolled underneath the bed pushing dust bunnies and himself as near the wall as he could.

"I'm dead," he thought. "The sawmill crew will find my mummified body under her bed and I won't have my pants on."

He tried to slip his pants back over his feet and legs, but there was not enough room.

The front door swung open and in came a man along with a little Pomeranian dog named Pug. He slumped into the chair at the kitchen table.

Burt heard him tell his wife, "I will only be here for three hours, I must continue with my run to Charlotte.

"Three hours," thought Burt, "I can't stay under this bed for three hours."

Stay or die were his choices. From his vantage point under the bed, he could only see two sets of feet. Burt began to sweat.

Suppose I sneeze? Suppose I cough? Suppose I need to relieve myself?

He heard her tell the man that Gentry had left the truck outside because he intended to return tomorrow to build the hog pens. Burt saw the man's feet and shoes when he walked into the bedroom. Burt also saw his life flash before him. He held his breath not to give himself away. It was a long three hours.

Pug, the Lindendahl dog, made a beeline for the bedroom barking, scratching and pulling at Burt's pants. He pushed Pug away with his hand but the canine would not go away. The dog growled and yelped as it circled Burt under the bed.

"You got a man hidden under the bed or something?" the man joked with her.

"Oh yes," she joked back, "I've got a man under every bed like you have a girl in every town." They both laughed. Mrs. Lindendahl pulled Pug out of the bedroom and gave him a scrap from the table, but the dog wouldn't settle down.

In the bedroom, under the bed, Burt lay in a puddle of his own water. His first encounter wasn't unfolding as he imagined. At one point Burt fell asleep and began to snore. Mrs. Lindendahl lost no time in giving the bed a resounding kick to awaken him. "What will I do if they decide to get into bed themselves?" Burt thought. Oh….. What a house of horrors!

At last he heard footsteps exit the front door and a truck engine fire up, then leave. Burt rolled from under the bed his body covered in dust bunnies. He put his pants back on. Mrs. Lindendahl gyrated through the door, shook her thighs seductively, and suggested they get on with their little affair.

"I'm too weak," Burt managed to say. He crammed his feet into his shoes and ran for the door. "Let your husband build your hog pens," he shouted. "Furthermore, he can eat all your damned Shoofly Pie, too."

Outside a roar of laughter rose from the sawmill crew. Gentry's men had set up the entire situation to tease Burt and they had all been outside watching the whole affair. One of the men had pretended to be Mrs. Lindendahl's husband. She had never been married. Burt climbed into his truck in a huff and threw dust rings from the truck tires as he roared down the dusty road. He mumbled something about never eating another piece of any kind of pie again.

Mrs. Lindendahl joyfully ran behind the truck waving her right arm in the air while holding her skirt hiked up above her knees with her left one, yelling, "Come back! Oh, do come back! I want to make love to you. I want to give you some more of my delicious Pennsylvania Shoofly Pie."

LINDENDAHL'S DUDES

Mrs. Lindendahl's cousins should never have come to our valley. Not that the valley was inhospitable, you understand. On the contrary, people there are kind and personable. But these cousins from Pennsylvania were criminals looking for a new location to set up their moonshine operation. They were big time operators desiring an out-of-the-way location for their operations. Knowing the terrain was a good locale for making moonshine, Mrs. Lindendahl suggested that they come see for themselves and perhaps they could live in her house. They brought with them their own moonshine equipment larger than anything the valley had ever seen. They brought with them Pennsylvania car tags and their atrocious accents, both alien to the valley people. Word spread quickly across the hills and hollows that new moonshiners were looking to set up somewhere in our valley. Farmers watched their fields and woods carefully lest the trespassers squat on their property. But these operators were slick. They brought with them street smarts and mercenary attitudes. The valley people referred to them as "Lindendahl's Dudes."

These intruders knew that they could not set up their moonshine stills on private property. They bought the old, abandoned gold mines and house above Lake McCall that had belonged to Raymond's father. They intended to work on their own property and not rile the locals. Their purpose was to make money from bootlegging, not to engage in a feud with valley people.

Lindendahl's Dudes took the moonshine business underground as Eli and Ottie had done when his house had burned down. There was nothing in the gold mines that could catch fire. They drilled holes down through the earth to the mines and inserted pipes so that oxygen could flow in. A second set of pipes carried waste and smoke to the outside. Seven moonshine stills eventually poured out dozens of quarts of liquor each day.

The leader of the Lindendahl's Dudes was named Lefty. Ironic as it sounded, it referred to the fact that he had lost his left hand in an industrial accident and now wore a hook where the hand once had been. He was far from handicapped inasmuch as he could use the hook as a weapon. Many an opponent went down at the end of his hook. He was street smart and he intended to become woods smart. He drove to Forest City to introduce himself to Sheriff Buford. He explained that his group was going to extract left-over gold from the old mines. Smoke and strange odors would come from the mines, but they were harmless. As he shook hands with Sheriff Buford, he placed a crisp one hundred dollar bill in his hand. "We'll call you if we need something," he told Buford.

At the end of the first month, the stills were producing quarts of moonshine. Using furniture trucks to allay suspicion about what they were doing, the Dudes set up a system that carried moonshine far and wide, even as far away as their hometowns in Pennsylvania. The valley people did not bother them until the day they decided to undermine Ottie's business. They boldly sold quarts of moonshine at the Boneyard effectively destroying her business.

Ottie was helpless in front of this steamrolling organization of Yankee interlopers. She considered her options of which there were few. She could not compete in production of "shine" because she worked alone in one small still. They were too powerful for her to fight. However, she refused to close down her operation and let these outsiders win. She went to Lefty with a proposal that they become business partners. He laughed at her. She asked him to hire her as one of his workers, since she knew more about making moonshine than any of them. She also knew the woods, the valley, and its entire people, not to mention Sheriff Buford. He accepted this proposal. She became an adjunct member of Lindendahl's Dudes.

Ottie was in a nest of vipers. These men had no morals, no sense of honesty, and no loyalty. Each made moonshine for his own personal money. None ever kept his word or promise. Their tongues clacked out lie after lie. These men would slit each other's throats for a dollar. Their conduct did not mesh with the moral conduct of the people of the valley. They treated Ottie as one of the men, subjecting her to all kinds of indignities and vile talk. Moonshine was her livelihood so she endured these scum. Everything changed when Lefty cheated her in her pay for the hours of work she had put in. He told her the small sum of money he gave her was all she deserved and was all she was going to get. Ottie suffered in silence. Little did Lefty know that Ottie did not forgive or forget those who trespassed against her.

The next day at work, Ottie stole a case of moonshine for herself. She hid it in the woods outside the gold mine and carried it home where she stored it in her own moonshine still. Every day thereafter she did the same until she amassed dozens of cases. This moonshine was payment Lefty had denied her. It would not be missed because it was her job to pack the cases with quart jars and record the total for shipment.

One day Ottie hid a nail in her jacket pocket and brought it to work. While everyone ate lunch outside, she quietly drove the nail into one of the copper coils, causing the moonshine to drip out on the ground rather than into the waiting quart jars. Then she grew braver. She brought a vial of turpentine the next day and poured it into the boiling mash ruining the entire run of moonshine.

Lefty discovered the empty vial in her jacket pocket. He became enraged. With his one usable hand, he hurled the empty vial across the room smashing it against the side of the rocky mine. He smashed the sharp hook on his left hand into Ottie's skull and twisted it clockwise across the thin skin covering her skull. He jerked the hook downward opening a long gash in her cheek under the left eye. When Lefty extracted his hook from Ottie's face, clumps of flesh and hair stuck to it. Ottie screamed in pain. Blood poured down her forehead blinding her momentarily. In darkness, she weakly clutched the sides of the goldmine seeking a way to safety. Lefty overtook her and grabbed her throat with his good hand. She smelled his hot, garlic-scented breath as his face neared hers. Cutting off the blood circulation through her carotid arteries, he caused her to fall into a dark, unconscious state. He left her there hoping that she was dead.

Ottie was not ready to die. When consciousness returned, the will to live and fight her adversaries rose like a mighty power in Ottie's being. She dragged her bloodied and bruised body along the sharp rocks lining the floor of the abandoned goldmine to the safety of a copse of trees outside. She lay there breathing heavily, feeling her pulse with her fingers to reassure herself that she was still alive. She crawled and stumbled through briars, over sharp rocks, and across small streams. She left trails of blood marking lines across the landscape. Three hours later she staggered into her farmhouse, grateful that Lefty had not killed her.

Word spread down the valley of the Lindendahl Dudes' vicious attack on Ottie. People were irate. The people of the valley would no longer tolerate these men in their midst. Valley men took their guns, donned black masks, and set out to ambush the Lindendahl delivery trucks. This group called itself the "Avenging Golden Rods." They stopped Lindendahl trucks as they slowly pulled over Bolding's Gap, beat up the drivers, and sent them back to tell Lefty that they had declared all-out war on "these damned Yankees." Lefty put armed guards on the next delivery trucks. The Golden Rods fired on the trucks all along the road. At midday, the Golden Rods gathered at Griff's Old House, put on their face masks, and marched through the woods to the gold mines. They disarmed the men working inside. They used sledge hammers and axes to break up the stills. They destroyed the entire operation. Men carried all the cases of moonshine home to Ottie.

Lefty brought in armed reinforcements. They went back to the gold mines in an effort to rebuild the operation. The Golden Rods decided that they would take back their valley. Many women gathered in a group headed for Mrs. Lindendahl's house to have a "calling out." It was the valley people's way of settling disputes. Ottie led them. They called Mrs. Lindendahl out on her own bad attitudes since she had arrived in the valley. They called the moon-shiners out on their violence toward Ottie and women.

Lindendahl let fly in return with a barrage of buckshot from her shotgun. She didn't care about their hayseed rules or a "calling out." The women scattered for cover continuing to berate her from their hiding places in the bushes.

"Did you live with pigs under your house up north?" one voice chided her.

"No, I only learned to live with pigs when I came to this damned valley," she screamed back.

"You misrepresented yourself as a missionary. I wouldn't follow your sorry ass through a bowl of grits," Ottie hurled these words with invective.

"Who would eat a dish like grits other than a bunch of poverty-stricken swine like you people?" Lindendahl said going for her jugular.

Beulah heard these sacrilegious words. Stung by this vitriolic attack on her beloved South, Beulah shouted through tears:

"I'll cut out your vile tongue and have the Golden Rods nail it to Independence Hall in your honkey state," Beulah hissed. "If I get my hands on you I will shove a bowl of southern grits up where the sun doesn't shine and where it can digest quicker."

Hearing the gunfire and taunts, Lefty and his men scurried to the cabin. There they made the last stand of the Second Southern Rebellion. The Golden Rods poured volleys of shells toward the cabin. The Dudes returned fire, knocking limbs and leaves off the surrounding trees. After thirty minutes of warfare and depletion of ammunition, Lefty signaled with his white handkerchief that he wanted to negotiate. He told the Golden Rod leader that he and his men were willing to close down operations and return to Pennsylvania. They agreed to take Mrs. Lindendahl back with them. (Keeping her word, Beulah did put the bowl of grits where Mrs. Lindendahl could not complain about their taste.) She had been a miserable failure as a missionary. No one would ever associate God with her again.

The Golden Rods escorted the Dudes to the county line where they informed Lefty that they would shoot him on sight if he ever returned to the valley. They used dynamite to close up the gold mines for good; then they set fire to the Lindendahl cabin. It burned to ashes. They proceeded to plough and salt the land so it was forever unusable. The people of the valley won their second Southern Rebellion in record time. And so, all returned to a state of peace. From that day forward, when people saw a car with a license plate from Pennsylvania, they all grabbed their shotguns and ran for the hills.

RAYMOND IS REAL

Raymond sat down on the window sill of the tavern letting his legs and feet dangle freely. The tavern opened at ten o'clock but it was just five a.m. He did not care. He drank enough alcohol from a small aftershave bottle just to keep his blood moving. The morning was cold and bleak. Steam blew up from a grate releasing stale air from somewhere beneath. A few neon lights blinked on and off. A sign in the distance intended to read "Welcome to Charlotte." But the burnt out letter "c" caused it to read "welcome to harlotte." Raymond felt like a harlot, if he felt at all. Life wasted, values prostituted, money spent, legacy squandered, these choices had marked his life. He lit up a cigarette and breathed the fresh tobacco smoke deep into his lungs. He coughed, blowing blue smoke out through his nostrils and mouth and then with nicotine-stained fingers, he pulled the collar of his light jacket tightly around his neck. A clock in the distance struck the half hour. The city began to stir. In the vastness of the city, Raymond was lost, just a number among thousands of people who walked by him pushing, bumping, shoving each other on their way to make money, like that that he had squandered. Most were middle class. This day Raymond remembered when he had lived an upper crust life among the elite.

Raymond was born into a family of wealth and means. His father, Mr. Potts, owned one of the active gold mines located on the ridge behind McCall's Lake. It produced enough gold to allow the Potts family to hobnob among the elite. They built an elegant mansion with one hundred fifty rooms in the mountains near Asheville. In our valley near their gold mine, they built a simple dwelling suitable for business visits during the week. Raymond was not born in this valley nor did he ever really become a part of it. Everyone knew him when they saw him, but few people ever spoke or associated with him. When he was a small boy, his father brought him to the second house near the gold mine. His father could not care for him while doing business so he hired Bertha to be his tutor and nanny during his daily visits. His father gave strict orders that he have no association with any valley children as he considered them to be lowly hillbillies not worthy of contact with his son. He wanted to shelter him in the elitism to which they were accustomed.

Raymond went to Bertha's house where he studied the classics and poetry. He could recite "The Charge of the Light Brigade" in its entirety. He read Latin fluently and spoke some French. He was an avid lover of math, doing geometry for pleasure. Bertha made him study the Bible in an effort to ensure that his spiritual growth equaled his secular knowledge. When time came for recreation, he chose to walk along the road outside her house where he could hurl rocks down the mountainside into a stream below. He wore the best of clothes, was exceptionally neat, prim and proper. He was also mighty lonely.

One day while throwing rocks at a stream, he heard the drone of the old school bus inching its way up the hill and around the curve at Bertha's house. Moving aside to let it pass, he looked up at many children hanging out the open bus windows waving greetings to him saying his name.

"Raymond, hello Raymond, how are you, Raymond?"

Sadly he could not say a single child's name in response. As he struggled to wave weakly at them, his father's voice washed over him, "Don't you dare associate with any of those valley urchins." The bus disappeared in the distance with him sadly staring after it.

The next day as the bus passed Bertha's house, Raymond was waiting on the side of the road. He waved warmly to all of us children. In his hand he held an orange with a white string tied around it. Attached to the string was a piece of paper. He hurled the orange randomly through one of the bus windows. It struck the middle seat near Phyllis and me so I grabbed it. Kids piled on top of me trying to pry the orange out of my hand. Phyllis fought for me. She bit into arms or hands or fingers, pulled hair, gouged eyes until they backed off. The only time valley children saw oranges was at Christmas so mine was a cherished prize. There was a greater prize on the paper attached to the string. "Come play with me," his note read. I couldn't believe that a rich kid wanted a boy like me with worn-out shoes and clothes to come play with him. It was my lucky catch of an orange.

I hatched out a plan. Eli's family lived across the road from Bertha. All these people were my aunts, uncles, or grandparents. I told the bus driver I wanted to get off at dad's house so he let me. I didn't go to Eli's house. I followed the bus around the curve and up the hill at Bertha's house. I saw Raymond staring at the back door of the bus driving away from him. He seemed very disappointed that no one got off the bus to play. As he started for his house, he saw me standing in the middle of the road. "Where did you come from?" he asked looking at my disheveled clothes and obvious poverty.

"Off the bus," I replied. "I caught the orange, read your note, and decided to come and play."

144

"My name is Raymond," he said.

"I am Fred," I responded.

"How do children play around here?" he asked.

"We let the play come to us," I said. "Whatever happens becomes our play. Let's go climb some trees."

We climbed trees; made stick horses and rode them, made tunnels through broom sedge grass, threw rocks in the creek, and wrestled each other all over a patch of green grass. Exhausted, I needed to go home. I did not go to Eli's. Raymond and I kept our play a secret to protect him from his father's wrath. Bertha knew but wisely remained silent. As long as Raymond was in the valley as a boy, I was the only hillbilly he played with. I was his only friend. I wish he had contacted me instead of going to the tavern in Charlotte.

Raymond grew up and moved on, or so we thought. Actually World War II came and he was drafted into the army. His father used his wealth and influence to keep Raymond at home, but he defied his father and went to the army anyway. Now he would stand shoulder to shoulder with common people from all over the nation. The hoi-polloi really changed Raymond. His father disowned him and never spoke to him again. He cut off all the money. When Raymond came home from the war, he was a changed man.

Unlike the biblical prodigal son, Raymond did not rise from his pig sty; rather he sank deeper into despair. He began to drink heavily. When he had no money to buy booze, he turned to Ottie for moonshine trading her sex for the alcohol he had to have. His family retired to the mansion in Asheville leaving Raymond in the dwelling at the gold mine. Ottie walked there twice a week to bring him moonshine and to roll in his bed for payment. He continued to deteriorate, becoming dirty, unkempt, and unwashed. Not even Ottie cared for that so she told him he had to pay her eight dollars per quart for moonshine just like everyone else. In desperation, Raymond got a job.

Actually he created his own business. He built a large square box truck on wagon wheels and turned it into a rolling store. Country people could not easily get to town to buy what they needed so his store would go to them. He filled it with basic items everyone needed and peddled merchandise to all houses up and down the valley. Many times he didn't quite make his rounds for he drank his moonshine and passed out, so customers found him, took what they needed, leaving payment in a glass jar on the wagon. People did not cheat Raymond nor did they steal his merchandise. Raymond built himself a second vehicle. It was a large sled with runners made out of two logs bent upward at the end. He nailed planks on top to form a carrying platform. Pulled by a horse, this sled could go anywhere across any terrain with ease. Sometimes when he used the sled, people would see him collapsed in a drunken slumber lying in the hot sun, other times in pouring rain. Unlike during his privileged childhood, he now knew the names of all the people in the valley. He even thought of some of them as his friends. I never stopped being his friend. He was now the official town drunk--outcast, nearly homeless, and sick, out of control. He would have died of alcoholism, leaving no memory or imprint of his life, had it not been for the snowstorm.

The snowstorm roared into the valley from the south on March 2nd, 1948. It pushed across Grassy Knob and Oaky Knob burying our farm under twenty-two inches of snow. The sourwood trees in the valley groaned under the weight of the snow. Some cracked and split as ice took them down. The entire valley disappeared under a white blanket. No road was visible, no road was passable. The temperature quickly dropped below zero leaving a frozen world in its grasp. Families did not have time to make preparations. Within a few days, they ran out of food. Both people and animals grew hungry.

In Griff's Old House above our farm, the Lindstrom family grew more and more desperate.

Carole told her mother, "I will not stay here dying of hunger and freezing from cold. I'm going to get help."

Every family in the valley needed something, be it food for themselves, their livestock, or some sort of medicine. Desperation grew. Carole made a pair of snow shoes out of two pieces of wood and strapped them to her shoes with rope. She bundled herself warmly against the wind and took off across the fields of snow guessing where the road might be. She planned to find Raymond's rolling store to buy flour, beans, eggs or canned food. But where was he? She headed for his house near the gold mine. He was not there; however, she saw sled tracks leading in the direction of Bertha's house. That is where he would go.

On the hill below the white church where Ottie pretended to be a Bigfoot and beat up Beulah, she found him asleep on his sled in a drunken stupor. He was wrapped in snow. Only the warmth of the liquor kept him from freezing to death. Carole wrapped him in a blanket she found on the sled.

"Where is your store?" she asked.

He pointed in the direction of the church. Taking the reins of the horse she straddled the sled holding herself in place with the home-made snowshoes, she pushed the horse onward up the hill to the church. There she piled the sled high with food and supplies. She revived Raymond from his drunkenness enough for him to drive the rolling store. He went south to assist people in that part of the valley as Carole drove the sled toward home.

She took food to her family first. Then she came to our house. We took what we needed. We had extra hay that we stacked on the sled. Some family would need it. Carole took off back down the road stopping at each house leaving food for some and bales of hay for animals at others. Whatever any family had extra, they piled on the sled sending forward to people in need. Carole and Raymond made numerous trips back and forth to his house to resupply. On one trip he traded the wagon for the sled for word came that a man at one of the houses had a heart attack and needed urgent medical care. Carole continued the trek to houses deeply snowed in as Raymond raced to help save a man's life.

Primitive torches and lanterns marked the way to the house of the sick man. Raymond pushed his horse at a fast pace up the driveway of a rich man's house. A lady ran out yelling, "He's in here. He's in here." Raymond ran inside to a man swaddled in blankets. He was moaning, barely breathing. When Raymond pulled back the covers to check out the man, he found himself staring directly into the face of his father whom he had not seen for twenty-five years. His father had been visiting a friend in this house when the snowstorm had struck without warning. Then he had a heart attack.

"We've got to get him to Forest City," Raymond urged.

Another man drove the sled as Raymond sat next to his father to keep him from falling off. Raymond gently reached down under the blanket and took his father's hand in his. The hand was so cold he already knew that his father had died. Raymond cried all the way to Forest City.

Carole continued driving the rolling store until every farm house had been visited and people's needs cared for. She then turned the horse toward Griff's House and home. When the snow melted, every person in the valley who took supplies from Raymond's store came to pay him in full. Letters of thanks poured in for Carole via Beulah's mailbox. When she was out and about in the valley, people gave her gifts, canned food, and even money. She graciously accepted their tokens of thanks.

Officials of the valley erected a plaque in memory of the snowstorm and to honor Raymond. It read:

"This plaque is raised with grateful thanks to Raymond and his rolling store. He saved us in our time of need. This valley remembers him warmly. Raymond is real."

The tavern opened at ten o'clock. Raymond staggered in. He stayed until late evening drinking until he fell into a stupor. He staggered down Tryon Street as a rare snowstorm began to hit the city of Charlotte. He became tired and disoriented. Finding a broken down bench behind a building, Raymond lay down to sleep. He dreamed of sourwood trees in bloom in his valley and of the warmth of his family and his father long ago. In his mind, he walked along the streams of his childhood and played games with me in the fields. In this eternal moment, there was no one there to ease his pain. Flakes of snow gently covered him as a mother wraps her arms lovingly around her child. A snowstorm had brought him his moment of glory. A snowstorm took him home. The police found his frozen body when morning broke. In his hand he held a faded photo of his father. The whole valley wept. Raymond was real.

OLD SWAYBACK

Half way down the valley on the main dirt road near where Eli lived with his real family, there was a pasture filled with crawdad holes and cow piles. Cows once had grazed here. The pasture was surrounded by a high barbed wire fence that had once kept the cows in check. In the warm months of the year neighborhood kids flocked here from all directions to play. They built a makeshift baseball diamond using old dried cow manure piles as the bases. The object was to touch each base lightly as you passed, but heaven help you if you ever had to slide to a base, hands first. There were never enough kids playing at one time to form two entire baseball teams, so everyone played on both teams.

There was another danger in the field where we played--- crawdad holes. Pesky crawdads with pincers dug large holes in the swampy ground and rolled mud out around the edges. Sometimes a person could see them, often times not. Many a kid knocked the skin off his toe when stepping in one of these holes.

A herd of cows had left the pasture long ago as the grown up grass attested. The only official resident now was an old swayback horse left there when its owner had gone to live in a rest home in Forest City. The poor horse looked as if it should be in a rest home too. His back swayed such that its belly almost touched the ground. Shorter kids walked upright beneath its belly without injury. It was an old pinto horse that someone had ridden when it was too young, therefore throwing its spine out of whack.

He was very gentle when he played with children. He allowed us to ride six abreast in the swag on his back. We rode around the edge of the pasture, the old horse content to be our taxi. A strange sight indeed was to see all those kids in tandem with their tiny legs and feet dangling off the horse's side. His ribs were a slightly bony yet the horse was fed often. He ate the green grass in the pasture and people brought him oats and hay in the winter. We took him apples from fruit trees that dotted the valley. Some men came and built a lean-to shelter out of cast off boards at the edge of the pasture so old Swayback could protect himself from bad weather. The horse was lonely so he warmly welcomed any human association. Mothers and fathers of us children deemed him worthless, a nuisance, and a possible danger to their offspring. They wanted to put him down and send his body to make glue in a glue factory. We children wailed and protested until the adult notions ceased.

The Lindstrom family moved into Griff's Old House one summer. We told the two girls to come to the pasture and play with us. One day Carole and Maureen walked down the dusty road to join us in our fun. Carole especially liked the horse. She spent lots of time with him, rubbing his soft muzzle, placing her hand playfully in his mouth, with no fear of getting bit.

He allowed her to place her arms around his neck and tease him by tickling his ears. She could walk directly behind him without getting kicked. Maureen kept her distance fearing that the horse would kick her with his feet. Carole lavished him with love and affection. Old Swayback followed her wherever she went in the pasture disallowing her playing games with other children. He wanted all of her time. He adopted her. It warmed Carole's heart to receive such unconditional love.

Everyone played until dark then went separate ways on tired little feet back to their respective homes in the valley. Old Swayback took on a forlorn look as the children rubbed his nose in departing. He wagged his tail from side to side and kept his eyes opened wide. There was a tint of sadness in them.

"We will come back tomorrow," Carole told Old Swayback.

What does a horse know or care about tomorrow? He understood that his playmates were leaving him now to be alone in the pasture, sad and lonely until our return. He watched until the last kid disappeared in the distance. He retraced the pasture path to the lean-to where he chomped on sweet grass until his belly grew full.

Half-way home Carole discovered that she had left her coat on the playground. This coat had been a gift from her mother. It had come to her at great cost in labor. She never let Carole forget that fact. Should Carole not go back for the coat, her mother would beat her. It was already dusk for long night shadows stretched through the trees and across the pasture land. Her sister Maureen walked home with us as Carole went back alone to retrieve her possession. She was not afraid of the dark. But Maureen twisted her hands nervously because she knew what their mother would do to both of them if Carole could not find the coat. Nothing in these fields and woods could harm her worse than an angry mother.

Carole retraced her journey down the road to the pasture. Upon hearing her cross the fence, Old Swayback came out of his lean-to to see who was there. In order not to disturb him further, Carole picked up her sweater and ran back toward the fence. All of a sudden her left foot got caught in one of the numerous crawdad holes. As she fell, she broke the bone in her left foot just above the ankle. She went down hard smashing her chin against the ground. The fall knocked her out cold. She lay there shivering, fearing that hypothermia might set in. Her mother assumed she was at home in her bed because Maureen did not tell her about the coat when she got home. Maureen climbed into her bed, pulled the covers up over her head, and gave thanks to Heaven that she was not in Carole's shoes. No help would come to Carole this night.

Rainfall toward morning awoke her to an ankle throbbing with pain; she cried as the pain was unbearable. She yelled into the darkness for someone to help her, but she knew no one would come, or so she thought. Suddenly she felt a gentle nudge from a soft, warm nose, warm with heat she so desperately needed. Old Swayback was there. He grabbed her shirt and arm in his huge teeth and slowly began to pull her across the pasture. Reaching up Carole used her last strength to grab the long hair on his mane with her hand. She held on with all her might as the horse dragged her into the protection of the warm, dry lean-to. Old Swayback stood over her so the rain would not hit her, his sagging belly only inches from her face.

In the morning Maureen cried as she explained to their mother what had happened and that Carole had not returned home last night. People gathered from all over the valley to search for Carole. They could not believe their eyes when they discovered her under the lean-to with the horse standing vigil over her. Old Swayback protested as adults moved him back in order to lift Carole into an ambulance for the ride to a hospital. The horse walked as far as he could go staring sadly as the vehicle carried Carole away.

Afterward, dozens of kids petted Old Swayback with their hands, gently touching his neck and head. People talked to him as if he were human and could understand language. Men rode up in a truck and built him a new, real stable. People brought him apples, carrots, hay and straw. As tributes poured in to Old Swayback, far away in a hospital bed in the city, a little girl named Carole lay in a soft bed, thanking Old Swayback for his miracle gift---her life.

WASH DAY

Dahlaree and her mother moved out of Griff's Old House not long after June Jr. stole their prize rooster and we ate it. True to his promise, June Jr. stole all of the chickens, one at a time, bringing them home to my mother to cook. Our family enjoyed chicken and dumplings more often than usual. People who live in Ottie's world on the edge of survival don't moralize about their actions. When food is available, they eat it. We felt no remorse or compassion toward Dahlaree's family or chickens. They had chickens, we did not. We were hungry, so we stole and ate them. Life was plain and simple. We would probably have killed and eaten Dahlaree and her mother had conditions gotten really bad. The desire to survive is strong in the human species, especially in Ottie's world.

Dahlaree and her mother made a pig out of clay from the creek bank, stuck bird feathers in it and placed it in the Devil's Creek Fork spring where we cooled our milk. They crossed two birch twigs in the form of a cross. As we had attacked their food source, they attacked ours. They left a curse on our milk. My mother averred that she did not believe in curses. She smashed the pig against the rocks, breaking it into hundreds of pieces. She kicked the birch twigs into the laurel. She spat on the rock and made a cross on it with her own foot, indicating a breaking of the curse. Just in case the curse was real, for the next several weeks, she had us put the milk in the creek near the barn.

Griff's Old House coughed up families as regularly as a volcano spews lava. This time, however, it did not stay vacant very long. Mrs. Lindstrom moved in with her two daughters Carole and Maureen. Mrs. Lindstrom and my mother could have been sisters, for life had forced them to be cold and hard. Rearing children by themselves exasperated their lot in life, leaving them indifferent to all but their own needs. Maureen was the softer of the two girls because long ago she had succumbed to the power and might of the mother. Carole decided not to capitulate to her mother, the bully, nor did she give in to her mother's boyfriends. Carole was a strong girl in mind and body. Maureen was not weak; she was just tired of all the fighting. Her kind nature had disappeared long ago under the rubble of verbal and physical abuse heaped on her by males and females alike. She protected Maureen as best she could as a surrogate mother. Carole was wise in knowing when to resist her mother and when to follow her dictums exactly.

Mrs. Lindstrom owned one prized possession---a washing machine. It was made of white enamel and rested on four legs with rollers on the bottom to move it about. There was a set of two ringers rising from the basin of the machine. They operated separately when one engaged them with a handle. In running clothes and sheets through the ringers, it squeezed out excess water making the drying process much quicker.

Mrs. Lindstrom's washing machine arrived on the back of a log truck where it lay securely tied with pieces of rope. It took a special place on her front porch so everyone passing would know that the family owned a status symbol. Mrs. Lindstrom boasted of buying the machine in Ritter, West Virginia, before moving to the valley. She shipped it all that distance not knowing that washing machines were available in Bostic only twenty miles from the valley. There was one major problem here. Griff's Old House had no electricity. Mrs. Lindstrom set about fixing that minor problem. She went to the office of the Rural Free Delivery (RFD) in Bostic. We never knew how she did it, but several days later the RFD men set up poles and strung a single electric wire to Griff's Old House. Mrs. Lindstrom plugged in her washing machine. It danced on the floor with a chugging noise. The RFD linesmen beat a hasty retreat.

Their mother laid down the law to Maureen and Carole that when they washed clothes and put them through the rollers; they were never to take the ringers apart. The company that had made the washing machines designed them so that the wringer and rollers came apart to allow proper repair and cleaning. It was virtually impossible for a non-mechanic to put the apparatus back together again so that it would work properly. Therefore, Mrs. Lindstrom warned the girls that under no circumstances were they to mess with those rollers. The girls knew that if they disobeyed, she would beat them severely. When she told you to do something, she would follow through on her threats.

One day Mrs. Lindstrom was away when my sisters and I went up to play with Carole and Maureen. Work and play were one and the same in our valley. If you visited a neighbor, whatever they were doing you joined in to help. When we arrived, it was Carole's wash day. The washing machine literally danced on its four legs as the agitator whisked clothes through the water. A strong musky smell of Octygen soap swirled up from the wash water. An occasional soap bubble formed, floating up toward the porch ceiling popping against a board. Carole busily sorted and stacked clothes, sheets, whites and darks all the while chatting and gossiping with us about everyone and everything. Meanwhile my sister and Maureen pushed brooms across the floor inside raising the cleanliness to that demanded by the mother.

The washing machine ran through its cycle and the clothes finished washing. Carole emptied the wash water through a side black hose attached to the side of the washing machine. Next, she poured buckets of clean water into the basin to rinse the clothes. With that done, she engaged the rollers on the wringer to wring out the clothes. She sent the edge of a sheet rolling through and I caught it on the other side. As the edge of the cloth came through, it was pressed flat with water in it pushed back into the basin. I heard Carole scream. Her fingers and hand had caught in the sheet and went straight through the rollers. They were already blue from the pressure of the rollers. She tried to pull her hand in reverse but the rollers would not turn. We thought about knocking the rollers apart but Carole screamed that she would rather cut off her hand than deal with her mother's wrath if she touched the rollers.

"You may as well go ahead and kill me," Carole said, "or cut the arm off."

Maureen already had an axe in her hand in order to do the deed.

"No, no," I yelled, "I'll go get Gentry to help us."

I ran down the dusty road past our farm in the direction of Skiff's Old House to find Gentry. My tiny legs left dust devils in the red soil as I literally flew through forest and over stream.

Arriving where Gentry lived, I yelled, "Carole's hurt. She's caught in a washing machine wringer."

Gentry grinned trying to form an image in his mind of what Carole looked like caught in the rollers. What did I want him to do, shove her on through? The two of us jumped astride his white horse and retraced my steps at a gallop. When he saw Carole, he thought out loud, "These new-fangled machines will be the death of us all." Gentry started to dismantle the wringer with its rollers. Maureen and Carole both yelled in protest.

Gentry saw Carole's swollen hand engorged with purple red blood. He took out his pocket knife and drilled a small hole in each finger so that the blood could drain, allowing the hand and fingers to be pulled in reverse through the rollers. Blood splattered everywhere as if someone had just successfully slaughtered a hog. Gentry gently pulled her fingers back through the wringer and bandaged them with some cloth. He sat Carole down in a chair where she closed her eyes, wondering what her mother would do. The other children who had been playing fled. Gentry stopped at our house to tell my mother what had happened.

Upon hearing what had happened, Mrs. Lindstrom examined her washing machine in minute detail to make sure it was not hurt and then she went into the kitchen saying, "I'm glad my machine isn't damaged." She never even looked at Carole's hand nor asked if she were fine.

Six months later the Lindstrom family left the valley at night. We heard the drone of the truck that took them away. We always wondered why they left. Maybe they encountered the Bigfoot, Knobby. The next day our group walked up the road to check out Griff's Old House in the event that there was something we could pillage. Surprisingly they left the washing machine on the porch. It was mysteriously broken. Someone had jammed a heavy stick through the rollers breaking them and ripping the whole apparatus apart.

"Carole got her revenge," I chuckled.

I lifted the lid that covered the wash basin of the washing machine and found a note in Carole's handwriting. It read: "You can have the washing machine. Goodbye. Gone to Oregon."

Forty years later I accidentally met Carole again in Winnie, Texas. She was selling used washing machines.

HAVE YOU SEEN MY SON

Winds of a far-away war swept across the valley. They took away six of our young men to the battlefields of France. One of the young men was Ephraim, a sweet country lad whose family lived on the south side of the valley. In his first three years of school, he had learned with Miss Lucy. In his second three, he had studied with Mr. Rawlins. He had gone then to high school at Sunshine. He had been too young to marry or move away, so he had continued to live with his parents and work on the farm.

Ephraim was such a gentle soul that he would not harm a human being or farm animal. In the fall when time came to slaughter the hogs, he would go away until the work was accomplished. He was kind and loving with children he met. He went to help another farmer do his work when he was sick. If there were an accident, he always went to the aid of the victim. How ironic it was that he was one of the six valley men the draft board chose to send away to war. When he left, a small group of his family and friends stood huddled at Stan's Country Store to see him off on his journey to the military and to a larger world of violence outside. As the

Greyhound bus pulled away, all his friends and family lifted their hands in a gesture of farewell. Ephraim pressed his face against the back window of the bus seeming to know that this valley and these people would never know him again. The horrors of war would guarantee it.

When he returned three years later, the entire valley turned out to welcome Ephraim back home. The crowd contrasted greatly with the handful of people who had watched him leave for they were now welcoming home a hero. As the Greyhound bus pulled into Stan's Country Store, thunderous applause greeted it. A choir sang "God Bless America" and a woman pushed an American flag into Ephraim's hand.

But it was a stranger who stepped off the bus, for the heart and soul of Ephraim lay on some foreign field along with his dead comrades. The horrors of war had taken away his youth, his innocence, and his warm heart leaving him a burnt-out shell. The visions of the many men and civilians he had killed paralyzed his brain. Ephraim was a broken man. He could not sleep. He could no longer work. He took to sitting hours a day on the bench in front of Stan's Country Store. He talked out loud as if carrying on a conversation with some unseen person in the air above him.

When my mother sent me to the store one day, I saw Ephraim on the bench, lost in his other world of war. I quietly sat down beside him looking admiringly into his deep, blue eyes.

"What do you want, kid?" he asked out loud.

"Nothing," I replied.

He no longer held a kind, gentle attitude toward children. He spoke a few more words to his unseen person then focused again on me.

"I didn't want to kill all those people," he agonized to me. "I couldn't even kill hogs on the farm."

Being a child, I could not possibly understand his pain. I placed my little hand in his as he began to weep, his shoulders heaving with sorrow only he understood. The emotion ran its course. Ephraim went into the store and returned with an R.C. and a moon pie.

"Here, this is for you, kid. I like you," he said.

I smiled as the fizzy R.C. burned my nose and the chocolate from the moon pie melted on my fingers and face.

"I'm going to tell you a story I've not shared with anyone since I got back home, because I can see that you do not judge people." He began:

"Love is the most powerful force in the universe. Not even Time and Space can withstand its strength. Unceasing, the bonds of love connect and bind to the ends of forever." I have seen the force of love in action and my life is forever altered.

As the fighting lessened in Normandy, I entered the small town of Ponterson opposite the magnificent medieval abbey of Mont-St.-Michel. The morning fog broke from the English Channel. I wiped sleep from my eyes and parked my vehicle next to the train station, or what was left of it after the fighting. I bought a brioche at a small bakery. People scurried here and there to board one of the few trains available. Suddenly, I felt a gentle tap on my shoulder. Turning abruptly, I looked down into the face of an elderly lady dressed in black.

Smiling at me, she said, 'Have you seen my son?'

"I'm sorry, Madam, I've just arrived here. I do not know him. I have not seen your son."

"Oh, thank you, sir," she said in a half dream voice. She walked to every person on the train station asking if anyone had seen her son. No one had. Each time I was in the vicinity of the train station, I saw the same lady. She appeared like a phantom among the crowd asking the same unanswered question, "Have you seen my son?"

Not until I was on my plane home to our valley did the meaning of the encounter with the lady come clearly to my mind. It was the war. This lady had lost her son in the war. He had departed this very train station. She, his mother, refusing to give him up, returned daily to search for him. She was an example of love in action, of unbreakable bonds of husband to wife, friend to friend, and mother to son. Maybe I killed him. My heart broke for her. I wanted to take her in my arms and say, "Yes, I have seen your son. I know him well. He is the symbol of all those who have perished in the holocaust of war. Your son was one of the Roman legionnaires borne home from a foreign country on his shield. He was one of the Crusaders desiring to retake the Holy Land. He drowned at sea in Spain's vast armada. He died before a firing squad in a concentration camp. He sat weeping for you in Flanders Field." At this moment I still hear her imploring plea. It will never leave me. When I stand before the Throne of Grace and lay my life before God for assessment, I will see again the lady in black and God will ask me in a loving way, "Do you know him, have you seen my son?"

Ephraim stood up, set me on my feet on the bench, leaned down and kissed me on my blond head.

"Thanks for listening to me, kid. I love you."

He marched down the dusty roadway, with lightness in his stride. There seemed to be a certainty in his gait. Ephraim had made up his mind. He was tired of life. He was tired of the war. He was tired of the madness that had seized his mind. So he went home and blew his brains out with his father's shotgun.

Each time thereafter when I sat on the bench in front of Stan's store drinking an R.C. and eating a moon pie, I remembered my friend. I cried for Ephraim.

FINAL JUSTICE

E phraim boarded the Greyhound bus at Stan's Country Store
to go to the army. It headed south to Shelby, then on to
Spartanburg. A young girl of eighteen got on the bus at the station
in Spartanburg. She sat across the aisle in the outside seat next to
Ephraim. He noticed that she was short, about five feet in height,
and approximately one hundred twenty-five pounds. Brown hair
fell down over her ears and forehead and she looked out at the
world through soft, brown eyes. Shy and retiring, she slumped
down into her seat as if she were hiding from life. She looked at
Ephraim, and then she quickly averted her eyes from his glance.
Taking a fashion magazine out of her handbag, she thumbed restlessly through it. She eventually leaned her head back against the
seat falling asleep. Night fell as the Greyhound bus pushed on
through the darkness toward Atlanta and points beyond.

The bright lights of Atlanta awakened her from her slumber.
Such a large city it was in comparison to Spartanburg and the valley. She was a city girl, (more sophisticated than Ephraim), who
felt comfortable among concrete buildings and crowds of people.

The bus driver announced that his leg of the trip ended here and that all passengers must change buses to cities farther south. The destination written on her papers read Fort McClellan, Alabama; as did the one on Ephraim's. She saw Ephraim go to the ticket counter and ask which bus went to Fort McClellan. She didn't quite hear the answer so she followed him out on to the bus tracks. He stopped at No. 42 placing his suitcase on the concrete.

She went directly to him and asked, "Is this bus going to Ft. McClellan, Alabama?"

"Yes," he replied.

"I'm headed there to join the army," she informed him.

"I've been drafted into the army, myself," he said.

"My name is Barbara," she extended her hand to shake his.

"I'm Ephraim. I come from Golden Valley about an hour's ride north of Spartanburg. Glad to meet you. Since we have the same destination, would you like to sit together?" he asked her.

"Thank you," she replied. "I'm a bit frightened about what lies ahead."

Nothing lying ahead could be more frightening to Barbara than what she was leaving behind her. In her eighteen years at home, she had experienced verbal, physical, and emotional abuse from a mother who lived in a world of non-reality and a step-father who treated her as a punching bag. The mother had signed papers for her to join the army only because one-half of Barbara's paycheck came to her each month. Unlike Ephraim, she had no family group to see her off at the bus station. No one came to say goodbye or to wish her well. Her suitcase was her only companion until she met Ephraim.

She was leery of him, as she was of all men, because they had always taken advantage of her. Maybe in the army there was hope for good, fair treatment. Maybe the men there respected women. Her heart was heavy as she looked back over her life. She had been denied love, warmth, affection, wealth and basic happiness.

A long career in the army was her present dream. It would be the pathway to a new life, so she intended to live fully. Her only option to the military was to stay home and marry Dean Pippers, a fate worse than death. They boarded the new bus and sped across the red clay earth of Georgia to the dark, Alabama delta and Ft. McClellan.

Sixty-five men and three women disembarked at the fort to the abusive shouts of Sgt. Jones.

"Get in line you assholes."

It was the beginning of the breaking down of raw recruits to rebuild them into solid soldiers. These abusive shouts and commands took Barbara right back to her family household. She had merely swapped the Devil for a witch. At this Induction Center, Ephraim left her because the army separated men and women for basic training. She had a physical examination, a haircut, vaccinations, and went to an assigned bunk in a barracks. For the next six weeks she was fairly isolated. They threw a G.I. party whereby the recruits mopped floors, washed windows, and set their living quarters in order. They all went to class to learn the way of the army---salute, rank, how to march, rules and regulations. At the end of basic training, Barbara went to Ft. Houston, Texas, to study to be a paramedic with the EMT. Men and women were trained together in this class. She could not escape the men. At home it was one man; here she must deal with dozens.

Barbara enjoyed her medical training. She looked forward to helping wounded people, but she never dreamed that life would wound her most of all. The destroying storm came in the form of a Sgt. Jones who commanded all the medical personnel. He singled out Barbara from the very beginning because he liked her looks. He was mercenary. During his long tenure in the army, he used his military authority over women to take what he wanted. He knew the male chain of command would not take punitive actions against one of their own. He cut Barbara from the herd by riding her case, verbally breaking down her resistance. One day he forced her to look through the window at a sign erected over the barrack gate.

"If you are looking for sex, use a G.I. for they are as clean as you are."

"I'm not looking for that," she informed him.

"I am," he retorted.

At those words, Sgt. Jones grabbed her around the waist, his hairy arms twisting her body toward him. She smelled his hot, spearmint breath from the stick of gum he had placed in his mouth moments before the attack. The sickening smell of his cheap, Patchouli aftershave perfume filled her nostrils, setting off the gag reflex in her throat. His large horse-like teeth became visible as his lips parted, forming a sinister smile.

He dragged her to his office and raped her. Afterwards, she fled back to her barracks where a fellow WAC found her weeping on her cot. She related the story to her friend who advised her to remain quiet. The men controlled the chain of command and viewed attacks on women as their prerogative. Barbara could not remain quiet. She had left her home because of this kind of treatment and would not accept it in her new place. Against the advice of all military personnel, she reported Sgt. Jones and what he had done to the Camp Lieutenant. He asked her for proof, for witnesses. She had none, not even a medical examination. Sgt. Jones denied any knowledge of an attack against her. In every weekly review thereafter, they rated her below standard on everything. Finally, the Captain's Court dismissed her from the army "for the good of the service." They ordered all soldiers to shun her. She left Ft. Houston on a Greyhound bus in disgrace.

Lady Justice laid down her sword, her shield, and her scales of justice, weeping at this travesty, this miscarriage of justice. Barbara was used, condemned, and thrown out for daring to declare her right to be a woman, one that refused to be used as a play toy by these ego-inflated men. Her soul cried out for fairness, for a balancing of the scales of justice, for her story to be told. Where were lawyers to take up her cause? Where were military men to rise and stay this unfair judgment against her? Where was the hue and cry from men and women back home that should not condone this type of treatment of women? They all sat in silence, their tongues frozen by fear, by disbelief that army men would behave in such a manner.

"Boys will be boys," they reasoned.

Men have their privilege. She had been raped. She had been violated. She was dismissed from her career for asking for justice. Then Lady Justice rose up striking her sword against the shield. She railed against this situation.

"This will not stand. I have not yet yielded my verdict."

There was no crowd to greet Barbara when she arrived back home. No choir sang "God Bless America." No flags were unfurled; only a derelict sat against a wall in a stupor. Barbara's life was now as empty and hopeless as his. Her heart weary, she did not return home nor did she go to marry Dean Pippers. Rather, she rented a room in a seedy motel at Fort Bragg and went to work as a waitress at a private golf club. It catered to active and retired military personnel. This club, known nation- wide, drew men from everywhere across the nation. Their golf tournaments were renowned. The highest ranking army men made it their goal to come here.

Barbara worked hard as she dealt with the sorrows of her life. It was a joy to meet and associate with military personnel, but a painful memory for her when some among them told her she ought to join the army. She had outstanding qualities the army wanted. What could she tell these hypocrites? I was in your army. One of your respected men raped me and drummed me out when I sought justice. Any and all of you would have done the same to me. She held her tongue and her anguish deepened.

Her boss asked her one day to cater a private party at the club. These men were important and powerful so he wanted his best waitress to serve them. She prepared the tables as cooks fixed special food such as lobster, pate de foie gras, escargots, paella, oysters on the half shell, and wild salmon. When the party began, she circulated, taking beverage orders. Such a military gathering she had not seen since Ft. Houston. One of the men in the group looked very familiar to her. As she took his drink order, she looked at his name tag. Sgt. Jones was now First Sgt. Jones.

"They rewarded him for crime," she thought to herself.

She studied him carefully. He was still arrogant, egotistical, relishing being a part of this distinguished company. He patted her on the buttocks when she brought him tea. First Sgt. Jones did not remember her because she meant nothing to him other than a moment of gratification. He laid her tip in a folded napkin on which he wrote, "Come to my room #213C. I think you will like what I have to offer you Jones." The full fury of her suffering rose to the surface. She screamed in her car on the way home. She broke out in hives. She threw up. Why could she have no justice for this evil man? Vengeance is mine says the Lord. Baloney! I will be my own swift sword of justice.

Barbara awakened from a troubled sleep one quiet Saturday morning. It was raining. She heard the raindrops falling against the metal roof of her apartment house. Her heart beat to the rhythm of the rain. Though sleepy, she felt a deep resolve within her. Today was the day Lady Justice had promised her redemption. Today she would strike from the depths of her wounded soul at the monster who had stripped her of her dignity. She hummed a military march in a soft voice as she dressed herself in a warm pink dress and overcoat. The soft pink made her feel like a woman again. Dried leaves stuck to the soles of her shoes as she made her way to a pet store where she bought a Ranitomeya Benedicta, a Blessed Poison Frog. She scraped from its skin some of the neurotoxic poison, placing it into a vial. Taking it with her, she went to room #213C.

Jones welcomed her enthusiastically. "Honey, come right to bed. I can't wait for a repeat of what I've had so many times in the military."

"I'll fix us a drink, first," she told him.

She went to the kitchen, placed the neurotoxin in a glass and filled it with vodka and orange juice making them a screwdriver.

Returning to the room, she placed the drink in his hairy, expectant hand purring "Do you believe in justice First Sgt. Jones?"

He swallowed the vodka. "Oh, yes," he said "I mete out justice to soldiers and men of lesser rank daily. As you climb in rank in my army, you have to dish out justice."

"Do you ever make any mistakes?" she asked him.

"Of course not," he snapped. "Any rank beneath you is beneath you. It comes with the territory. Who gives a damn about grunts?"

"Do you get to have a lot of sex in the military?" she quizzed him.

"All I want," he bragged arrogantly. "If the women don't consent, I coax them with my charm and endowment." His speech began to slur from the effects of the frog neurotoxin. He continued, "Occasionally one of them will squeal. I fixed one woman's ass at Ft. Houston when she squealed on me. Busted her rank and sent her packing. The army is a man's world and it will never punish one of its own for screwing a woman." His body began to freeze in place as his muscles stopped working. Soon only his eyes moved, his knees buckled, and his voice quivered into a freeze.

She sat beside him now to have her say:

"My name is Barbara. It is I that you forced to consent at Ft. Houston. That forcing is called rape, my dear. You had me thrown out of the army when I sought justice. I have come back, Sir, as my own avenging angel. The paralysis you now feel is from the Blessed Poison Frog who has become my friend. You killed my spirit. You injured my soul. You took from me my dignity and self-worth, slowly, piece by piece as this frog poison now disintegrates you. How could I ever be the same? I was a Judas Goat on your alter of pleasure. There are still so many men like you in the military and I intend to destroy all of them. I have a name. I am a person. I am a woman. I stand equal to you. You took my life, I now demand yours. I want you to see every woman you 'forced to consent' as your sorry life slips away."

She stared into his eyes as life left them. She rose, took her glass and vial, wiped everything free of fingerprints, and departed. No one saw her or would ever know that she was there.

A hue and cry arose when maids found the sergeant's body, cold and stiff, the following morning. Assuming a heart attack had taken him, the doctors performed no autopsy. They gave him a high ranking funeral eulogizing him, speaking of his outstanding diligence to duty, especially his concern for the welfare of women in the military. In her apartment far away in the seedy motel, Barbara mixed some new vials of neurotoxins. In front of her lay a list of army officers who had sat on military courts where officers had been accused of rape and set free. Lady Justice took off her blindfold and winked. Final justice would come.

MISS LUCY

A feeling of nervousness and anticipation ran through our small group as we jostled each other for viewing position at the six oversized classroom windows. Everyone was straining to get a glimpse of Miss Lucy as she slowly made her way down the path that led from her house to the two-room school. Dressed in overcoat, scarf, gloves and boots, she made this grand walk every day for twenty-five years. To a traveler along the highway, she seemed no more than a country housewife on her way to the store, but to us she was a Grande Dame walking along the boardwalk of her kingdom. She was Miss Lucy, our teacher, and we loved her.

Miss Lucy's reputation as a teacher was established long before most of us came into this world. She taught all our mothers and fathers before us because the community was small and there was no other school but hers. There was no rule but hers, too, and no one rose to question her authority. She had no formal degree or certification but such was of no consequence. The rising educational quality of the small community was the only necessary testimony of her right to be in the classroom. She served as school board, superintendent, principal and teacher. On cold mornings she was the janitor, for she arrived long before we did in order to build a coal fire in the pot-bellied stove that occupied one corner of the classroom. At noon she was the cafeteria staff. Moving efficiently from desk to desk, she distributed the free bottles of milk provided us by the state. Two days each month she was our nurse for she took responsibility for checking for bad tonsils, body sores, head lice, yellow teeth, and dirty hands. True to her duty, she was as accurate as a computer at spotting any health offense and a curt note went home in the lunch pail of any offender. She was our counselor, our surrogate parent and our counselor when we cried. She also found time to teach.

It was the autumn of 1949 when I first came under the guardianship of Miss Lucy. I cried as I walked with my older sister up the interminable wooden steps that ended at Miss Lucy's room. Somehow I just knew that when that big oak door opened, my life would never again be the same. The hinges creaked; I cried even louder, but my sister pushed me into the room and into the omniscient presence of Miss Lucy.

"Child, this classroom is a place of happiness. There is no need for tears here. Blow your nose," she said as she handed me her delicately embroidered handkerchief.

I blew my nose, stopped crying, and took my seat with eight first graders who, no doubt, had experienced a similar trauma.

Over the next two and one-half years, Miss Lucy opened the world to us. She took me from the first awkward attempts at printing the alphabet to beautiful, flowing cursive sentences. I learned to read in the "See Jane Go series" and to spell from the old Blue Book Speller. We learned to count by using objects in the classroom. Our excitement with learning moved with the seasons. For Halloween we drew bowed-up cats and pumpkins. At Christmas we made cards and stockings. Hearts and cupids were online for Valentine's Day as were black, cardboard silhouettes of Washington and Lincoln on their birthdays. Spring brought St. Patrick Day green with shamrocks and leprechauns. There was an annual egg hunt at Easter. In June, we had a farewell party with cupcakes and milk.

We chanted parts of our language daily in unison like a children's choir: go, went, gone.....see, saw, seen. At the time we did not understand the finer points of grammar. However, in later life the musical sound of that rhythmic chanting alerted us to the correct usage of verbs. And, worst of all, when we had difficulty with a subject, Miss Lucy made us write it out. Many are the nights I sat up late writing out words I had misspelled and poems for memorization. No one ever questioned Miss Lucy's wisdom.

In February of my third year in her school, June Jr. stole a car and my family had to move to Burke County, so I said goodbye to Miss Lucy on my last day. She walked me to the door of the school, said goodbye as the big orange bus pulled away. Looking back through the rear window, I saw her standing like a marble statue; arm outstretched waving a white embroidered handkerchief, the same one that welcomed many terrified first graders into the exciting world of formal education.

Years have come and gone now. Good teachers have come my way since, but it is Miss Lucy who has forever remained my idol. She was very special because she taught by example, never asking her students to maintain standards that she herself did not have. She never complained of working conditions, salary, nor long hours of work. She showed no preference for creed, color, or social standing. We were all her children. Hers was a high calling. Her work continues through me and the hundreds of good citizens she helped produce. We are all the notes in her song of life.

As I now labor to solve the problems life brings, discouragement sets in. I waver in my faith in people. I complain of the vicissitudes of life. Sometimes I cannot find my way to a better level of living. Then Miss Lucy's voice comes ringing across the years. "Find a way, child, or make one." I've made a way, Miss Lucy, thanks to you. You are the person who taught me how to read and write. This book is my gift back to you.

VAMPIRES

No one will ever convince me that vampires aren't real. They exist. I have seen them. They are mostly tall women dressed in white with long capes outlined in blue. They wear square, starched caps across the front of their hair. They have long, sharp incisor teeth that stick down over their lower lips. They carry a wooden picnic basket covered with a white cloth and it smells like rubbing alcohol. In their baskets they carry extra teeth they stick in your arms to extract blood. They wear white stockings to cover hair on their legs and white shoes to cover their cloven hooves. These vampires I've seen and felt come out at midday unafraid of presenting themselves to small school children. They prefer it that way. When they appear, kids hastily seek out dark places in which to hide as if they were their victims. Miss Lucy called them "nurses" but we did not believe her. They were vampires.

My first encounter with a vampire happened when my older sister took me to school when I was five years old to get diphtheria and smallpox shots so I could enter school the following year. The first time the bus stopped for me, I was too little to get aboard. I tried to climb up on the bus step but my body was too small. My sister lifted me up the two steps and sat me on the first bench seat. The bus driver waited patiently and even smiled as I climbed on board. I spent the school day with my sister waiting for my first vampire visit. In the afternoon Miss Lucy called my name. My sister walked with me down the sixteen steps to the basement of the school building where the vampires waited. They grabbed me with their winged claws and they inserted two extra fangs into my arms. One fang carried the diphtheria vaccine and the other carried the smallpox. I cried a little because the fangs hurt. Both my arms swelled. I resolved to go to war with vampires from that day onward.

A year later in the first grade, I was an old pro at being in school. I loved learning in Miss Lucy's class. I was a good reader. I hated math. But there was so much more. There were no boring days. We had lunch and playtime at eleven o'clock each day. Miss Lucy turned us loose to create our own play as we wished. The boys in all grades claimed the broom sedge field and pine trees behind the school building for themselves so these spots were off limits to girls. The girls claimed the huge wild grape vines growing between trees where they could sit and play house. We boys pretended to be ape-men by climbing up the pine trees until we could swing from one to another. We traveled the length of the field in the treetops. We built grass forts in the broom sedge field. It was great fun to navigate the field via the tunnels. Inside the school building at the side a door opened to a stairway which led into an unfinished dirt part of the basement. It was a dank, dark, dirty place. Kids rarely ventured into this area for it seemed to be a natural habitat for vampires.

We were having a wonderful play day together. Some kid noticed a slant-back 1940's coupe ford enter the road to the school. It moved slowly with intent. Imprinted on the side was a huge blood drop surrounded by a circle. Tinted windows prevented anyone's seeing the occupants inside. Every kid on the playground froze in place like statues in Pompeii. As the car stopped and the first vampire emerged, a hue and cry, a yelling and moaning rose from the throats of the children.

"Vampires," somebody yelled shrilly, "Vampires."

The words flew across the broom sedge and up the pine trees, across the wild grape vines and through the hallways. Kids ran in panic. Some hid themselves in the grass fort and tunnels. Some climbed as high as they could into the pine trees holding on to the limbs like leeches. Several fled into the dank, dark basement to escape. Girls huddled in the outhouse. Boys hid under their desks in Miss Lucy's classroom. Some slid away into the closets. In five minutes, not one child remained visible. The school was vacant, abandoned except for Miss Lucy, Mr. Rawlins and the vampires. How could they welcome these hated blood suckers into our inner sanctum?

Mr. Rawlins rang the bell to end lunch and recess. No one returned to the building. The two teachers called out for us to come back inside. No one responded. These teachers were not accustomed to walking into the fields and pines so they did not know our secret places. The vampires ignored us all and set up their laboratory in the old cafeteria in the basement of the building. Our two teachers enlisted the aid of the vampire nurses in trying to lure us back into the building. What a mistake. Miss Lucy took the area that included the girls' outhouse and play station in the vines. Mr. Rawlins took the basement area and the pine trees. One vampire went to the classrooms while the other headed for the broom sedge field. I was hiding in the broom sedge field. She was too large to crawl through the tunnels like we did and we were not answering her calls to surrender.

This one was clever. She took a long stick and proceeded to jab it into the grass tunnels every two feet. She looked like Old Granny Seever gigging for frogs. Boys dodged left and right to avoid getting gigged, but she finally caught me. She dragged me and another victim to the vampire den and set us up for examination.

Meanwhile Miss Lucy nabbed two girls in the outhouse and three more in the wild grape vines. The second vampire pulled two kids from the pine trees. We yelled and screamed not wanting to go willingly to have our blood and brains sucked out. A line now formed outside the basement room. It consisted of us kids they had already caught.

Mr. Rawlins used his flashlight to clear out the opposite side of the dark, dank basement. One vampire returned to the pine trees where she proceeded to shake several boys out. They fell to the ground like giant apples from a tree. The grass tunnels and fort lay in ruins. Upturned chairs littered the classroom. We all stood in line now defeated. The vampires had won the war.

Word spread down the line of kids that "they're giving shots with a needle" in there. Wailing broke out anew. Kids lost their lunch. Some passed gas. Some pooped. Some peed in their pants. Others grew weak and just sat down accepting their fate. An un-pleasant smell of vampires filled the area. Kids emerged from the vampire room pale as a ghost, eyes frozen like the proverbial deer in the headlights. Their arms bore needle or bite marks covered with cotton and tape. Kids inside the basement room cried and screamed. We could bear it no longer. The line broke and we all fled. This time kids headed for the hills, the road, the cemetery, for home.

Miss Lucy, Mr. Rawlins and the vampires tried to corral us, but they were left high and dry, alone at the school. Kids sought ref-uge in any house that opened its doors to them along the main highway in the valley. Some even ran as far as Stan's store. How do we get these children to come back, they pondered? Parents fil-tered into the school laughing at the humorous event. One smart father brought a case of moon pies and RCs. He rode up and down the highway yelling into the woods, across the fields, and houses that they had a free moon pie for anyone who would come back to school. Kids slowly crawled from their hiding places to accept the treat.

The vampires packed up their wares and returned to Forest City. In order to educate us children about health and to show us that nurses were kind and helpful, Miss Lucy organized a program. All of us knew and loved her mother and recognized her on sight. Miss Lucy asked her mother to dress up as a nurse and stand on stage so we would associate her kindness with that of nurses. When she walked out on stage in that nurse's uniform, some dumb kid seated in the back yelled out, "Oh, hell, her mother is a vampire." Looking up Miss Lucy saw that the auditorium was totally empty. Not a kid in sight.

GOMER'S KITTY CAT

I t did not bother Gomer Glitch one bit that he was repeating the third grade for the fourth time. He was making progress. Now he could say his ABCs, write his name, and do his three times three multiplication tables. He could read from the Second Grade Series of books quite well. Gomer could not do academic work from books. Letters and numbers simply did not resonate in his brain. His parents wanted him to quit school, but the Know-It-Alls on the school board in Forest City said no. Splendora told him he needed to learn the curriculum to get into college. "What is college?" he asked her. Anyway, he could quit school in the Fifth Grade because he would be sixteen years old at this rate. Gomer liked school. Mr. Rawlins built him a special large table desk standing on four legs so his knees could fit underneath. They gave him an adult chair to sit in. Miss Lucy furnished him with regular crayons which made him feel proud. She placed his table near her desk so she could give him special attention.

When playing baseball at recess, all students wanted Gomer on their team because he was the home run king. His powerful arms easily sent the ball across the home run line. He held the school record for grand slam home runs. Younger children clung to his hands and arms like baby ducklings bonding with their mother. He was their hero. Gomer also held the distinction of being the only student in school who could carry a bucket of coal by himself. Miss Lucy sent a student to accompany him to make sure that he came back to the classroom. When she had to leave the classroom for a moment, she left Gomer in charge. He didn't bother to take names. He walked around the classroom slapping offenders on the tops of their heads. He took his work seriously.

Everybody forgave Gomer his shortcomings except for one curious one that no one could understand. Gomer loved the smell of skunk. When he found where a skunk walked, he would follow its trail until he found the critter. He would pick the skunk up to pet it. Of course the skunk sprayed its scent all over him. It didn't bother Gomer. His mother made him sleep in the barn until the scent wore off. It is impossible to wash off the scent of a skunk with ordinary soap and water. Old wives' tales indicated that tomato juice was the only substance capable of neutralizing the odor of skunk. His mother kept some juice on hand so he could bathe in it after usual encounters. She washed his clothes in it too.

At recess one day th3 kids came charging back into the classroom yelling that Gomer had caught a kitty cat and was intent on bringing it for Show and Tell that very afternoon. Mr. Rawlins grabbed his keys and locked the two front entrance doors to the school building. Everyone gathered at the tall, glass windows in Miss Lucy's classroom to watch Gomer come out of the woods with the kitty cat.

It was a small skunk with a white stripe from the nose crossing the back ending at the tip of its tail. Gomer held its jaws closed with his hand to prevent getting bit as he petted the animal with his other hand. It continued to lift its tail spraying scent all around.

Gomer did not care because it was like perfume to him. Miss Lucy yelled for him to put the kitty back in the woods. She moved his table and chair outside the building next to the outhouses where the skunk odor wouldn't matter so much. Poor Gomer sat alone doing busy work for the rest of the day. The bus driver made him walk home.

Gomer was dumb as dirt at school work but when he was in the woods, he was a master. Miss Lucy let him teach us about natural science. She accompanied us outside the school building where Gomer became the teacher. He led us into the woods and fields near the school. He showed us different trees: pine, birch, maple, oak, and hickory. He made us stand quietly listening to bird calls. He named them for us: finch, cardinal, woodpecker, mourning dove, and robin. He pointed out squirrels, rabbits, chipmunks, and two wild turkeys. We saw turtles and small fish in a stream and two toads on the path. Gomer turned over a log so we could see termites, larvae, worms, and ants. This was his world. We all felt dumb as dirt in Gomer's world as he must have felt in ours. He showed us edible plants. He insisted that we gather enough to make salad for the whole class on our return there. We picked wild lettuce, cattails, creasy greens, dandelions, young polk salat, and wild garlic. He broke branches from spice wood trees to make us a sweet tea. We took all our greens back to the classroom and washed them well.

Miss Lucy broke the spice wood branches into a huge, iron kettle, and added water almost to the top. She placed it on the pot-bellied stove to boil. When the food was ready, we each got a paper plate filled with wild greens seasoned with vinegar. We drank sweet spice wood tea from our own cups. Everyone in the class looked at Gomer in a new way knowing that he was far in advance of all of us in real, useful knowledge. Upon hearing of the incident with the skunk, school board member Splendora wrote a letter telling Miss Lucy and Mr. Rawlins to calm that dumbbell down or she would rate both of them below-standard. Upon hearing of the letter, some kids at the school sent her one of Gomer's kitty cats in a box.

We loved Gomer. He was our mascot. Kids brought him fruit, sweet potatoes, even moon pies and baloney sandwiches. He, in return, brought kids in the class pretty rocks, leaves, bird feathers., moss, bark, pine cones and pretty weavings he made out of broom sedge. Gomer loved to play marbles. At recess kids would rush to the playground to draw circles putting their cat-eye marbles inside. Gomer cleaned them out in no time at all with his giant shooters. He balanced them between his thumbnail and index finger. With a powerful thrust he let fly with the shooter, usually clearing out most of the marbles in the circle. Gomer had the biggest collection of marbles in the school. No one really minded losing to him.

One day Gomer decided to reign in some of the bullies in the school. He intended to have a "calling out." There was a hundred percent attendance on the announced day of the "calling out." It would occur at recess. Miss Lucy decided to allow extra time for him to get the job done. He called out June Jr. and Redtop. Kids gathered around the playground forming a semicircle. Gomer stood in the center. He called for Redtop to come stand opposite him. Redtop defied him choosing to stand on top of a small hill. He called Redtop out on his mistreatment of Little Eva. He ordered Redtop to faint like one of the goats when he clapped his hands. Redtop refused calling him a dumb, skunk-loving retard.

"I'll settle with you later, spider-lover," he told Redtop. Then he called out June Jr. for stealing Miss Lucy's money. June Jr. told him to go stuff it. He wouldn't allow the school's village idiot to tell him what to do. June Jr. intended to stomp his dumb-as-dirt ass. "We'll see," said Gomer.

The 'calling out' ended in a draw but animosities grew more intense. The three enemies returned to Miss Lucy's classroom all three loaded for bear. Within minutes a fight started. June Jr. walked to Gomer's large table and knocked him flat with one blow.

"That's my calling out card, you big dufus," June Jr. mocked him.

Redtop came over and beat Gomer in the head with his fists knocking him deeper into unconsciousness.

"Now you are a fainting goat," he yelled.

At that point all hell broke loose. Little Eva hit Redtop with one of her textbooks. Phyllis and I went after June Jr. with our chairs. We pummeled him good. Some of the second graders hurled books, chunks of paper, shoes, anything they could find. Redtop and June Jr. fled the scene with their egos bruised and their bodies bloodied. Gomer awakened with his head covered with knots from the beating. June Jr. and Redtop did not come back to school for a while. Tensions remained in the air until the spring picnic.

The entire school went to Lake McCall on the annual picnic in the spring. Children were enjoying themselves in various activities. In years past some remembered Harold Cody saving June Jr.'s life and Redtop's harassment of Little Eva. This year everyone hoped for a quiet, uneventful day. Not to be. Girls playing hopscotch looked up to see Gomer emerge from the woods carrying a baby skunk.

"Come see my kitty cat," he yelled to the girls.

They screamed and ran as the skunk lifted its tail and sprayed them all. Gomer walked over to a group of boys playing marbles saying, "Come pet my kitty cat." The boys left their marbles in the ring scrambling to get out of the skunk's range. It was too late. It covered them with spray. Not at all deterred, Gomer walked the skunk over to a group of children eating at the picnic tables. "Come play with my kitty cat," he invited. They overturned the tables trying to get out of the way, but the skunk got them all. Bodies lay everywhere around the lake some vomiting, some writhing in pain, others crying from the awful smell of skunk.

Mr. Rawlins bribed Gomer with a moon pie to take his kitty cat back into the woods. Kids went to get Raymond to load his sled with three large wooden tubs and go down the valley asking for donations of tomato juice from farm wives to wash off the skunk odor. Raymond drove his sled from door to door explaining the emergency at the lake, asking farmwives to donate tomato juice. They ran to their cellars and emptied quarts of juice until the tubs were filled. He drove them back to Lake McCall. They set up a triage center on one side of the bushes for the girls and a second one on the other side for the boys. Students stripped off their clothes and bathed in the tomato juice. Afterward, they plunged into the cool water of the lake to rinse off. The teachers burned all the clothes that were covered with skunk odor. Tom T. Tuttle from Forest City donated clothes to replace those lost. The kids grabbed Gomer and dunked him in the tomato juice head first all the while chanting, "Here kitty, kitty."

The year Gomer turned sixteen he had made it through the fourth grade, so he decided he needed no further formal education. He was probably right. The school decided to give him a graduation party. They made him a cap and gown with a gold tassel. They hand painted a special diploma granting him fourth grade status. He marched down the aisle of the auditorium by himself feeling proud of his accomplishments. The kids chanted in unison:

"Gomer, Gomer he's our man
If he can't do it, his kitty cats can."

As a graduation gift, they gave him a barrel of tomato juice.

Gomer Glitch grew up to become a multi-millionaire by selling de-scented skunks as pets all over the country.

HONEST ABE WAS NOT SO HONEST

It was the first week in February and Miss Lucy had us busy learning about Washington, Lincoln, and Valentine's Day. She passed out patterns of Washington and Lincoln face silhouettes that we students traced and cut out of black paper. She had us write a short paragraph about each and glued it on the back. Miss Lucy lined the classroom walls with our artwork. She brought out a large, brown, cardboard box which the class covered with bright red construction paper and cut out lace doilies to glue on it. She cut out a slit in the top and decorated it with hand-cut valentines. Kids made valentines, addressed them to classmates, and placed them in the box. A party was coming on Valentine's Day with the distribution of the contents of the box. The classroom blossomed with art and color.

Our teacher lectured on Washington and Lincoln as great Americans that we should emulate. We learned about Lincoln's birth in a log cabin in Kentucky, that he walked miles in the snow to return borrowed books, that he was the great Emancipator. We believed this story because we trusted Miss Lucy. When the lesson was over, Crawford, one of the third graders raised his hand and asked Miss Lucy, "Is this story of Lincoln really true? My parents and adults in my community told me that Lincoln was not born in Kentucky at all but here in our county, Rutherford County, in North Carolina." The next day Miss Lucy smiled as she told us that today she would teach us the, "real story of Abraham Lincoln."

"How many of you have heard the story of Lincoln being born here in Rutherford County? About half the students raised their hands. "Yesterday we talked about the version of Lincoln's life taught in history books. Let's contrast the textbook story with the traditional story told in the valley. According to history books, when was Lincoln born? "

Feb. 12, 1809, came the response.

"What does our tradition say?

"1803"

"Where was he born officially?"

"Hodgenville, Kentucky."

"What do we say?"

"Puzzle Creek, Rutherford County, North Carolina."

"Who was his mother?"

"Nancy Hanks."

"Well, on that point both versions agree. In textbooks, who was his father?"

"Thomas Lincoln."

"Who do we say was his father?

"Abraham Enloe. "

"Crawford, you asked the question yesterday that brought us to this discussion. Why don't you tell us what you know about Lincoln?"

Crawford stood up nervously twisting a tuft of hair hanging over his ear as he spoke. "My father told me that Abe's mother,

Nancy Hanks, came from Gaston County where her mother had left her and her sister because she could no longer care for them. She made her way to Rutherford Co., where the Enloe family found her sitting alone at one of the stores. Abraham Enloe, the wealthiest farm owner of the area took her in to rear with his own children. She had a baby with Mr. Enloe, even though she was not married to him. Isn't that wrong, Miss Lucy?"

"They thought it was at that time," she said. "Mr. Enloe paid Thomas Lincoln, a man who worked for him, to take Nancy and Abraham out of the community to Kentucky and marry her. Their situation was a scandal to Enloe's wife who refused to have the girl and her baby boy around her Thomas Lincoln was a poor cattle drover, yet without any education, history tells us he became the fifteenth wealthiest man in the state of Kentucky. How did he manage that? It seems Enloe continued to pay him his entire life not to divulge the secret of Abraham's bastard birth." Crawford sat down.

"You told the story well, Crawford," Miss Lucy told him. "Does anyone know where Puzzle Creek is?" she enquired.

"I do, I do" Peggy raised her hand enthusiastically. "It's about ten miles east of Rutherfordton. Turn right at Washburn's Store and continue until you reach the creek. Above the creek is Lincoln hill and the remains of the cabin in which he was born. That's it." "Correct," said Miss Lucy.

"You can still see the rocks from the foundation of the cabin in which he was born," added Rex. "There is an historical marker there."

"One thing about life," Miss Lucy told us, "don't believe everything you hear." She could just as well have added the warning that everything you learn is a lie, especially if it comes from a public school system textbook. Those who write the textbooks have an agenda. Those who teach must follow that agenda. Truth gets lost in the shuffle. "In tomorrow's lesson we are going to look at evidence for both stories. What does the word 'evidence' mean?" "Proof," students shouted the answer.

"Go home tonight and interview the old folks in the valley about what they know. Write down what they tell you. We'll contrast and compare what you learn with the official version in history books."

Ottie told me that night that she had heard for years the story of the Lincoln birth in Rutherford County. I anxiously wrote down what her parents had told her. She explained that Concord Baptist Church had Nancy Hanks and her son listed on their church roll. Abraham Enloe took Nancy Hanks into his family when her mother could not care for her. She came as an indentured servant but the Enloes accepted her as a family member. They taught her to read and write. Nancy Hanks became pregnant by Abraham Enloe and birthed a son whom she called Abraham.

Mrs. Enloe became furious at her husband and Nancy. She insisted that he send Nancy and her son away. Enloe paid Thomas Lincoln to take her to Kentucky where they were supposedly married. Many women in Rutherford County knew Nancy and her son. They were present when she left for Kentucky with little Abraham sitting on her lap.

"Why is this story not in history textbooks?" I asked my mother.

"Historians believed Lincoln's version of his early life and chose not to hear what people of Rutherford County had been saying for years."

The next day broke rainy and cold. Everyone did not much care because we were so excited to share what we had found out about Lincoln. Some students made Lincoln top hats out of black construction paper and wore them to class. Miss Lucy stepped to the chalk board and wrote these words on it: "Old Abe Was Not an Honest Abe." "What did you learn that supports this sentence as true?"

Students shared what their parents, grandparents, and people of the valley had told them. It seemed as if Lincoln had to cover his illegitimate birth in order to be successful in politics. But, so what did that matter to us? Many of us sitting in the classroom discussing Lincoln on this day were also illegitimate.

Miss Lucy noticed how the discussion had affected the class.

"You can believe what you want to believe," she told us. "Because of his assassination in office, people of his era made Lincoln greater than life. If what we wrote here is true, then Lincoln had lived a lie and had deprived us in the valley (as well as the rest of the world) of knowing we produced him. Kentucky gets to honor itself as his place of birth."

Adults in the valley began talking again about Lincoln. He did not own up to whom he was nor did he acknowledge where he originated in order to cover up his illegitimate birth. Valley people disdained this attitude. When Miss Lucy took down the silhouettes from the wall, we threw them in the trash. We trashed the top hats too. How could people be proud of this man when he disowned Rutherford County and North Carolina? He was president. So what? He was never president of our valley. He was never president of Rutherford County or North Carolina. When he was in office, we were part of the Confederate States of America. Jefferson Davis was our president. Lincoln had had no authority over us.

Miss Lucy felt like an iconoclast at what she had done. She had broken some sacred beliefs and had made some children uncomfortable. She did not kill Bambi; she just showed principle in that she would not live a lie as Lincoln perhaps did. Education is about searching for truth and accepting what you find until another truth upsets the previous one. She refused to let her students live a lie or believe that because something is in a textbook it is true. "Leave your minds open to any and all possibilities," she told the class.

School board members love to get embroiled in controversy. The less they know about an issue, the more fervently they prosecute it. The three Know-It-Alls in Forest City, Saccahrina, Splendida, and Aspertid heard about the lesson Miss Lucy had taught. They knew these same stories about Lincoln because they had grown up in the area. However, they would not allow her to teach information that was not in a textbook or approved personally by them. Already they had made her teach the creationism theory of the earth and that it is flat. She had to include that storks bring babies, unicorns live at Lake McCall, and pigs can fly. Not to mention that the sun moves around the earth, the earth is only 6,000 years old, and the moon is made of green cheese. As members of the school board, it was their duty to preserve the status quo. Keep students barefoot and ignorant, then they will not cause trouble. No one would leave the valley with an open mind. They would ensure it.

To punish Miss Lucy for her open-minded, excellent teaching, they docked her one month's pay, suspended her one month from school, and brought Teresa Whitrock back for a second reign of terror over us. Splendida, who took her duty ultra-seriously, could not find a category on her rating sheet that was low enough. She made up her own. Below Frog Level. She actually rated Miss Lucy below frog level. None of their antics changed one bit of the facts about President Abraham Lincoln.

The next year Miss Lucy made no mention of Lincoln or his birthday. On February 12th, Miss Lucy taught us about Bigfoot. His name was Knobby and many people had seen him around the valley. Ottie knew, for she had met him up on Devil's Creek Fork. Curtis shot at him through the kitchen door one night. We renamed Lincoln's Birthday, "Bigfoot Day." Kids wore huge cut-out feet over the soles of their shoes from that day forward. Miss Lucy put more focus on Valentine's Day. This wonderful day was about Cupid, love, hearts, valentines and cinnamon candy that burned our noses. We children became mean in our attitudes toward

Lincoln. We made up malicious rhymes and chanted them down the hallway:

> Old Abe Lincoln we can't abide.
> His place of birth, he had to hide.

Underneath the large portrait of Lincoln hanging on the wall beside George Washington in our classroom, someone glued the following sign: Abraham Enloe, 16th President of the United States.

Thirty years later Lydia Clontz led educators in establishing the Boston Lincoln Center in Bostic, North Carolina, to preserve the Lincoln Tar Heel tradition. Richard Eller and Jerry Goodnight told Rutherford County's version of his birth masterfully in their book, THE TAR HEEL LINCOLN. DNA testing will ultimately settle the argument.

SOMETHING DREADFUL THIS WAY COMES

The killer wind came in from the south across Spartanburg and Chesnee, South Carolina. No one suspected that it would come until they saw falling barometers indicating bad weather. TV stations in Spartanburg and Greenville were in their infancy and meteorologists drew weather patterns on primitive chalkboard maps. They could not see storms much in advance. The storm front formed out on the flat plains of Texas and moved at a rapid pace across the Mississippi River. Cotton farmers in Alabama ran for cover in their cotton sheds but the winds took off the roofs sending fragments of rusted tin skyward. In Georgia the winds downed centuries-old oak trees while lifting roofs heavenward. They splintered peach orchards and water towers in South Carolina. They reserved a savage fury for the hills and hollows of our valley.

Farmers working outside in the south side of the valley noticed long finger-shaped clouds floating northward. By noon the sky grew dark. Animals began to move from their open pastures to a copse of trees or to their stables. Flocks of birds flew in disturbed patterns skyward then swirled toward the ground as if they were controlled by an unseen force. A hush fell over all of nature. In the waning light, chickens went to roost. Something dreadful this way comes. Farmers unhitched their plough horses and brought them back from the fields. Those with tractors drove them under barn sheds and covered them with leather blankets. The sheriffs working southward sent telephone and telegraph messages along the string of small towns alerting them to what had happened in Alabama and Georgia. Worried mothers began to think of their husbands and children because there was no way to reach them easily. Sheriff Dawson heard a report from the sheriff's office in Chesnee that threatening weather was moving northward. He drove to Miss Lucy's school and told her to be alert to the clouds and gathering storm.

"Take the children downstairs if the skies turn greenish yellow or if you hear a roaring sound like a train."

She thanked Sheriff Dawson assuring him that she would be vigilant.

Eli and his road crew cut bushes along the CCC road, then shoveled sand out of the side ditches. They dug a ditch and put in a metal culvert to carry water under the roadway. It was four o'clock and the crew looked forward to packing up their tools and going home. The boss gave them a fifteen minute break so they opened their thermoses to drink water or coffee. Some ate left-over biscuits from their lunch pails. Eli sat down on a tree stump and wiped sweat from his brow with a handkerchief. The temperature suddenly turned colder and all the men felt it.

"This weather is strange," Eli said to all the men. "Look at those black clouds gathering on the horizon. It doesn't feel natural."

"Yes," replied one of the men, "the wind is picking up in the distance."

They called their boss over, asking him to assess the weather. He, too, felt uneasy about the changing conditions, so he gave orders to load up tools and personal items. They all climbed aboard the truck and set out down the CCC road toward the main highway.

Hustlebutt walked across the Boneyard with wind whipping her hair in wisps around her head and ears. Pieces of loose paper moved like tumbleweeds across the empty lot. She tied down her tables and merchandise with rope, then bolted the door to her storage shed. There was a heavy quiet over the Boneyard. The wind died down, leaving her with apprehension and expectation. Thunder sounded in the distance as a strong flash of lightning broke across the dark clouds. Hustlebutt decided to seek shelter from the coming storm in the Choo-Choo Diner next door to the Boneyard. She bought some coffee and sat on one of the swivel stools where she could watch the gathering storm through the cafe's windows.

"It could get rough," the waitress whispered to her.

Gentry watched the sky from his sawmill in the woods. He did not like the greenish-yellow clouds. Instinctively, he recognized that the building storm would not be a normal one. He shut down the saw motor and blew a sharp blast on his whistle to call the loggers and woodcutters back to the saw mill.

"Men," he addressed them, "unhook the horses and let them walk on their own back home. They know where to go. Pack the saws and axes in the truck, and then all of you get in it. I don't want any man trying to outrun the storm on foot."

The truck engine fired up and they all moved quickly down the road toward safety. Loose work horses ran across the fields and in front of the truck. When they reached home, dark storm clouds were rising and hail was beginning to fall.

Eli and his crew left the CCC road turning in the direction of the schoolhouse. The storm bore down on them from the southwest. Golf ball size hailstones pelted the truck cab, windshield, and the unprotected men on the back. A huge hailstone hit the windshield cracking it like glacier ice. The stretched fingers of the thin crack ran the length of the windshield. Eli's crew yelped from the force of the hailstones. They tried to protect themselves by throwing their folded arms over their heads. The driver of the truck pushed the gas pedal to the floor in an attempt to outrun the storm. In the distance, Eli recognized the ominous form of a funnel cloud. It dropped, striking the ground, ejecting flotsam and jetsam skyward. The truck driver careened in at Miss Lucy's school and sped the truck to the entrance of the building. The men rushed up the sixteen stairs, streaked down the hall, and burst, shouting, into the classroom.

"Tornado coming," they yelled. "Get the children to safety."

Children began to whimper and cry, and some froze in their chairs from fear.

"Line up, lineup," Miss Lucy ordered.

"Where do we go?" Eli's crew asked.

"To the unfinished basement under the school," she screamed.

The men grabbed the students frozen in fear out of their seats and carried them over their shoulders or under their arms down the hall to the safety of the basement. The entire group huddled against the basement wall covering their heads with their arms. Hail and high winds struck the upper floor windows shattering the glass out of the classroom. A deafening roar assaulted their eardrums as the pressure outside the building dropped, causing Miss Lucy's classroom to explode outward pulling desks, chairs and the pot-bellied stove with it. Huddled in fear in the basement, the children and adults wept and prayed for deliverance.

At the Choo-Choo Diner near the Boneyard, Hustlebutt slurped her coffee and watched the sky turn a sick green-yellow. She saw people scurrying into buildings for cover. A line of trees at the edge of the town bent to the ground as straight-line winds pummeled them, while chairs, barrels, and cars rolled across the street under the power of the raging wind. The owner of the diner opened the freezer where meat was stored and told patrons to take cover there. Hustlebutt ran with the rest into the locker. No sooner were they inside than the lights went out. They sat in a fearful darkness. They heard the glass in the restaurant windows shatter and the entire diner rocked as if they had been hit by a train. A tremendous force sucked at the freezer door, and those inside screamed from the pressure on their eardrums.

Gentry and his men tethered the loose horses that had followed them home. He drove the truck behind the protective walls of the house. The men started to run inside the house, but he stopped them.

"It's a deathtrap," he yelled. "Come back. Let's take cover in the deep ditches across the stream."

They followed him across the creek and lay down in the deep ditches which an earlier farmer had dredged to funnel water from a meadow to the creek. The ditches were now dry.

"Lie flat on your stomach," he ordered.

Large hailstones pummeled them on their backs and heads. Wind blew debris into the ditch. Gentry saw entire trees flying over them. The roar of a train approaching popped their ears and the pressure lifted their legs and feet into the air. They held on to each other to prevent being lifted into the air. Horses broke their tethers and broke for the open meadow. The wind picked up one horse and set it down a mile away, unhurt. Strangely, they did not hear shattering glass or splintering wood from their house.

Three tornadoes struck the valley that afternoon. One went over Miss Lucy's school. One hit the Choo-Choo Diner. The third swept over Gentry's place. In a moment's breath, the storms were gone.

Miss Lucy, Eli, and the crew, stepped cautiously out of the basement. All windows in the building were shattered. The roof was gone. The contents of the classroom lay scattered across the broom sedge field; some were hanging in the pine trees. The school bus lay on its side.

Eli and his crew loaded children on the DMV truck and began driving them home. They saw lines of broken trees and destroyed buildings in the wake of the storm. Wounded farmers and their families wandered around destroyed property. Neighbors would come to help, for the devastation was great.

Hustlebutt and group emerged from the freezer to a destroyed diner. Only torn window curtains flapped in the empty spaces where glass windows once had stood. She thanked the cafe owner for the place of safety and made her way to the Boneyard. It was unrecognizable. It was a pile of mixed debris. No tables left. Her storage building had been demolished. Split electrical poles lay strewn over the field. She trudged over to the main street of the town and saw that the storm had missed the downtown area. All buildings stood intact.

Gentry pushed broken limbs and trash off him and scampered over the ditch embankment. The men followed him back across the stream. The house was undamaged. It was a miracle. A mile-long path of broken trees spread apart as if cut by a knife. The horses slowly returned.

"We dodged a bullet," Gentry mumbled.

There were numerous injuries, but death did not come to the valley this time. Farther south, towns were not so lucky. People wailed and mourned those whom the storm took. Help came from Charlotte and compassionate neighbors in South Carolina.

Parents walked among the ruins of the school and gave thanks for deliverance. Those who surveyed the diner gave thanks for the survival of those trapped inside. Gentry and his men paused in the forest, looking up at a clear-blue sky, and gave thanks for their deliverance and that of their animals. In large letters, someone wrote on the remains of the chalkboard left standing in Miss Lucy's classroom:

"With grateful thanks for deliverance from our killer storm."

REIGN OF TERROR

A week before Christmas vacation, Miss Lucy brought a strange-looking woman with her to our classroom. She said the woman's name was Mrs. Thelma Whitrock and that she would be our substitute teacher from January to May. Miss Lucy explained that she must undergo a gallbladder operation and would not be able to return until the next school year which would start in September. We didn't know what a gall bladder was, so she brought pictures in a health book to show us. She taught us new words such as surgery, ether, and recuperates. She assured us that she would do well and would come back to us in September. Merry Christmas, Miss Lucy.

It was a cold day in early January when the bus driver delivered us into Hell. He did not know it at the time; neither did we. Children ran up the sixteen stair steps toward our classroom as usual only to hear a troll-like voice yell, "Go back to the door and walk up the stairs. There will be no running in the hallway." Back at the base of the stairs we all stood shivering, afraid to go back up the stairs to see what the voice came from. The crowd pushed me forward step by step until my head peeked over the top stair. Looking down the empty hallway, I saw Mrs. Thelma Whitrock standing in Miss Lucy's spot holding a paddle under her folded arms. She meant business. "I see you," she said to me. "Bring that group up the stairs, down the hallway, into the classroom. Don't say a single word," she barked. I complied with her orders. We went directly into the classroom and sat down in our seats. The bell rang to start the day. Mrs. Thelma Whitrock took over our school.

Never in our lives had we dreamed that someone like her existed anywhere on the planet. She was a Devil's disciple straight from the fiery furnace. Her wiry body rested on two spindly legs ending in two tiny feet stuck into oversized witch's shoes. She was barely taller than the tallest third grader. Frizzy hair stuck out from all sides of her skull while two beady eyes focused like radar beams on anything in their path. On her cheeks she packed thick rough to indicate there might be some life under the wrinkled face. Lipstick outlined two razor-sharp lips through which blistering, caustic words flew at any kid that crossed her. She was all about academics. No warmth. No kindness. Just-the-facts madam. In her mind, we had learned nothing in our three years with Miss Lucy so she intended to rectify that situation from the very first day of her tenure.

She restructured the entire classroom. She placed her desk next to the exit door so she could throw kids through it into the hallway as she saw fit. She built semi walls between the first, second, and third grade tables so they were not visible to each other. One could hear voices and see pieces of colored clothing through cracks in the wall. It was as if she wanted a separate classroom for each grade.

She required us to stand in the morning when she entered the room and say in unison, "Good morning, Mrs. Whitrock, we hope you are well today." We truly wished her dead but none dared express it. Woe to any kid who did not pay homage to her. No one could say a word without first raising his hand and waiting to be recognized. She assigned individual quiet work for second and third graders while she read aloud to first graders. Anyone who spoke without permission got to stand with his nose stuck in a corner of the room. At recess we lined up like ducklings in order of physical height in order to march in silence to the playground where we played games she prepared for us. Pine trees and broom sedge fields were strictly off limits.

At lunch she made us all put our long tables together like a main dining table in a monastery. She provided a napkin which we put in our laps and then placed our right hand on top of it. We ate with our right hand holding a fork properly between our fingers rather than stab with our fists. No one must ever talk with food in his mouth. She watched us like a hawk and upbraided any offender with her selective vocabulary through those razor lips. After lunch, she marched us in two lines to relieve ourselves in the outhouses. The only times we could go was at recess and after lunch. That was it. Any kid who could not adjust to her schedule was out of luck. You sat in your pee or poo until recess or lunch came. It was a part of her plan to instill discipline in all of us.

In the classroom she drilled us unmercifully in academics. Learn multiplication tables by heart or stand in the corner. Learn principle parts of verbs or stand in a corner. Learn to spell words or plan to write them ten times each. Addition must be done in your head, not on paper. When you read a paragraph for her in the history book, you had to paraphrase what you had just read or do it over. Kids had to prove constantly that they were learning the lessons.

Francis was a cute, little blond girl liked by all kids in the school. She loved to talk, all the time. It was inevitable that she would lock horns with Mrs. Whitrock. The curmudgeon sized Francis up with her beady eyes clicking her teeth together in disapproval of what she saw. Francis was what she never was in childhood. No one had liked Mrs. Whitrock when she had been a child and none would ever call her pretty. Mrs. Whitrock looked for chances to punish Francis. She slammed the door too hard, stand in the corner. She didn't do her homework, stand in the corner. She talked out of turn, stand in the corner. Francis' nose began to grow crooked from having to stand in the corner. It was at recess one day when Francis sat playing with some of her friends on the steps leading into the building. Mrs. Whitrock came down the stairs, stopping briefly beside the group of girls. Looking directly at Francis she hissed to her, "You don't deserve to be an American. You don't deserve to live in this great land of America." Without any explanation, she exited the door and walked to the playground to find some other kid to intimidate. Puzzled, Francis began to cry because she just knew Mrs. Whitrock had the power to revoke her citizenship and her passport. If Mrs. Whitrock did not like you, she punished you.

Not realizing that Miss Lucy was on sabbatical, June Jr. and Redtop returned to school. Upon seeing Mrs. Whitrock, they snickered thinking she was an ordinary substitute teacher. They began making mocking noises with their lips. Here was fresh meat for them to torment. Poor guys did not know they were marching into the jaws of Hell.

"And who are you?" Mrs. Whitrock asked June Jr.

"Puddin and tane, ask me again, I'll tell you the same," he giggled looking back at Redtop and the boys in the class for support.

"Who are you?" she asked Redtop, "puddin and tane too?"

"No," he said, "I'm Little Red Riding Hood and you are my mother." He slapped his knee with one hand and howled with laughter at his own joke.

"Oh, no," she replied, "I'm the big bad wolf and I eat kids like you for supper." No truer words had ever been spoken. "Sit down," she said to June Jr.

"I sit wherever and whenever I want to sit," he retorted.

She walked directly to him, grabbed his neck between her thumb and index finger squeezing hard. He began to yell. She walked him to her desk, took out Miss Lucy's Doomsday paddle with holes bored in it, and proceeded to whack him on the buttocks.

"The first whack is for disrespect; the second is for talking back; the third is because you don't know how to act in class; and this fourth one is because I don't like puddin and tane jokes" she explained.

June Jr. yelled for her to stop. "I've just started in on you," she told him. "When I have finished with you, you will be a new man." She shoved him into a seat with instructions not to move without her permission.

She then turned on Redtop who sat snickering in a corner. Her nose blew fire, her eyes honed like sonar on him, she breathed heavily through clenched teeth. Her frizzy hair stood out like snakes on Medusa's head. She grabbed Redtop by the hair of his head, pulling it as hard as she could. She laid four swift whacks of the paddle to his rear end. "How does that feel, Little Red Riding Hood?" she sneered. "The wolf likes it rough."

"No more, no more," he surrendered.

"Oh, yes, there's going to be plenty more of this until you learn to behave."

She sat Redtop in a chair daring him to move. She lined boys and girls up in two separate lines, led us outside and for the next hour we marched military style around the playground yelling, "Yes, madam, no madam." She made June Jr. and Redtop stand on each side of her desk looking straight ahead listening to all the lessons from all three grades. She started the next day by bringing the two boys to the front of the class where she whacked them twice with her paddle. "If I can't reach you through your brains," she said, "I will surely reach you through your butts."

From that day onward, the school became a model of decorum. Everyone did his homework. Children ate lunch with perfect manners. No one spoke out of turn. June Jr. and Redtop began to make progress academically. June Jr. was good at math and Redtop read the most books in the class. Children began to be happy under Mrs. Whitrock's rules. They finished the entire spelling book, finished all their readers and even Gomer finished his three times three multiplication tables

Phyllis and the outcasts no longer had to worry about persecution because Mrs. Whitrock tamed their tormentors. Little Eva looked forward to school and rarely fainted any more. If any kid clapped his hands to make her faint, Mrs. Whitlock whacked him with the paddle the same number of times. Time passed. The end of the year came too quickly. Since January every single student in class had made progress and felt good about it. Mrs. Whitrock's paddle ensured movement forward.

To our dismay, Mrs. Teresa Whitrock announced that there would be no picnic at Lake McCall this year. Children wailed upon learning there was no picnic. How cheated they felt. Hard work all year and no picnic. No Harold Cody, No Gomer's kitty cat, no Little Eva fainting, the end of a tradition was at hand. We were doomed to spend another day in Hell

When the day of the picnic arrived, we sat in our seats sad and dejected. Mrs. Whitrock told us to put away our books and come with her. She led us down the sixteen steps to the old cafeteria that had been closed for years. None of us had ever been inside the room.

When she opened the door, we were shocked. Inside there were ten woodstoves with blazing fires. On kitchen tables stood five hand-cranked ice cream machines. Some of our mothers were there helping out. Girls divided into groups and began mixing cookie dough to bake fresh cookies for all of us.

Soon the smell of spice cookies pierced the air. Boys crowded around the ice cream buckets mixing milk and strawberries, milk and vanilla, milk and chocolate so there would be a variety of flavors of ice cream to eat with the cookies.

When the first cookies and ice cream were ready, the boys and girls traded places. The boys baked cookies and the girls made ice cream. Every kid in the school ate as much as he wanted. Even Mrs. Whitrock ate a cookie and some strawberry ice cream.

Our parents were impressed with what we could do. Mrs. Whitrock just smiled because she knew who worked this miracle. As per instructions, we cleared everything spotlessly then went outside to play. No one wanted to go back to Lake McCall.

Miss Lucy had successful surgery and was well enough to return to school on the last day to say farewell to us all for the summer. She and Mrs. Whitrock sat side by side, one at the teacher's desk and one in a borrowed desk.

It was customary for us children to bring farewell gifts to the teacher to show our appreciation for her work during the year. After the bell rang, students readied their gifts. The first groups laid their gifts in front of Miss Lucy saying their thanks. When it came turn for June Jr. and Redtop, they walked over and laid their gifts in front of Mrs. Whitrock.

"Thank you," they mumbled.

Phyllis, Little Eva, and I also laid our gifts in front of Mrs. Whitrock for it was she who brought an end to our mistreatment. Child after child laid their gifts on the desk in front of Mrs. Whitrock. When all had finished, Miss Lucy rose, picked up gifts left for her, and laid them on the desk in front of Mrs. Whitrock.

"In appreciation," Miss Lucy said to her.

The Reign of Terror was over.

NOT CHOSEN

One who touches the heart of a child immortalizes himself, for that child carries the memory with him into eternity. It becomes a part of his emotional DNA, wherein his descendants tend to be more joyful and more likely to reach out to touch another in a loving way. Thus the good deed moves on into perpetuity. Mrs. Whitrock was rough on us kids, but she lifted many a child to a better place, to a better life. She protected those in her care and taught them conscientiously. Everyone knew of her tough reputation. I knew another side of her which appeared at one of the most disappointing episodes in my life.

Fifth grade, where she taught, is a special transition time in a child's life. Academically, he is leaving foundation learning behind to challenge tougher courses in history, literature, and math. He begins music education formally and gets a chance to be part of an athletic team representing his school. At least he should be given an opportunity. All teachers are not fair and this is a real-life experience to show that teachers can have a devastating impact on the lives of students.

Mrs. Whitrock announced that all fifth graders could choose to try out for the basketball team. Our training, if we were chosen, would lead to a possible spot on the high school team some five years later. Excitement ran high. On the appointed day, each prospective player should bring tennis shoes, shorts, and a white pull-over shirt. That within itself was challenging for many of us, because we did not have those items.

I told my mother, Ottie, what I wanted to do and that I needed these extra clothes items, but she told me to forget it. These are luxury accessories when one is poor. I loved basketball. I would not let such a technicality as poverty stop me. I borrowed a white blouse from my sister. I asked a neighbor if one of her sons had perhaps a pair of shorts I could borrow. The neighbor looked through her laundry and found a pair a size larger than what I required, but that mattered not. A securely tied safety pin over a doubled crease in the shorts would make them fit.

Getting a pair of tennis shoes was a different matter. "I'll play barefoot if I have to," I thought to myself.

I went to the Eagle Shoe store in town and asked the Jewish couple if they could donate me a pair of tennis shoes. Despite all their suffering and poverty themselves, they refused me. I looked at the dozens of pairs of tennis shoes lining the shelves in their store and wondered how people could be so stingy and unkind.

June Jr. went to their store to steal me a pair. But the couple recognized him from before and refused to let him come in.

"Ingrates," he hurled an insult at them. "Go back to the soup kitchen."

The pursuit of money warps some people to the extent that their hearts freeze up. I was at the end of my rope. All I had left was hope and, maybe, a little luck.

I walked home from Melvin's house, where we had been playing. I decided to take the main highway, instead of cutting through Burley's field where the cows were. I passed the road leading to

God's Pinnacle Church and made a right turn on the road to God's Salvation Church. At the base of the next hill lay the bridge over Silver Creek where June Jr. almost died in the car wreck and where we fought with the Piggott boys. I stopped to look at the rebuilt section of the bridge and to peer into the water below. A strong odor of tar and turpentine, used to preserve the wood in the bridge, burned in my nostrils. One of the outside car mirrors from June Jr.'s wreck lay stuck in the muddy creek bank. I noticed it when the rays of the sun struck it, lighting up my face as if someone were pointing a flashlight at me. Broken pieces of the windshield lay scattered over the embankment. I shuddered at the memory of his near death.

Something caught my eye as I turned to continue my journey. I saw a tennis shoe hanging by its string from one edge of the bridge. I climbed down through the weeds on the embankment for a better look. l waded into the cold water of Silver Creek and saw, not one tennis shoe, but two dangling from one of the original bridge supports. Lifting the shoes from their perch, I carried them back upon the bridge and examined them in detail. They were in good shape still. I eagerly tried them on. Though a size too big, they were usable. I could stuff newspaper in the toes for a better fit.

I sat down on the bridge railing, drifting into deep thought. How did a pair of tennis shoes come to be hanging on a country bridge? They were exactly what I had hoped for. I listened to the rippling water in the creek below. Its waters smelled fresh and crisp. A bird chirped in the grass as a group of crows quarreled above a nearby field, their caw and cackling breaking the reverie of the moment. I looked up at the blue sky, wondering if some guardian angel had sent me to walk to the bridge this day. Had my longing and desire to play basketball manifested this gift? My heart filled with gratitude. These were my magic shoes. I did not tell my mother that I had managed to amass the items that I needed.

I could hardly pull open the heavy, oak green door to our classroom on the day of the tryouts. I wore the shirt, shorts, and shoes as my regular school clothes that day. Those students who showed up with brand new outfits and knew they would make the team, smirked and made caustic comments as they viewed my clothes. Two kids wore official team uniforms from the high school for their parents knew the coaches and had requested them.

It was hard to concentrate on the early lessons that Mrs. Whitrock was teaching, for my mind anxiously awaited the ten o'clock hour. I day dreamed. In my mind I saw myself on the high school team, chosen captain, maybe. I saw myself winning games with last second shots. I was most valuable player. I won the state championship for our school team with the game tied and two seconds left to go on the clock. The crowd erupted with a thunderous roar. I was a hero. I made the last-second shot. The buzzer ending that game was the clock striking ten o'clock. The principal's deep voice resonated on the wall loudspeaker, "All boys and girls who wish to try out for the basketball team, please report to the gym."

Students from all the fifth grade classrooms pushed, jostled, and ran excitedly into the hallways, expecting to go to the gymnasium to try out with Coach. But there he stood in the middle of the hallway waiting on us. Like most coaches, this man was a legend in the community. People spoke his name reverently, as if they were speaking to God himself. Whatever this man wanted, the community delivered it to him. He was not required to act like ordinary teachers, for he was elevated to a godlike status. He did whatever he pleased. No one could touch or criticize him, for he stood like a Greek god astride Mount Olympus.

We younger students adored him, too.

He told us to form a long line along the hallway, to stand against the wall. My heart was so filled with excitement and anticipation that my stomach was upset. He said not one more word to us beyond the command, "Form a line." He signaled a student from our classroom to come to him. This student named Newell was from a well-to-do family with privilege above and beyond the rest of us. His family lived next door to Coach. His dad and the coach were best friends.

"Newell," he said, "I am going to let you pick out the students you know best and the ones you think can play ball." Newell proceeded to name his friends, those in his little clique, those with money and influence, and himself.

"You fifteen come down to the gym with me and the rest of you can go back to your classrooms. You are not chosen," Coach said to the rest of us very coldly.

I could not believe what had just happened. I stood frozen, my feet paralyzed from sheer disappointment. I could not believe what this beloved coach had just done to us. We revered him. We thought he was a fair man who dealt fairly with students. Today, however, we got to know exactly who he was and that he did not give a damn for anyone except those who could do something for him. He stacked his basketball program with kids whose parents had influence. Coach designated a fifth-grade kid, a classmate, not an adult, not a teacher, but another fifth grade student to decide everyone's fate. My respect and love for Coach died on the hallway floor. The chosen group, and Newell, slapped each other on their backs, whooped and yelled as they exited the building in the direction of the gym.

Coach turned his back to us with no word of consolation, no apology. He showed no sensitivity. He did not know how hard I and others had worked to come up with the shirt, shorts, and tennis shoes just to make it to this hallway. He followed his chosen few out the door moving to lead them to the gym, like Jesus leading his special few into the mythological heaven.

We ten-year-old fifth graders had just been served a dose of reality. We had expected to go to the gym, where Coach would give us all a chance to demonstrate our skills and potential. Then, he would fairly choose the best, make a list of their names on paper, and post the list on the doors of the fifth grade classrooms. That way, those not chosen could back down gracefully. However, his little pet had made the decision. He chose people on the basis of who they were, not what they could do. In that moment I hated that little jerk that was given life or death decisions over my dream of playing basketball.

My head bent low. Feeling ashamed, I started the long, heavy walk back to Mrs. Whitrock's room. In my mind I went over my struggle just to come up with the clothes required for this day. All my years of practice with a make-shift goal were in vain. All my love for this game disappeared. I felt judged for whom I was, for my poverty, for all the mistakes and shortcomings of my mother's life and for the fact that I came from the valley. I had just seen Coach, an adult, a teacher abrogate his responsibility to all of us adoring fifth graders to a privileged classmate.

When I entered my classroom, Mrs. Whitrock looked up puzzled. "Why are you back so soon?" she asked me. My pride wounded, my heart broken from not even having been given even a chance, I mumbled, "I was not chosen."

"It has only been five minutes. There was not time for you to go to the gym. Did you not go to the gym?" she persisted.

"No ma'am," I replied. "Coach let Newell choose who would go."

There, I had told on him, and it felt good.

Mrs. Whitrock's face turned crimson red. Her beady eyes forced inward like a cobra ready to strike; she breathed hard and her nostrils flared.

"Continue your work, students," she instructed us.

We would do our work for we feared her wrath. She went to the gymnasium and observed the chosen ones already practicing, running drills, acting as a team. How could this be, if they had just been chosen? She understood what had happened in the hallway. The coach and Newell had chosen their people in advance, so Coach could avoid any work or responsibility for himself. Mrs. Whitfield summoned Newell and the others from her classroom to her.

"Come back to class this very minute."

"But we've been chosen to be on the basketball team, and Coach wants us to practice now."

"You should be ashamed of yourself, Newell, for participating in such a diabolical scheme. Practice on your own time. You are in my classroom until three o'clock."

The gym door slammed shut behind her as she moved the little group like a mother hen back to the classroom. When reassembled, she sat a long time in silence, thinking. She periodically glared at Newell who knew he had no special place with her now.

"Children, close your books, sit up straight, and hear what I intend to tell you. Life can be hard at times. Life can be terribly unfair. Sometimes, adults are the worst offenders when fairness is on the line. We are not all born equal. I show no favoritism to any of you, for I value all of you equally. What has just happened to some of you in this class is a travesty and those who perpetrated it should hang their heads in shame. Those of you whom Newell picked to play basketball will not be excused from my class to do so. Those not chosen, I apologize for what happened and I ask you to use this pain you now feel as a stepping stone to greater achievement." She had finished talking.

Just as she went silent, Coach opened her door without knocking, poked his head in, did not even say "excuse me" and blurted out a command, "I want my players back on the gym floor right this minute."

Mrs. Whitrock looked at him in disbelief. "Fred," she said, "please tell this man the manners we use when we wish to interrupt a class."

I looked at Coach with disdain. I knocked on my desk, pretended to open an imaginary door and said, "Excuse me, Mrs. Whitrock. I'm sorry to interrupt your class while you are teaching. May I speak with you?" I sat back down.

She stepped outside the door and spoke to Coach in a loud, angry voice as she chastised him, "You cheated my students earlier this morning. They came with an expectation of trying out for basketball. They expected to go to the gym with you and be fairly assessed. You cut it all short by allowing Newell to do your work for you. You are unfair. This treatment of my students will not stand. The chosen ones did not get chosen fairly either, so they will not leave my classroom to practice with you. They are assigned to me and I will say what they may do and with whom. Your conduct is despicable and I'm ashamed to work with the likes of you."

She closed the door and sat down at her desk in silence for a while. She poured herself a cup of hot coffee from the thermos to rejuvenate her spirit. At this moment, I began to love Mrs. Whitrock. What a human being! No one had ever stood up for me before. And she was right in all that she said and did. She lived what she preached to us. After a long period of thought, she rose and spoke to us again, "I'm organizing an intramural basketball team for all students not chosen today. Newell and his friends will not play on this team. I'll talk with other fifth grade classes to see if they wish to participate." She was done. She was the only teacher that ever had the nerve to stand up to Coach.

This was a side of Mrs. Whitrock she had never presented before. She did organize intramural basketball. We had six teams.

The basic rule was that everybody played. No one warmed the bench. The program spread into the community. She organized a committee of parents to formulate rules for choosing basketball players. Every child must be considered. Every child's skills were evaluated. Coach would not make the choice in such a manner ever again and no student ever again stepped forward to act as God over his peers.

When I went back home that day, I placed my shorts and shoes in my dresser, where they remained for many years. I never played basketball again. I did not want to. The unfair treatment cut too deeply.

Newell went on to succeed in life as well he should, for he learned how to cheat early. Had there ever been any honor in him?

Sixty years later Final Frontier High School played for the state championship in basketball. As I dressed to attend the game in Chapel Hill, I accidentally opened the drawer where my shorts and shoes were still lying. What memories flowed through my mind! I wondered why I had kept them so long. I took them with me to the game for good luck. I placed them on the floor of the gym next to my shoes at the Dean Dome and laid the shorts on the back of the seat in front of me. The game unfolded as I had day dreamed it long ago before basketball try outs. With the game tied, a student made a basket with two seconds remaining. We won the game. They carried the hero off the court.

"That could have been me," I thought, "had it not been for an unfair coach and an ass-kissing kid." Big tears ran down my cheeks. I grabbed the shoes and shorts, waving them up in the air as a joyous victory sign.

I saw Mrs. Whitrock's smiling face and heard her say, "They did not choose you, Fred, but I chose you. Newell cannot hold a candle to you, never could."

I hugged the spectators around me. We formed a circle, jumped up and down and yelled, "Champions! Champions! We are champions!"

Sixty years of a broken heart, of a wounded spirit dissolved. I let go of my bitterness and hatred of Coach and Newell. I forgave myself for my hatred. I felt it rise upward through the Dean Dome and float away on the noise of the crowd. I felt like a champion now in my personal life. My shouts joined with the joyous cries of other adults celebrating around me, who probably had not been chosen in their fifth grade classes either.

THE NEW GIRL

Golden Valley, our valley, once rang with the sounds of people. Gold was discovered and hundreds of prospectors and their families flocked here in search of riches. New houses went up, three country stores were built. Churches dotted the landscape; valley craftsmen even built a new brick schoolhouse with six classrooms, an auditorium, and cafeteria. Dozens of people moved daily along the dusty dirt road in wagons, model Fords or on foot. The place was alive with activity and life. Then the Great Depression and World War II arrived. The gold fields petered out. Remnants of mines, still visible today, look like large, excavated holes in the mountains. People lost their jobs, homes, and livelihoods. Then the draft in the war took the very best of the valley's young men. It showed them new places, new people, new ways of living and doing. They went to Paris, Berlin, London. Life offered in the valley became too slow, too provincial and backward even. So they never came back home. People left in droves. They left abandoned houses like the Wright Old House, Ida Place, Griff's Old House and Skiff's Place. Broken-down wagons and automobiles littered front yards. Two country stores closed as did all but two of the churches. The new school building was too big so Miss Lucy and Mr. Rawlins combined all the students into two classrooms. She taught grades 1-3 in one classroom and he taught grades 4-6 in another one up the hall. Families in the valley grew poorer, most reduced to subsistence farming or making moonshine. My family did both.

Most neighbors around our farm departed leaving numerous houses vacant. My family became more isolated and more provincial in our attitudes and actions. No influx of new life existed to alter the status quo.

The situation changed right after Christmas. Rumors circulated at school and on the bus that a new family was moving into our valley. Since ours was the only bus, they would ride with us. Kids fear anything different or any change in their routine. We had our hierarchy. Tougher kids bossed us weaker ones around as those with more economic clout paid off the bullies to leave them alone. Incredible lies circulated about this new family. They probably had lice. Someone knew for sure that one of them had scabies, whatever that was. Someone said the oldest girl had just gotten out of reform school. One had a baby when she was nine. Another had a clubfoot and limped. Child rumors and fears cut through the school and church atmosphere like a cold knife. People believed their own lies.

What brought this plague of new kids, this curse on our valley? Had we not already suffered enough? Some children even suggested that we slip down at night to burn down the house they were renting. No one had the courage to do that.

Days went by with nothing happening. Some of the bigger liars with the most preposterous tales accused everyone else of having made up a big lie. No new family was coming.

That notion quickly changed when our bus stopped at an unfamiliar bus stop not usually included on our daily journey. All eyes strained in the direction of the house where four stair-step children emerged bundled in hats and coats. Each followed an older girl like ducklings following their mother. On the bus children scurried to sit close to each other. They pulled books and lunch pails over the seat so the new people could not sit next to them. A hush fell over the bus as the driver opened the door. The oldest girl got on first, her eyes lowered, looking at the floor of the bus. There was no scarcity of seats since all of us huddled at the back or front of the bus. Middle seats were empty. The four of them huddled in the middle of the bus gazing at their feet.

I watched them intently from my perch between my sister Gertie and a pile of textbooks. The oldest girl had a strange ritual. Summer or winter she wore a long coat and headscarf. Each time she got on the bus, she sat down and placed her books in her lap. Then she took off her coat and pulled it around her shoulders. Next she removed the headscarf and folded it neatly leaving it to rest on the top of the stack of books. Upon arriving at school, she reversed the ritual. As she boarded the bus for the return trip home, she followed the same ritual. It was as if she were stuck in a time warp on a day of tragedy when something horribly unforgettable happened in her life. Fate doomed her to repeat these actions to eternity. She never wavered from her ritual.

On the return trip, all the children rushed on the bus ahead of me filling all available seats. When I got on the bus, there was only the middle bench seat with space to sit, but it was already occupied by the four new, outcast kids. The oldest girl dared me with her eyes to sit in their territory.

The school buses of the 1940s did not have individual seats that held three people. They had three long bench seats that stretched the length of the bus, two along the rows of windows on each side, and one down the middle aisle. There were no handrails or straps to hang on to. When the bus put on its brakes, everyone slid forward into a pile. When it accelerated, everyone slid toward the rear piling up there. My fate was sealed. I held on to the seat for dear life each time the bus stopped to let someone off or as it lurched forward again. All eyes were on me. Don't you dare bump into that crew of new people. All my well-being in life rested on this bus ride. I failed. The bus stopped, lurched forward, tumbling me backward down the seat squarely into the midst of the pariah children. A gasping sound tore through the bus from a dozen throats. My doom was sealed. I began to cry as I slid down the seat toward the front of the bus. Children cringed away from me lest they touch the person who touched (them). Wherever I walked, children parted like the Red Sea when Moses lifted his rod. No one played with me after that day. People at church said they were glad I stayed in the car because they didn't want to catch something from me. I may as well be a member of the new family. Everyone ostracized me.

For the rest of the year the new family sat in imposed exile huddled on the middle seat. I sat a few feet to the left of them in my imposed exile. Daily life at school saw three groups form: the new family, me, and everyone else. At recess and lunch I found my own spot where I ate and played alone. The four new kids did the same. Everyone else spread out into the broom sedge field and pine trees playing cowboy.

One sunny day as I sat eating my lunch in my spot of exile, I felt a warm hand touching my shoulder. Looking up, I stared into the face of the new girl. God, I thought, she has put the kiss of death on me for sure. She was smiling. In her extended right hand she offered me a slice of homemade apple pie. Looking around I noticed that the other children were busy in the pines. No one was looking at us. I took the apple pie. She walked away quietly. I did a lot of thinking from that time until the end of the day. I made a fateful decision. As everyone boarded the bus, I intentionally waited until last.

"I am just like these new children, forced into exile through no fault of my own," I thought.

I boarded the bus pausing at the front. Lifting my head proudly, I walked back along the aisle and sat down next to Phyllis, pushing my body close enough to touch her and her family.

"Hi, my name is Fred," I said. "I'm Phyllis," she replied.

We chatted softly until they got off the bus. As other children exited the bus, they intentionally stepped on my feet, kicked my legs, or bumped me in silent revenge. Every day thereafter I sat with the new group. We ate lunch together and formed our own group at recess. I needed these new friends and they needed me. On Feb. 2nd, 1953, my family left the valley and took me to a new life, to a new school. Since June Jr. stole a car, we left in a hurry so I never said goodbye to Phyllis and my new friends.

Years later I was teaching in a very large, comprehensive high school with 2,500 students. One day at the beginning of the new school year a tall, beautiful, imposing lady, wearing a long coat and headscarf, walked into my classroom with her teenage daughter in tow.

"Since I signed my daughter up for your class, we came to meet and say hello to you," she said. "I wanted her to have you as a teacher." Looking at her daughter she advised, "This man will be good to you. Let him help and care for you."

Extending her hand to shake mine she said, "You won't remember me. My name is Phyllis. I gave you apple pie when you befriended me and my family long ago in the valley. I have never forgotten you. I wanted my daughter to know you; to know that you are filled with courage and goodness."

When she left the room, I sat down at my desk and I cried.

GOD MAKES ALL THINGS RIGHT DEO VINDICE

My grandmother strode through the log cabin door carrying a small Confederate battle flag in her hand. The flag was red with a St. Andrews Cross and eleven white stars. In her other hand she held a bouquet of flowers made out of various colors of paper. She wore her long, brown floor-length dress with a calico pocket. A white apron hung over the dress. These were her daily work clothes, her uniform for farm and housework. There would be no work for her today for this day, May 10th, was Confederate Memorial Day. She was on a mission to remember the men who had fought in the War as valley folk had done for over eighty years. When people experience devastation of a civil war, they never forget. The experience is imbedded in their DNA and is sent down the centuries to be forever relived and remembered. This valley lay in ashes and ruins in 1865 after the Northern armies marched through. Many of its men died fighting to protect their homes. Many died of starvation thereafter. This destruction is the reason so many people lived in log cabins in the twentieth century. It is not that they were ignorant; they were poor from war's devastation. Recovery was not complete and forgetting the war would never be complete. One should not forget his loved ones no matter how they have died.

I poured her a cup of coffee and put a piece of persimmon pudding on a plate decorated with red roses. She set her treasured flag and flowers on the table, then drank the coffee and ate the dessert. I studied her in detail as she sat at the table resting. She was small in stature, but physically strong. Having faced many of life's harsh challenges, she was mentally and emotionally like steel. This was Mary, my grandmother, of German descent. She wore her Teutonic heritage like a trophy. She was hard-working, moral, disciplined and strong. Like many of the valley women, she held the society together.

Finishing her coffee, she stood saying to me, "You will come with me today. I have much to teach you."

Useless it would be to refuse her. Had I done so, she would have paralyzed me with her gaze and admonished, "You will come with me today. You will learn what I have to teach you. And you will like it. We have our ways of making you like it."

"It is a pleasure to go with you, today, Grandma," I said.

She tied the ribbon of her straw hat beneath her chin, picked up her flowers and flag, took a crooked walking cane from behind the door and struck out down the path in front of the cabin toward an open meadow at the base of a small hill. I followed behind trying to keep pace with her dignified gait. She was more than eighty years old, yet strong and purposeful in her walk.

Hills rose above us melting into higher mountains with broad shoulders. Hawks flew in circles, slowly moving eastward in the blue skies above, as if they were guiding the way forward. The woods smelled of pine and warm, rotting leaves. In the distance I heard the roar of the waterfalls we called the Pots. It roared and gurgled like the low, throaty sounds of a wild animal. The path diverged; one prong led to the Pots, the other went up the mountain toward a church. She took the one leading to the little, white church built of wooden planks resting at the edge of the woods. The War had destroyed the original building and this one had been hastily rebuilt to replace it. I began to ponder why the Northern armies would have burned a church? Were they afraid God would hold them accountable for their wanton destruction? This church made of cast-off planks and lightly white washed with donated paint, was our humble cathedral. No stained glass windows were here. No gargoyles. No flying buttresses. No massive spires pointing upward toward Heaven.

Should God pay a visit to this simple church, he would probably say, "These people have religion right. I like their spirit. If I exist, I live in your heart. I wouldn't be caught dead in a grandiose cathedral or sumptuous palace. Besides, I love to smell the sweet sourwood blossoms and redbuds in spring around here."

On the east side of the unobtrusive structure was a small graveyard. Most of the tombstones were plain field rocks with name, birth date, and death date scratched on them. There were a few professionally-made stones with names and designs artistically etched on them. My grandmother focused on one tombstone with a small circle on the front. The circle contained two crossed military flags of the Old Confederacy. One had two large stripes, one red, and one white with a circle of stars on a blue union. The other one was white with a large, vertical red stripe on the end and the stars and bars in the upper left-hand corner. The soldier's name was emblazoned on the stone along with his dates of birth and death. What surprised me is that he had lived forty years after the War of Northern Aggression had ended, so he had died in 1905.

Grandma placed the small Confederate battle flag on a plaque put there by Burke County Tigers, a group of Sons of Confederate Veterans. She laid the paper flowers in rows across the top of the grave mound. Halfway down the tombstone, under his name, someone had written the Latin words, "Deo Vindice."

"Look," she pointed to it, "that was the motto of the South. It means 'God makes all things right." And so he does. "That is your great-uncle Dave."

She sat on the soft grass seeking to be more comfortable.

"Listen to my story, son, for those who write history books tell only lies about the War of Northern Aggression. Our story never gets told, so I share this family story. Burn the words on your heart and tell them unto the last generations of valley people."

I remember Dave well. He was just a plain, uneducated ploughboy who grew up in this valley. Like us today, he toiled at hard labor to eke out a living from these reluctant mountains. He knew nothing and cared nothing for politics. He knew nothing of plantations and slaves for no black people ever lived in this valley or these mountains. He knew nothing of eloquent parties, Mint Juleps, or cotton fields for all that happened in Charleston and Savannah. He knew a pine cone fire and a banjo plunking in the night. He cared naught for political strife between North and South. Dave and the rest of the Southern soldiers cared about their homes, their families, and their land.

The news that a federal army had crossed the Potomac, invading Virginia and the South, swept like wildfire across the hills and hollows of our valley. Men huddled in small groups talking and worrying about the fate of their homes and families. There was no other decision to make, they had to fight. Dave left with the other men with his hunting gun slung over his shoulders."

"We will keep you safe from harm," his words rang with assurance in our ears. He fought for us, for his home, and for no other reason.

"They walked over the mountains to be trained at Camp Vance in Morganton. I did not see him again for four years. Only one letter from him made it to the valley. He returned home gaunt, sick, broken from a Yankee prison at Point Pleasant. At least he came home. The only words I ever heard him utter about the war was an apology. "It breaks my heart that we could not protect our families and keep you safe."

That feeling, shared by all Southern soldiers, was the greatest hurt of the war and is probably the reason the South will never get over the experience. So many families died in the conflict.

I'm here today to remember this fine man, to express my gratitude, to let him know that he will be remembered until the rocks melt and the seas burn. If ever I had a friend on this earth, it was he. God has made it right, Dave, she addressed him personally. The South has risen and we are proud and safe in our homes tonight. You fought a valiant fight against insurmountable odds. We hold our heads high. Our loyalty is not bought at the end of a gun. Our loyalty lies with heroes like you. This flag I place on your grave now has the colors under which you marched and these flowers are the tears and remembrances of what was lost."

A profound silence settled across the cemetery. Just the singing wind moved among the gravestones. I thought I heard the rat-ta-tat of snare drums and the booming of distant canons. Maybe it was just thunder rolling down the mountains. I felt proud knowing that this man's blood ran in my veins.

"I will sit alone a spell," Grandma said to me.

I understood. I left her there and walked the path further up the mountains to a point where I could see twenty miles across the South Mountains. The mountains rose one after another, each higher than before. A blue haze hung over the more distant ones. I gazed at this magnificence.

"These are my mountains," I thought. "My people have lived here for centuries. This is my land. The South is my country. It belongs to Dave, too, and his sacrifices have pledged it to me.

He lies sleeping on the hill. His legacy is mine. His love of the South holds steadfast in my heart. Whatever you feel you may have lost, Dave, it is not so. Deo Vindice. God makes all things right."

MISSIONARY ZEAL

Those who lived in far-away states of Missouri and Pennsylvania must have thought of us in our valley as backward heathens in dire need of salvation. That was the major reason three missionaries came to work among us. Many valley people thought they probably came to get husbands. At least two of the women succeeded. Bertha and her sister married Moose and Marvin. They were my uncles, brothers to my absent father Eli. Since sisters married brothers, a situation arose about kinship which was hard to figure out. I was probably my own grandpa anyway, so it didn't matter. My father, it is said, would make love to a woodpile if he thought there was a snake in it. True again.

Mrs. Lindenhardt, the third missionary, came from Pennsylvania and lived in a log cabin near Lake McCall. She kept her pigs in sties built under the dwelling. The cabin was built on raised pilings. She was rotund, really very fat with a mean, nasty, Yankee disposition. She looked down on the local people as if her fat belly and nasty temper were superior to anyone. That is the reason no valley man ever married her.

She quarreled with her neighbors refusing to be a part of the ways and customs of the valley. She spoke English with an atrocious accent, wiped her nose with her dish towel, and threw garbage into the woods behind her house. Yet she considered herself superior to the local yokels. She found out about our valley from my mother who sent her boxes of holly at Christmas in exchange for used clothing for us children. Holly trees did not grow where she lived up North. Nothing loving and kind seemed to grow up North.

Mrs. Lindenhardt criticized how the local women raised their children and kept their houses. She had a better way of doing everything up North but she never seemed to get around to demonstrating it. Hers was the dirtiest house in the valley. Soon no one opened his door to welcome her in nor did anyone stop in to socialize with her. Her missionary work fell to the way side for no one wanted to hear what she had to say about God. Even my mother turned away from her, shaking her head sadly that any human could be so sarcastic and mean. We were happy as we were. She had nothing to offer the valley for we chose not to live our lives the way people did where she came from.

Bertha and her sister were kinder and more successful. They brought a Midwestern sweetness and caring for others with them. They taught by example visiting our homes, mingling among us, appreciating who we were. Bertha sang in church on Sundays with a beautiful soprano voice. She looked ethereal with her gray hair as she stood in front of the velvet red curtains in the church pulpit.

She taught my Sunday school class telling us Bible stories illustrating them on a large board with cut-out felt figures. Unlike Clyde's church, this one was quiet. No one dared shout or create a disturbance. The only time someone danced a jig here, Bertha, the preacher, and deacons escorted them out of the church suggesting that they go join up with Clyde and Jesse Pearl.

Bertha kept the youth involved. She gave parties in her home for all the children who attended church. She organized home-coming festivities each year where the women fixed their best dishes of ham, chicken, green beans, biscuits, mashed potatoes, and much more. Chocolate cakes, pies, cookies would fill our sweet tooth. We ached for the preacher to stop his droning sermon so we could attack the tasty food on tables sagging from the abundance.

For some reason, Bertha took a special interest in the children in my family. She was an intelligent, well-educated city lady. She made sure we were included in all church activities. For that reason, I never missed a church service. She did not approve of Ottie's world. She considered her as neglecting her children. She viewed her carousing with Gentry and his sawmill men as immoral. Her relationship with Eli, a married man, was downright sinful. The fact that my mother made and sold moonshine was a scandal. There was nothing in Bertha's life in Missouri---well-ordered, financially secure, and educated---that could possibly prepare her for meeting my mother.

My mother was a survivor. She sent us to Bertha's church because we got clothes and food. She went to Clyde and Jesse Pearl's church because she could shout and be with Eli. My mother viewed life with the attitude, "Whatever it takes." Born in a log cabin at the turn of the century, uneducated, dirt poor she lived life on a daily basis only, for unlike Bertha, no silver spoon stuck out from her mouth or experience. She was fiercely independent. Though life was hard, she held on tenaciously to her children and the single unit they formed.

Bertha did not understand that poor people have pride. They are independent and stubborn. Their poor station in life is all that there is. Pride and independence are the only values others could take away from them. My mother did not particularly care for Bertha, because she had succeeded in marrying Eli's brother;

whereas my mother never succeeded in marrying Eli. Bertha represented what my mother could have been, had she had Bertha's advantages in life. Bertha was beyond child bearing age when she married Moose, so she would never have children of her own. Bertha formulated a plan to take over the rearing of some of Ottie's children.

Bertha wanted to experience a family vicariously. She zeroed in on my sister Carrie and me because we were five and seven years old and we could still be molded into virtuous lives. She had a friend, Mrs. Palmer, who lived and did missionary work in California.

Mrs. Palmer was filthy rich. She had so much money that diamond and gold rings dripped off her fingers. She had her hair done weekly and ate expensive Swiss chocolates with chubby little fingers. She was chubby too. Her dress fell down her fat body leaving ridges along the way, not unlike the feed sacks we bought our cow feed in at Tony's Country Store. Unlike my mother and Bertha, Mrs. Palmer was born to the upper crust. In our valley culture she was a pig out of the trough. An invitation from Bertha arrived in California asking Mr. Palmer to help with her project. Mrs. Palmer licked her fat lips as she sent back her response: "Yes, I'll come."

These women formulated their plan to nudge us away from my mother into their custody. Intentions were noble. They would find gainful employment for Ottie in one of the textile mills in a neighboring town. She could have a steady income without making liquor and it would pull her away from the men as well. Carrie and I would go to live with Bertha and Mrs. Palmer while the other children would go to public school. It was their plan to give us the best of everything---school, church, worldly goods. As recompense, each of them would have the child to rear which they lacked in their regular lives.

Bertha and Mrs. Palmer threw an ice cream party, inviting many of the valley children so Mrs. Palmer could meet us and set their plan in motion. We arrived early. Bertha took Carrie and me into the bathroom where she bathed and dressed us in new clothes that Mrs. Palmer had brought from California. They passed out party hats and paper whistles that elongated when one blew on them. Then they broke out the homemade strawberry ice cream, scooping it into cones. I dug my fingers into the cone licking the sweet cream off my fingers.

"Don't put your fingers in the cone," I heard Mrs. Palmer say.

She didn't know that's how we ate it where I came from. I did not like her. With my luck, she would probably adopt me. Then would come the beatings and I would only have exchanged Ottie for a rich version of my mother.

Everything was well planned but the women forgot a very important detail---they did not consult my mother in the plan. They merely told her what they intended to do.

The party was proceeding joyfully when some kids came running into the kitchen, yelling that the corncrib was on fire. Sure enough it was. As I ran outside to see the fire, I saw my mother standing in the road with a kerosene can hanging from her hand. She tossed the can aside as she approached the main house. Bertha and Mrs. Palmer fled out the rear door running to the safety of the little white church on the hill nearby. My mother grabbed up the ice cream churn and smashed it against the kitchen floor.

"Come on, kids, we're going home," she hissed with fire in her eyes.

I looked back at Bertha's big white house on the hill as we crossed the bridge of the creek and headed for home. I dreadfully wanted another cone of strawberry ice cream. And maybe Bertha had a daddy for me waiting in the wings.

"Nobody is going to take away any of my children," Ottie huffed.

Ottie meant business. As difficult as life was, she would not give away any of her children.   As much as I wanted a better life, I knew I had to throw in my lot with her and live in Ottie's world.   So, I tore off the new clothes brought me from California, threw them in a ditch, and walked naked all the rest of the way home.

THE CALLING OUT

Disputes, quarrels, and arguments arose from time to time among the residents of the valley. Some quarrels were fresh, having broken out recently, while others were decades old. Nothing seemed to last longer than a perceived wrong or injury. One family kept an intergenerational quarrel going for years over the theft of a plow. Dahlaree and her mother left the valley quite angry at our family for June Jr.'s theft of their prized chickens and they struck back by cursing our milk spring. They carried their ill will with them. I stayed angry at my mother for years because of having to carry milk to the spring up Devil's Creek Fork. No family in the valley escaped conflict. It was a natural part of living.

No one escaped the desire to tell another off, to curse them at times either. Our people developed a rather unique way to defuse the anger brought on by disputes, quarrels, and arguments. This unique custom arose from earlier fighting in which people got seriously hurt. Everyone knew the commandment not to kill another. No one could find in scripture where giving someone a good cursing was forbidden. Rebuking was acceptable. Most likely the custom of "calling out" originated when someone acted on impulse and went to an adversary's house to vent. Rules for the engagement rose of their own accord and everyone knew and accepted them.

If a conflict reached a breaking point, the aggrieved party could opt to use the custom we named "calling someone out." The rules were simple. Go to an enemy's house; call him out on his porch or into his yard. He could not leave the bounds of his property and you had to stay in the public road. Yell out emphatically the nature of your grievance against him. All words in the English language may be used, including the most vile and vulgar, especially the most vile and vulgar. Curse him out with all your might. Read his pedigree from the biblical "begats" down to the present. You do not have to tell the truth for this is an exercise in emotional release. One may gesticulate with his fingers, arms, hands as well as make facial expressions.

The adversary is allowed to respond in kind. Such encounters were often dramatic. They sounded like wild animals of a jungle. When both parties had exhausted their emotions, they retreated to their respective domiciles. It was over, finished. Nothing more could be done or added. Valley people shunned any party that brought up the issue again. Thus individuals settled their differences without harm. It was high entertainment, better than a physical fight.

When word spread of a potential "calling out," dozens of people showed up at the assigned house to watch the event. In that way, they kept abreast of what was going on in their society. It was every bit as entertaining as a hanging. People chose sides. They applauded their side and gave encouragement as well as insults to it. They placed bets on the outcome risking their money to see who would walk away first.

In the wake of a "calling out," the valley settled down. People had been entertained. Some even went away with money jingling in their pocket from the money they had wagered. All were witnesses to the fracas and that ensured that there would be no recurrence of hostilities.

At the end of August word went out that Ottie intended to "call out" the two missionary women over their attempts to adopt two of her children. Stan's country story buzzed with inquiries from those wishing to be entertained, so much so that he put up a big hand lettered sign over the area where he made baloney sandwiches. It read, "Calling out, end of August, missionary's house." People cancelled appointments, hired babysitters, packed picnic lunches, and prepared chamber pots because no facilities are set up for any "calling out." Children skipped school. Miss Lucy and Mr. Rawlins called in sick knowing that this one event was for the history books. People chose sides. The God-fearing fundamentalists naturally backed the missionaries. Clyde and Jesse Pearl were right there. The heathen, hedonistic, hard-drinking fornicators pulled for Ottie to win. Naturally Eli was there in his element.

At the end of August the main road through the valley was cluttered with cars, wagons, people on foot, all headed north toward Bertha's house. The two opposing camps had already staked out their turf with the pro missionary group guarding Bertha's house and yard. The pro heathen group occupied the road in front of the house on the spot where Ottie burned down the corncrib. Old folks said this was the largest crowd to attend a "calling out" in their memory. Bertha's crowd opened with "The Lord's Prayer." Their adversaries responded with the chant, "Don't steal Ottie's children." From the yard came the hymn, "Thou Art Good and Holy," answered by a chant, "you are neither good nor holy." Both groups enjoyed taunting each other. Ottie was not even there yet.

A voice yelled out, "Here she comes." A hush fell over both groups as all eyes focused on the small road leading from Bertha's house to the white church on the hill. Ottie attended this church from time to time. Today, however, it served as nothing more than a milestone on her journey to settle accounts. Hundreds of eyes turned toward her still distant figure emerging from the trees. She carried two large leather bags bulging at the sides with something she decided to bring along. June Jr. came stumbling along behind her carrying two large leather bags as well.

Ottie was in a huff as she approached her destination. Nostrils flaring wide, mouth held tersely open, lips pulled tightly across her teeth, she breathed hard and fast from the passion of the moment. She had fire in her eyes. Putting the heavy bags down on the ground, she opened one and took out a fine specimen of white lighting made in her moonshine still deep in a hollow near Devil's Fork.

Turning to her supportive audience, she announced that this liquor was for sale at a cost of eight dollars a quart, a rather large amount in the 1940's. There were many takers and soon June Jr. had his fists full of dollars from the sales. Those who bought the quarts of liquor passed them through the crowd so everyone could slack their thirst and embolden their courage.

Many got tipsy. Ottie opened her own quart jar taking several swigs from it. She rolled the liquor across her tongue before spitting some out in a forceful stream. Enough went into her bloodstream to bolster her courage.

The crowd moved back to make room as Ottie stepped forward toward Bertha's house. They waited breathlessly for the first words. Ottie let fly with the first salvo.

"Come out of the house on to the porch you miserable Midwestern missionary bitches," she yelled. Her crowd roared in approval as their lips echoed the word "bitches." "I have a bone to pick with you."

Bertha had to come out or violate the rules. Bertha came sheepishly through her screen door on to the porch but Mrs. Palmer slunk behind the screen door with only her silhouette visible to the crowd. Neither woman had any concept of what was about to happen. Nothing in their Midwestern culture operated this way.

"I'm calling you out for trying to take my children away from me."

Bertha raised her hands to silence her crowd. Then she spoke. "Miss Ottie, we only wanted to help you with your children, to give them a better life and education."

Ottie spewed a large stream of snuff from her mouth then rinsed it out with a generous drink of liquor. Stamping the ground with her right foot while pulling at her hair vigorously with both hands, she resumed her diatribe.

"If you wanted to help, why didn't you bring us food? I needed help with hoeing and picking the cotton. My cows have to be milked twice a day. There's plowing to be done." Ottie's anger caused her entire body to gyrate in the same manner as when she shouted at the church.

"We don't know how to do those jobs," Bertha retorted.

"Damn right you don't" replied Ottie. "You missionaries aren't worth your salt. You can drone on and on about God and religion and the Bible, but can't milk a damn cow. You are useless. What makes you think you can raise my children better than I can?"

"We only wanted to help give you more than you have," said Bertha.

"Why don't you get married and have your own children. No man would have either one of you, that's why. If you would put out a little more than religious dogma, men might be interested in you" replied Ottie.

Bertha became a little miffed at the last comment and thus replied, "Mrs. Palmer and I don't care to sleep with all the men in the valley like you do."

"You're as cold as a nun's crotch in the Klondike," yelled a half-drunken yokel from somewhere in the crowd.

"More like a witch tit," snarled another.

"I've got more to offer between my legs than you do in your whole wretched missionary existence," said Ottie. "And you don't have to wait to go to Heaven to get at it either."

"Sleep with us, Ottie---Sleep with us Ottie," yelled the drunken crowd.

The pro missionary crowd bowed their heads repeating Psalm 23. "Turn from your wicked ways, Ottie," they beseeched her.

By this time Ottie's moonshine was doing its wondrous work. She was tipsy and her words began to slur. She was not as bright and clear in her intent as when she arrived. Her supportive crowd became less interested in her cause as they conversed among themselves.

From down the valley came the wail of a siren. The county sheriff sped toward the crowd with urgency. Stepping down from his car, he walked directly to Ottie grabbing both her arms, placing handcuffs around them.

"It's a calling out, it's a calling out," roared the crowd. "You know the rules, sheriff."

"There's moonshine here," he said, "all know the rules about that. You are under arrest, Ottie, for inciting a riot and for public drunkenness."

"Go to jail, go to jail," Bertha's crowd roared.

"Go to hell, go to hell," Ottie's crowd responded.

"Repent, repent, repent," Bertha's crowd replied.

"Long live sin, long live sin," chanted the heathen.

The sheriff drove Ottie off to jail in Forest City. Both crowds, having had their entertainment they had come after, slowly mingled with each other, where Ottie's white lightening found its way into mouths and pockets of Bertha's supporters as well. Even Clyde and Jesse Pearl bought a quart for themselves---for medicinal purposes only, you know. A few months later Bertha and Mrs. Palmer got their husbands. They married Eli's two brothers. Both crowds from the "calling out" attended the wedding, socializing with each other as if nothing had happened. Saved remained saved; heathen remained heathen. The only person they did not invite to the wedding was Ottie.

The money Ottie and June Jr. made from the sale of her moonshine at the "calling out" was just enough to pay the fine to get her out of jail. In leaving the jail, she made a hot date with the sheriff. He accepted.

FEAR IN THE NIGHT

Mountains surrounded Ottie's world on all sides so that no one could come in without a considerable climb. Very few people thought it worth the effort to make such a climb because only my family lived up here on an isolated farm. All the other houses were long abandoned.

Griff left his house to build a new one next to his two brothers on McCall's Lake. These men were my uncles although they would not admit it openly because my dad, their brother, coupled illicitly with my mother. The Ida Place nourished several families over the years and collapsed in on itself. The Wright Old House was only a memory by the time I was nine years old. Skiff's House still stood and housed Gentry and his sawmill crew. These old houses took on personalities and stood as landmarks in the evolution and demise of life in the valley. There was not a large population left. Most people knew each other and made it a point to know every-one's business to the most intimate detail.

In the vastness of nature surrounding our farm one could still encounter something of the unknown. People spoke of an un-known animal or creature that lived up Devil's Creek Fork.

Ottie embellished the story to frighten intruders away from her moonshine still. The animal was rarely seen, but people smelled and heard it. At times the area around the milk spring smelled rotten, a smell between wet dog and unwashed human. On the rare times that strangers ventured up the fork, they always said that they felt watched and followed.

Ottie and Beulah saw the creature once. People in the neighboring county reported seeing it, too. They gave it the name Knobby because it was seen lurking around the tops of the low-lying knobs.

It was described as seven feet tall, with excessively long arms hanging to knee level, and it had hair covering all of its body. It had a cone-shaped head. It never really harmed anyone. Farmers lost a goat or a pig from time to time, but otherwise, whatever thing it was, it lived in harmony with folks in the valley. Ottie found large footprints along the creek and at the tree line.

Valley people held their tongues or spoke in hushed tones around their tables at night and kept a sharp eye as they walked through the woods or worked in their fields.

My mother laughed at the idea of a wild man.

"I'd cold cock him with a stick of wood if he came around me," she bragged.

I never doubted for a minute that any creature or person that messed with my mother would end up cold-cocked on the floor. We children took all the tales in stride as went about our business.

It was a mile from our farm to the main road where the bus picked up us kids for the ride to Miss Lucy's school. Long ago we made a path through the woods to avoid muddy roads and cut time off the walk. On a particular rainy morning in March, Gertie and I left the house ahead of Curtis and Justine on the trek to school. We threw an old coat across our shoulders to prevent the rain from running down our clothes. We were about eight minutes ahead of our siblings.

Following the path up the hill past the Wright Old House, we walked down the muddy road for a brief moment, then down the hollow filled with rotting leaves. Gertie and I emerged in front of the Ida Place and skirted the edge of a cotton field. As we began to cross a log bridge over a gully, a movement caught our eyes back up at the Ida Place. I stared in disbelief at a very tall figure. It stood there in the rain staring back at us. It was dark gray with long arms and a pointed head. The two of us picked up our walking pace leaving our brother and sister to deal with whatever it was.

When we all met at the bus stop, Curtis swore he had seen nothing. What would valley folk be doing there at a collapsed house in the rain at seven a.m. in the month of March? On the return trip, all of us walked rapidly past the spot, listening to any sounds from the woods. My mother reassured us that she would check the place out, but she never did.

Summer came and went with everyone forgetting the incident of the unknown person. Autumn came. The family went to dig sweet potatoes in the farm field at the base of Grassy Knob. The fat, red sweet potatoes rolled out of the ground as we pushed our shovels under the rows. The boys filled several baskets and carried them on our heads. My mother told us to wash them in the creek. Next we dried them with a cloth. Ottie built a roaring fire in the woodstove and put a generous number of potatoes in the oven to bake. The family gathered around the stove in the warm kitchen to smell the aroma of the baking potatoes. The kitchen became a spot of contentment.

Outside dark night fell as black as velvet curtains. No moon came to break up the darkness. One could not see his hand in front of his face in such blackness. There were no city lights, no flash lights, and no artificial lights to break the void. The wood fire in the stove and two kerosene lamps threw shadows along the wall.

Curtis was uneasy about something for I saw him get up and bolt the door. I focused my gaze on what he was doing. He leaned forward in his chair listening with his right ear. He became agitated while rubbing both hands together as beads of sweat rose up on his forehead. Curtis was an expert woodsman. He hunted often and he knew the sounds of animals in our forests. He was not afraid of any of them. Tonight, however, there was something nearby that he could not identify. He leapt from his chair, ran into the living room, and grabbed his shotgun from off the mantel.

Returning to the kitchen he whispered to all of us, "Be quiet. There is something out there."

Focusing our attention outside, we all heard movement. Curtis was right. Whoever it was walked with very heavy footsteps around the house. We were all frightened. Even my mother cowered behind the stove with a huge stick of wood in her hand.

Our hearts sank in fear as something opened the gate to the kitchen porch letting the latch fall down with a metallic sound. It bumped against the metal dipper in the bucket. Heavy footsteps raced past the boards on the porch.

June Jr. ran to the living room and returned with his .22 rifle. We gasped in horror as the doorknob slowly turned with a raspy sound. Something wanted into our house.

Curtis let fly with two bursts from his shotgun. One volley of gunshot hit the wood frame around the door and the other splashed around the doorknob. June Jr. shot directly through the door.

Whatever was there leapt across the porch over a five foot fence and landed on the ground below. This unknown entity raced toward the barn seeking safety up on Old Grassy.

None of us dared go near the door, much less open it. I sat trembling in fear. My mother moved nervously about the kitchen opening the stove door occasionally to check on the sweet potatoes.

From time to time, she cocked her ear to the side listening for any unusual sounds coming from the outside. She stared inquisitively at Curtis and June Jr. who sat glued to their guns resting them across their knees. None of us felt much like eating baked potatoes when they were ready.

The two boys kept vigil for the rest of the night as the remainder of us tossed and turned in our beds. My mother suffered a disturbed sleep.

When morning broke, she went outside to examine the scene of our great fear. On the path to the barn, she found footprints eighteen inches long. With a handful of broom sedge she quickly wiped the footprints away so none of us could see them. She told us everything was fine and not to worry.

Then she announced to all, "I've decided we'll keep the milk here at the house for the time being. You won't have to take it up to the spring at Devil's Creek Fork."

Fear had cold-cocked everyone in Ottie's world.

THE FIRST SALVO

Little Eddie was a full-fledged bully although he was only eight years old. He belonged to the Piggott family who were our nearest neighbors when we arrived at our new house with June Jr. and his stolen car. They heard our vehicles as well as our loud voices as we shouted to each other unloading our belongings from the truck. Little Eddie, his father Cleetis, his mother Emmer, his sister Philomena, and brothers Rake and Coy crept through the pine woods until they could see our house and moving truck. They concealed themselves behind bushes and some of the larger trees so we could not see them. Like us, they were survivors who lived on the fringe of life. They were opportunistic; taking whatever presented itself to them or whatever they wanted. They were brazen in overpowering weaker individuals.

Little Eddie was the terror of the third grade in his school. He took lunch money from the first and second graders leaving them to go hungry. Those who refused to surrender their money, he beat severely.

Daddy Cleetis went about the neighborhood stealing tools, food, and clothing from clotheslines where they hung drying in the sun. He took bales of hay from farmers' fields before they could be stacked in the barn as winter fodder. Farmwives, returning to the spring house where they had stored milk to cool, found no milk. It was going into the stomachs of the Piggott clan at supper along with some cornbread and onions. Little Eddie's sister, Philomena, fancied herself a Gypsy maiden dressing in frilly skirts with bodice tops and pretending to tell people's fortunes. Her fortune telling for the men of Frog Level included baring her naked breasts for a fee of twenty-five cents.

The whole family was highly adept at picking pockets of anyone who allowed them to get close enough. Their mother Emmer came to heal people when they were sick. She used herbs and the laying on of hands. With one hand on a person's head supposedly extracting their bad energy; she slipped the other hand into his pocket relieving him of his wallet. Rake and Coy always worked as a team. Neither one had enough intelligence to operate alone. Together, however, they presented a rather formidable threat to any person or property that came their way. It was this group that had terrorized Frog Level for many years. They were on the verge of crossing swords and purposes with Ottie and her family of moonshiners.

Ottie and her family were weary from the sudden upheaval from the valley. Each of them fought a solitary emotional battle of being torn from a life and routine to which they were accustomed. Here, now, an unknown presented itself with nothing certain printed on its card. They knew no one here.

The house was big and old. It was not warm; rather it was cold and aloof. Their meager possessions salvaged quickly from the farmhouse in the valley only partially filled the rooms of the new abode.

In walking through the living room, one could hear the echo of his own footsteps because there was very little furniture to absorb the sound. The kitchen had three doors, two that opened to the outside and one that led to the living room. All doors in all rooms opened either on to the dogtrot or to the outside. Two upstairs rooms opened to the stairs that descended precipitously to the dogtrot below. To feel safe, Ottie needed to control exits and entrances to wherever she lived or worked. No feeling of safety was available here.

Ottie called her group together to inform everyone that she was hungry; therefore, we would find food. She acted selfishly inasmuch as she thought of food when it concerned her. If the children had been hungry, she would have told them to wait. Unless life affected her directly, she took no action. The boys pooled their sawmill money and decided that all would eat baloney sandwiches and, perhaps, two moon pies split among the eight. Each person may have his own R.C.

My two sisters, June Jr. and I walked the one-half mile to Pop's store. We took a short cut down the path along the hillside behind our new house. The path wound under gigantic cedar trees at least a century old, past sweet-smelling boxwoods that were taller than we were. It crossed a small stream of water, proudly displaying a small waterfall, and then connected to the main gravel road at a place that someone long ago had used as a vegetable garden.

As we walked through this new territory for us, we heard movement in the trees and bushes on each side of the path. Whatever it was walked with a regular cadence on two feet and it was careless. Twigs broke under its weight and it occasionally stumbled. We were somewhat uneasy, not really afraid, and just cautious.

Our feet kicked dry dust from the roadway and sent small pieces of gravel flying. After rounding a big curve with a high bank on the left, we crossed over the bridge on Silver Creek where June Jr. would soon have his wreck.

Pop's store stood at the top of a hill. It was a tiny building about thirty feet by thirty feet. He did not open the store on a regular basis. Clients knocked on his door, and he opened the store to serve them, then locked it back and returned to his house. We whistled to let him know he had customers. My lips were dry from the dusty walk, so all I could do was pucker. June Jr. deftly placed his thumb and index finger under his front teeth letting fly a shrill whistle that caused us to stuff our ears with our fingers. A solid, white head appeared through Pop's kitchen window. "We want in the store," June Jr. yelled to him.

In a few minutes a very elderly, plump man waddled toward the store. In his left hand the man carried a huge iron ring filled with dozens of keys. He licked his fingers to pull the keys apart and came up with a tiny one that easily opened the lock on the oak door of the small store. Pop was eighty-eight years old and feeble.

"I want baloney enough for eight people, a loaf of bread, some mustard, two moon pies, a jar of peanut butter, crackers, and eight RCs," June Jr. told him.

"I only accept cash," Pop told him.

"I only pay in cash," June Jr. told him.

"Let me see the money first," Pop said.

"Let me taste your baloney first," June Jr. argued. "The stuff you sell in this rinky-dink store might be out of date and no good."

"Who are you people?" Pop wanted to know.

"We are eight hungry people who just moved into the house on the hill. We have money to pay for these groceries. We are tired and hungry. Our lives have just been torn to hell moving up hyar. We are not in any mood to be hassled by some geezer as old as Santa Claus and as ugly as home-made sin. So give me my damn food or I'll hang your sorry ass alongside the Coca-Cola sign on the wall over the cooler," June Jr. cussed him. June Jr. would have carried out his threat. Pop gathered the items and put them in a well-used paper sack, handing them to us to carry. Pop turned his back for a moment to close the lone window to the store.

In a flash, June Jr. stole an entire box of moon pies and ran out the door with the rest of us on his tail. We trotted back down the road toward the bridge laughing at the theft. But our laughter abruptly ended as we saw three strangely-dressed kids playing in the sand along the roadway beside the bridge. Their clothes were in tatters and they were gaunt from hunger. We moved to the opposite side of the road and continued in silence. All three of them locked their piercing eyes on us and our groceries as if they were serpents and we were their prey.

As we crossed the halfway part of the bridge, one of the older boys spoke, "Where do you think yer are going?"

"Who's asking?" June Jr. hissed derisively.

"Rake and Coy Piggott and Little Eddie," he snarled. "This is our bridge and you have to pay us to cross over it. This is the second time you've crossed it today, so you owe us double."

"What do you charge?" June Jr. asked. "Give each one of us one of 'em moon pies," Rake replied.

"Somebody forgot to tell you boys, but my brothers and sisters and I now own this bridge. We claim it right now, "June Jr. informed him.

Rake stood up. He was short like June Jr. Coy Piggott was taller but skinny. Little Eddie, only eight years old, was plump but agile.

"Get off my bridge," Rake ordered us.

"No, you get off our bridge," June Jr. told them.

We set our groceries down on the wooden planks forming the bridge in anticipation of the coming conflict. Rake jumped with both feet striking June Jr. with a tremendous dropkick in the chest. It sent him sprawling against the bridge railing almost toppling him into the creek. June Jr. sat dazed against the bridge railing. Little Eddie grabbed me in a headlock, spinning me around three times making me god-awful dizzy. He pushed me down on the roadway at the edge of the bridge. My ears rang like a church bell.

Then the Piggotts attacked my sisters. Gertie fought like a man. She opened a deep cut on Rake's cheek with her fist, simultaneously kicking him strongly in the groin. He slumped down on the bridge.

Meanwhile, coming to my senses with my bloodied nose, I realized I was lying on a piece of wooden stick torn from the bridge by an earlier storm. I grabbed the stick and thumped Little Eddie on his left temple. He crumpled down and did not get back up. June Jr. rallied from the initial dropkick administered by Rake, who was now rolling on the bridge from my sister's savage attack. June Jr. grabbed Coy by the front of his shirt, slamming him in the nose with his balled-up fist. Lights out. Coy went down for the count. We were bloodied and bruised, but victorious.

June Jr. took three moon pies from the box and laid one each on the bloodied faces of the Piggott brothers. "That's the last damn fee you'll collect from us. Now get off our damn bridge." As we turned the curve and looked back, the Piggotts lay motionless as if they were frozen in time.

Ottie did not bother to ask us why we were bruised and bloodied. She wanted to know what took us so long because she was hungry. Initially we planned to share two moon pies among the eight of us, but June Jr.'s talents provided each one of us a treat of our own. None of the adults asked or seemed to care how the moon pies got on the table.

We took our food outside and sat down under a gigantic spruce tree to eat. The baloney between two slices of bread with mustard made an exquisite taste for our hungry stomachs. Peanut butter crackers made up our second course, followed by moon pies for dessert. These large chocolate-like cookies filled with marshmallow filling were a delight to Southerners. Mostly poor people ate them.

As we sat eating, we finally told Ottie about the fight at the bridge with the Piggott brothers.

The only comment she made was, "No one should have to pay to cross a public bridge."

She obviously had not heard of the state of New Jersey. We did not tell her that we had laid claim to that same public bridge and now planned to exact tribute from anyone who crossed it.

Ottie finished eating and went back into the house to resume work.

She came out within minutes yelling at all of us, "Where did you kids put the churn, the rocking chair, the clock, the kitchen table and chairs and all the other stuff?" she demanded.

While Rake, Coy, and Little Eddie Piggott were keeping us in conflict at the bridge, Cleetis, Emmer, and Philomena Piggott had gone in the back doors of our house and stolen items as soon as they had been brought in. Ottie had brought in the churn; Emmer had taken it out the back door. Curtis had brought in the rocker; Cleetis had taken it out the back door into the woods. Willard had brought in the clock; Philomena had slipped it through an open window and taken it to the Piggott house. These Piggotts moved quickly like shadows unseen by my family. After all our work, our house remained as empty as the moment we had arrived. The Piggotts were richer by virtue of theft. We never stopped to consider that a family might exist that was more clever and adept at theft than we were. It takes a thief to recognize one and catch one.

Ottie walked around outside the house looking at footprints everywhere. She followed them into the woods where she came upon some of our furniture piled in a heap. She retrieved most of it but left one piece as bait. Hiding among the trees, she waited until the Piggotts came back for the piece. She followed them across a broom sedge field, down through a pine thicket to their ramshackle hut in a meadow. She noticed much of our belongings sitting haphazardly around their yard. Ottie took note and returned to our house with the news. "Boys, we are going to war with these damn Piggots."

THE FIRST PIGGOTT WAR

The fight at the Silver Creek Bridge with the Piggott boys equated to the shot heard around the world at Concord Bridge. Both events signaled a desire for freedom to be left alone by burdensome people. The Piggotts were certainly not ruling royalty, nor were we. They were bothersome gnats that one wanted to slap at and crush. They were miniscule enough to be practically invisible, yet they irritated to the very soul. Ottie gathered us all together and we marched en force out the dirt road that ran to the Piggott's house. The woods on each side of the road were scavenged clean of all pieces of fallen, dead wood because the Piggotts had no axe with which to cut real wood from trees. They had a cow in a nearby pasture whose ribs showed through her sides. Their house was a hovel. At one time it had been a real house, but now it was so often patched with cast-off pieces of rotten boards that it looked like a heap of wood left in a dump pile. The night was cold and a line of blue smoke curled from the chimney slowly upward toward a flock of buzzards circling high in the sky. They awaited the loser of this confrontation. The house had a very small porch, just enough for two to stand on. We were careful to keep our distance and stay planted firmly in the road.

Ottie yelled for the "low-down" Piggotts to come out on the porch. Emmer emerged followed closely by Cleetis, who carried his shotgun under his right arm. "Put the gun down," Ottie told him. He hesitated. Ottie told him again. Once again he hesitated. Then the sound of gun triggers cocking came from behind Ottie. Cleetis saw Curtis and June Jr. pointing shotguns directly at his head. He retreated to the safety of the interior of his house.

"I'm calling you Piggotts out for stealing from us and for fighting with my kids," Ottie began the conversation.

Emmer sat down on a chair and rocked back and forth. She seldom spoke, but when she did, it was only in a one or two word sentence. "Who?"

(Ottie intuited that she was asking, "Who are you?")

"Ottie," she said.

"What?" Emmer asked. (She meant, "What is your last name?") Ottie meant not to reveal the truth of who she was, so she made up a last name, "Smithjonesjohnson," Ottie said.

"Long name," Emmer commented.

"You have our furniture and I want it back," Ottie told her.

"Don't have it," Emmer told her.

"It's sitting all around us right here in the yard. There's my churn, rocker, chairs, and table," Ottie's voice rose.

"Bitch," uttered Emmer.

"Bitch I may be," Ottie said between clenched teeth, "But you are one of God's half idiots. I intend to have my things back or you won't have a lying tongue left in your mouth."

Cleetis, Rake, Coy, Little Eddie, and Philomena stood behind Emmer's chair, making derisive comments and vulgar signs at Ottie and her clan. June Jr. punched the air with his fists imitating the beating we had given the Piggotts at the bridge. Philomena pulled her blouse down revealing her breasts to the three boys. Rake and

Coy turned their backs to us, dropped their pants revealing their naked buttocks to all of us.

"Chew on this," they yelled at us.

"You put all my things back in my front yard by tomorrow evening," Ottie told them.

"Go kiss a pig," Emmer yelled at her.

"You are the only pig I see to kiss here, Mrs. Piggott, and no, thanks, I pass," Ottie chided. We withdrew to our own turf leaving the Piggotts laughing in our faces.

Ottie was angry at being outwitted by a bunch of dimwits. She told us to find a couple of flashlights and dress in dark clothes for we were going back after midnight for our belongings. Our group set out like special military forces toward the Piggott house. Curtis and Willard carried a bundle of paper and rags to burn as a decoy. They slipped behind the corncrib piling their bundles together. They were going to set it ablaze. Ottie placed each of us kids near a piece of our furniture in the yard surrounding the Piggott house. On a given signal, when the fire blazed, we were to grab the furniture and head for home.

The night was as dark as a cypress swamp in summer. Not much moved in the stillness. An owl hooted on a hillside in the distance. The boney cow moved about in a nearby pasture. The Piggott house creaked as someone walked across the floor to the kitchen to get a glass of water. We could hear our own heartbeats and breathing as we waited to get the war going. Ottie carried her own shotgun under her arm. Each of us carried a large stick of wood in the event we might need to pound on the Piggotts. We looked like a scene out of Planet of the Apes. In reality, we were all a group of low-class people acting like apes. A glow came from the area of the corncrib as Curtis and Willard lit the decoy fire. The glow turned to flames, then a blaze that leapt upward, filling the night as a starburst. The Piggotts stirred from their deep sleep, trying to grasp what the light in the corncrib was. Cleetis yelled out, "far!" The prospect of fire terrified the Piggotts, because theirs was a true ramshackle house. In various stages of dress, they grabbed buckets of water and raced to pour them on the fire. Back and forth between well and corncrib they ran silhouetted against the glow of the fire like athletes painted on a Grecian urn.

In the distraction of the fire, I grabbed the churn, June Jr. took the rocker, Ottie and my sisters picked up the table and chairs. Willard left the fire burning, slipped into the Piggott house, and retrieved our clock. Placing it securely under his arm, he fled into the night back toward our house.

One by one, my family members returned home with our possessions on their backs. We placed them in their proper places in each room. Then, in an act of defiance and humiliation, Ottie told us to come with her to help the Piggotts put out their fire that we had started.

She kept her shotgun in one hand, but in the other she placed two quarts of canned tomatoes. The Piggotts did not mind us helping with the fire. However, we watched our pockets while around them. I was surprised that we returned home with our clothes still on our backs.

When the flames were extinguished, we said not a word. We just went back home and went to bed.

Realizing the Piggotts were hungry, her action unseen, Ottie placed the two quarts of tomatoes on their front doorstep. Like great military leaders of old, she was magnanimous in victory as we won The First Piggot War.

GETTING OTTIE'S GOAT

Ottie hated goats. In her youth, she had taken care of Cainey's goats on the farm where she lived. She had fed them, milked them, washed them and led them out to pasture. She had helped deliver the babies when they had come in the spring. She had staked them on a long chain in the yard where they could eat the wild honeysuckle vines that had tried to overgrow the place. She had shoveled the pellets from their sheds packing them into the wheelbarrow; then, she had emptied them as fertilizer on the bean field. When the goats had escaped from their pens, it was she that had spent the morning running after them.

"When I grow up, I will never own a goat," she had told Cainey and anyone else within hearing distance.

She had grown allergic to the rank smell of the billy goat urine which they constantly sprayed all over their pens and barnyard. The goats had taken a severe dislike to Ottie, too. She had beaten them with a stick at every opportunity and they had returned the favor by charging at her, knocking her on her back with their horns. She now bore many a bruise and scars rendered by a sharp goat horn or head butt. The big spotted billy goat named Pellet because of his abundant output of goat dung, squared off with Ottie at every chance. He looked for opportunities to ram her with his horns which circled his head like two wheels. Ottie had had to watch him constantly. If she bent over to place food in the goat bins, Pellet had rammed her at top speed usually sending her sprawling head first into the food bin. She had carried a long pole with her and had struck him with it. At times she had whacked him right between the horns leaving him bloodied and bleating in the fields.

She had decided one day to get rid of the goats. While selling moonshine at the Peddler's Stump, she had taken Pellet on a chain with her to sell him to the highest bidder. She had told One-eyed Sam if he bought a full case of shine, she would throw in the goat for free. He had declined. She had offered the goat at various prices to the men who stopped to buy moonshine-twenty dollars, fifteen, ten, and five. No takers. While she chatted with a customer, Pellet knocked over a quart jar spilling its contents on the stump. He lapped all the liquid up. It wasn't very long until he walked with a staggering gait. When going home, Ottie had tied him to a tree in the woods and had left him to survive on his own. The next morning Pellet stood in his usual place at the goat pens waiting to be fed. Ottie whacked him with her long goat stick just for good measure. She decided to take the goats high upon Grassy Knob and set them free. She tied five of them on ropes and led them along a logging road up toward the higher mountain meadows. They took their time for it is useless to hurry a goat. It was long past noon when Ottie turned the goats loose in the mountain meadows where fresh water and green grass were plentiful. She sat a while with them, and slipped away when they moved into the shade of the trees.

Ottie felt a sigh of relief as she made her way back down the mountain. She thought about her life without goats. Her time now belonged to her. She could sew, bake cakes, take long hikes and have many pleasures that goat sitting had taken away from her. She crossed the creek and took the logging road back toward the farm. She was tired from the day's exertion and just wanted to go to the kitchen and brew a fresh cup of coffee. As she sat drinking the fresh coffee at the kitchen table, she heard a familiar sound coming from the goat pens. Looking through the window, she saw Pellet and the four female goats standing in their regular places calmly chewing grass. The goats had taken a shorter route and had beaten her back to the house. Ottie began to cry in frustration. What does it take to get a goat's goat? When she came to Frog Level, she left the goats behind on the farm.

Burley bought some goats and put them in the pasture with his cows. Going back and forth from the Mill Shoals, I now had to maneuver around cows and goats. The day I came back from the shoals when the sudden storm struck, I did not know that when I crossed the barbed wire fence, the wire broke loose from its post, leaving a large gap. The goats found the opening and climbed through from the pasture to the woods. They wandered home behind me but I did not see them. The next day as Ottie drank her morning coffee; she looked out the window and saw a bunch of goat eating honeysuckle vines next to the barn. It was deja-vu from former days. She felt sick on her stomach. A feeling of rage rose within her at the prospect of dealing again with goats.

"Did you bring those damn goats in here," she demanded.

"What goats?" I asked.

"The ones in the honeysuckle patch," she replied.

"They are Burley's goats," I told her.

I heard her dialing on the old black phone wheel. I guessed she was calling Burley. She ended her call saying to someone on the other end, "Tell him to get his goats out of my yard or I'll be eating goat for supper." That afternoon the goats were gone.

The next day Ottie drank her morning coffee and went out to her vegetable garden to hoe and weed. She whistled as she picked up her hoe and walked through some bushes to the garden. There they stood, Burley's goats, grazing on her garden. She looked out the bean row and saw only stubble where her lush beans had grown yesterday. All her hard labor was lost to a bunch of aggravating goats. She yelled, threw rocks at them driving them back into the woods. Burley came for his goats again returning them to the pasture. He did not know yet that there was a gaping hole in his fence.

It was morning again. Ottie buttered a biscuit and added some peach jam. It tasted so good with the morning coffee. Her day was off to a good start. She felt happy inside. Then she heard a "baaa" from the direction of her rose garden. "Please, God," she prayed, "Don't let it be a goat." Opening her front door, she saw it. There stood the despised goats enjoying their breakfast in her roses. Ottie stamped her feet; she pulled her hair in frustration. She babbled like a lunatic uttering nonsense syllables. "Burley, Burley, Burley, Burley," she said over and over like a mantra as if his name would remove the goat infestation. It dawned on her that Old Pellet from the valley had put a goat curse on her. Because of her dislike of the original goat herd, the goat gods would not let her go. She sat down on the front porch steps to think, while the goats finished off her roses and then went for her marigolds. How could she appease those old goats? Then the answer came into her head. She would adopt the damn goats.

Ottie did not call Burley again to complain about his goats. They were now her goats. She took them to her barn and put them in the cow stalls. She fed them. After having her coffee the following morning, Ottie took the goats out to the woods to let them graze freely. At night the goats returned by themselves to the stables. Ottie began to develop a fondness for these cursed goats. She even named each one: Daisy, Mooky, and Betty Sue, Spot, and Spike because he had only one horn.

Two months passed and Burley did not inquire about his goats. On her path to get the goats one morning, Ottie did not realize that she stepped over a copperhead snake. She opened the gates and let Spike lead the herd to graze. Instead, he charged Ottie, knocking her sideways to the ground. She watched Spike as he trampled a tuft of grass beside the path. The attack hurt Ottie's pride for she had begun to care for those goats. The goats calmed down. She rose from the grass wiping dirt from her clothing. Then she saw the dead copperhead lying pummeled in the grass. Ottie looked at Spike with wonder. He just had saved her life. She went to him and hugged his neck despite the wretched smell of goat urine that emanated from his body. She felt gratitude as she realized that this animal understood the danger facing her. She revised her opinion of goats on the spot. She whistled and hummed as she led the goats to their pasture. The warm sunshine spread over the hollyhocks, the larkspurs, and iris. Bees buzzed in the blackberry blossoms. The pungent smells of summer permeated the earth. Spike had lifted Old Pellet's goat curse.

FIRING THE OLD GOSPEL GUN

There was a difference between what the people of the valley believed about God and what they practiced in their daily lives. "Do unto others," "forgive thy neighbor," "judge not" were great sounding philosophical phrases that were found in religious teachings, yet couldn't quite seem to find themselves into daily practice of the populace. People spouted these verses to support their points of view or arguments or to make a point. Beulah never missed a church service. She spent Wednesday night and twice on Sundays sitting in the front pew of the church where she could hear every word the preacher uttered. Then she would go home to spend the remainder of the week gossiping about every family she knew, judging, condemning their way of living life, telling vile stories about those of whom she did not approve. Come Sunday, she was back in her front pew being filled once again with old time religion which she had no intention of applying in her own life. People referred to such as her as "firing their old gospel guns." One year the church chose her as the "member of the year" citing her love of people and good work in the community.

My mother was a scared religious person. She never missed a Sunday service. "She's eating the preacher" people said of her, "trying to ride his coattails into glory." I was never able to understand what drove my mother to her fanatical church attendance. Perhaps she was just bored and wanted to be around people. Maybe she was terrified of God and tried to appease Him by showing up where she thought He hung out. (Not in any of these churches, he wouldn't). A fear of God did not affect her when she was sleeping with Gentry and his sawmill gang nor when she forced us to take the milk to the Devil's Fork spring. Did she instill any fear of God in June Jr. to stop his juvenile behavior? My mother was not able to read well enough to understand what the Bible said or meant. Everything she thought she understood was imparted to her through some neighbor or itinerant preacher whose knowledge was little above her own. The blind leading the blind it was. The ignorant educating the ignorant. Anyway, going to church mattered to her. She laid down the law to all of us that we would be in church with her every time it opened. Such was the law in Ottie's world. That is the time in life when I walked out on God.

The lucky church that got her as a member was a primitive, fundamental, missionary one. The size of the church building was as miniscule as the minds of the people that attended it. They broached no foolishness in what they believed and how they chose to express their beliefs. Every word in the Bible was true, including any wrong punctuation marks or misused grammar. If someone spilled water on the Bible, that was part of what God intended. They yelled, shouted, danced up and down the aisles. They spoke in tongues, prophesized, washed each other's feet. Thank God they did not handle snakes.

For the first time in my life, I made up my mind to defy my mother. This action was tantamount to defying God because she sat on his exalted throne with Him. I realized that her retribution would be swift and sure for my indiscretions because that is how she believed that God operated. This horse she could drag to water, but I would not drink of these waters. She could drag me to this church, but I refused to be like the people there.

The fateful Sunday arrived. Eli picked us up in the model-T Ford and headed down the road toward the church. My courage wavered with each mile we travelled. She would hit me for sure. Upon arriving at the church, she ushered us into the sanctuary. I moved along with my brothers and sisters, my plan of defiance utterly defeated. I was going to fight back anyway if I could.

The congregation rose and sang the song, "Will There Be Any Stars in My Crown?" singing slightly out of tune.

"Nay not one" I intentionally yelled out loud taking a cue from June Jr.'s book of behavior.

My mother smacked me across the left ear with her hand. Everyone sat down. A murmur went through the crowd and all heads turned toward the rear door of the church. Clyde, the preacher, and Jesse Pearl, his girlfriend, walked down the aisle toward the pulpit. They were well-dressed and lived in a lavish brick home built from funds taken from the collection plate. Clyde sat in the large chair behind the pulpit wiping fresh, wet lipstick from his neck and collar, a residue from the sexual encounter he had just enjoyed with Jesse Pearl. They were not married.

Jesse Pearl was not a true blonde. Dark roots protruded at scalp level. Long, dyed curls fell loosely around her ears down across her shoulders. Religion disallowed her cutting her hair. Her skirt came below the knees and wrapped tightly around her hips, accentuating the pear shape of her buttocks and thighs. Jesse Pearl took what she thought was her rightful place in the comfortable chair behind the pulpit on the stage opposite Clyde. She crossed her thin legs provocatively teasing all the men seated in their regular pews. Jesse Pearl had them on the verge of firing their old gospel guns.

Clyde lost no time in stirring up the crowd for Jesus. He reminded them that they were all sinners, having fallen short of the glory of God. They yelled in agreement, implying that only Clyde had risen above original sin. (His sins were both original and man-made.) He smiled at Jesse Pearl pursing his lips as if to throw her a kiss. He then promised the congregation eternity in Hell if they did not come to the altar in front of his pulpit to renounce their sinful ways. Overcome with religious fervor and emotion, Sister Poindexter rose from her pew yelling in an unknown tongue at the top of her lungs. She danced down the church aisle toward the door, turned and retraced her path to the altar where she lay prostrate on the floor. God blessed her with an ample girth and weight, so her footsteps shook the floorboards of the little church. If she had worn high heel shoes at the beginning of her dance, they would have been flip-flops by the time she made it back to the altar. She fired her old gospel gun until she passed out.

Brother Eller was sitting beside the window, his eyes rolled back in his head frothing at the mouth. Words of praise escaped from his drawn lips as his feet tapped out a cadence with meaning known only to him and God. A cacophony of sounds swept through the little church: singing, shouting, yelling, floor tapping, and praise. It rose in intensity. My mother stood in the midst of this commotion, raised her hand toward Heaven, swayed back and forth as if moved by an invisible force. Her voice rose above the din of the crowd,

"Praise God, Praise God, Praise God, and Hallelujah."

She clapped her hands in time to an unsung hymn, her knees lifting up and down. She broke free from the confines of her pew and danced out into the aisle of the church. Everyone clapped hurling their hosannas toward Heaven. I sat on my bench in disgust.

All this noise terrified me. I was only six years of age. It reminded me of the physical fights that I had observed among adults.

My brothers Curtis and June Jr. had almost killed each other. My mother had beaten on Eli with a stick of stove wood. They had yelled and beaten each other periodically with their fists. They had beaten on me as well. I had no tolerance for physical fighting, yelling, and cursing that usually accompanied it. For me there was no difference between fighting and the yelling in the church. How could God like this nonsense? How could people love and praise God in the same manner as they fought each other in the woods?

I put my original plan to defy my mother back into action. I screamed in fear, dodging the shouting faithful as I fled out the door, down the steps into the darkness. My mother opened her eyes long enough just to see my exit from the church.

I raced in the darkness toward the safety of the model-T, opened the door, and dived under a blanket in the back seat. Her big hands came and yanked me out of my hiding place by my hair. My body resisted, becoming rigid as my feet dug deeply into the gravel. Like ship's anchors, my feet cut a furrow right to the church steps. My mother's religious ecstasy turned into rage against me. She struck her hand across my head, back, and face as she shook me violently. She dragged me down the church aisle.

All the God-loving, God-fearing, Heaven-bound adults watched approvingly as this assault waned. Not one of them came to my defense. "Spare the rod and spoil the child," they believed. That is how one administered punishment in Ottie's world. They just beat the crap out of you. My head felt dizzy from the beating. This Godly congregation resumed its praise and adoration to a God that I would never worship.

In days to come my mother and I fought the endless battle over church attendance. I agreed to go, but I would stay in the car the whole time. If God wanted to see me, He could just come out to the car.

At times, my mother seemed to acquiesce, other times she yanked me from the car and pushed me toward the church. I screamed, kicked, defied. When congregation members began to stare at her, she let go of me and I returned to the back seat of the car. We settled into a nervous truce. I wrapped up in my blanket and slept while the rest of my family praised God by dancing a jig. I never understood how my mother managed to save face with church members after beating me severely. My view of God became tainted. I disdained these ignorant bumpkins, as well as my mother, and their wretched attempts to tell people about God. I chose to go it alone.

The road in front of the church rested on an incline. Eli put wooden blocks under the front wheels of the car to keep it from rolling away. One dark night, someone opened the passenger side of the car. I heard someone open and begin eating a cake my mother had brought along. Then he reached toward the back seat looking for something else to steal. His hands touched my warm face. Slamming the door, he ran away into the night. When my mother discovered the theft, she blamed me. Then came random blows across the seat aimed at my head.

"You did this. I can't trust anything around you, you little heathen. I'll show you."

At least she got the heathen part right. I cowered on the floorboard dodging the fury, waiting for her anger to abate. I licked my wounds.

My mother sat up front beside Eli bragging, "Wasn't that a wonderful sermon about love and forgiveness? Praise God. I just love going to church."

My dad Eli and my mother were never married to each other. The Bible instructed them to be fruitful and multiply, so that is what they did. Eli had a wife and family of his own. Nonetheless, on Sundays he left his family, came for my mother and us, took us to church. In passing his house, we waved at his real wife and family as we drove to worship. How did Eli get by with this? God would have to sort it out. Eli, like me, was not at all religious. He went to church to please Ottie. Like me, he would have stayed in the car if he could. However, this Sunday, God turned his attention to Eli. He would take the beating instead of me. When the family entered the church, Eli insisted on sitting in the last pew. My mother agreed, because the women of the church had to turn all the way around to look at her. She strutted around with Eli as if she was married to him, yet everyone knew that his real family stayed at home. Eli had no shame. Ottie had none either. He chased petticoats. He made conquest of any willing woman. Unlike my mother, he did not strike me. He did worse: he ignored me. Eli did not have any beliefs about God. He viewed himself as outside the "begats" and "thou shall nots," endlessly intoned by the ignorant church members who thought they understood the Bible. His job was to get us to church on Wednesday nights and twice on Sundays. My mother rewarded him well.

Clyde and Jesse Pearl carried the congregation through songs, Bible verses, and prayers. The faithful danced and yelled up and down the aisle. Now Clyde had not saved a soul in a long time. This very night he decided that that statistic was going to change. Along the front of the church was a long bench known as the "mourner's bench." That is where they dragged sinners to scare them to accept God and be saved from eternal damnation. The red velvet covering of the bench was stained from the tears of those who had already made the trip. Clyde wiped sweat from his forehead and lips with his white handkerchief as he locked his beady eyes on Eli seated in the back pew. He slowly made his way from the pulpit down the aisle to where my family was seated. Eli began to fidget. Small beads of sweat came out on his forehead. The faithful of the congregation got up and moved to the "mourner's bench" in anticipation of saving Eli's soul. They openly roared supplications to Heaven on his behalf. The piano blasted out the song, "Just as I Am." Clyde took Eli by the hand, forcing him down the aisle to the bench. Eli gave way for a brief moment, wavering in his resolve not to be saved.

"Brother, let God come into your life," said Clyde softly in his ear. "He will take away your sins and burdens."

He pulled Eli down on to the mourner's bench where arms of the congregation piled around his shoulders. They moaned, cajoling him to surrender to God.

Eli had had enough.

"Get your hands off me, you damned hypocrites," he yelled loudly bringing the salvation drama to an abrupt halt. He flipped the mourner's bench upside down with one hand toppling several of the faithful on their heads.

"Surrender, my ass," he cursed stomping the floorboards as he made his way to the door. "Surrender to what?"

"I'll get my soul saved, Clyde, when you stop humping Jesse Pearl without benefit of marriage," he hurled the invective across the church.

My mortified mother raised her hands toward Heaven in silent supplication. Eli came out to sit in the car with me. The little congregation had fired its gospel guns to no avail. Furthermore, now two men defied my mother.

In the weeks and months that followed, Eli never again went back into the church. I slept warmly in the backseat of the Model-T as he walked a half mile down the road to a country store. He arranged a poker game with a group of his unsaved buddies while my mother and the faithful poured out judgment on him and me, praying for our souls.

At times Eli slipped into the back room of the store to have a roll in the hay with Gumtooth, one of the local strumpets who hung out there. He paid her with snuff. When church service was over, he came back to the car. On the way home my mother chatted animatedly about how going to church had made her such a better person. The love of God warmed her heart. She felt love toward everyone.

"Except me," I said out loud.

She reached back and slapped me.

"Our church is on the move. We are saving souls. People everywhere are firing their old gospel guns. Some haven't been fired in forty years," she bragged.

At that moment Eli farted quite loudly. "That's about the best I can do with my old gospel gun, Ottie," he smiled.

I split my sides laughing.

I'LL KILL YOU IN THE MORNING TIME

E lam did not like to go to church. As a matter of fact, he didn't go except for special occasions like Christmas and Easter when the mundane, boring services added something of interest such as treats and Easter eggs or at homecoming when he could see old friends and enjoy a good meal with others that he knew.

Elam was thirty-five and unmarried. He was good- looking though he didn't believe it himself. He stood five feet nine inches tall and had a stocky, muscular body built up from years of heavy farm work. Farm work was all he knew. He was kind and he was lonely. His loneliness drove him to come out into public more often than usual. More than anything he wanted a woman, a warm companion to share his life. That is why he resumed his habit of going to church. Women went there, some single and available, some not. He cared nothing for the church services or the dogma that drove them. The church was his hunting grounds for a mate.

Grady and Coleen lived on a wealthy, productive farm on the south end of the valley. It spread over a hundred acres of rich farm and pastures made more fruitful by Grady's never-ending work. He toiled ten hours a day cutting hay, planting fields, feeding cattle. He poured his whole life into the farm.

Coleen took care of a tall, lovely two-story house as best she could. Like Grady's work, hers was overwhelming. Daily work was endless. Her body ached from exertion and exhaustion as did his when he returned home at the end of the day. She begged him to use some of their hard-earned money to hire a handyman or woman to lift some of this burden from their shoulders. Grady was too stingy to spend the money. They were not true misers but poverty in their youth left its harsh mark on them, especially Grady.

What had once been a marriage of warmth and intimacy grew cold. The two of them barely associated now; each was tied to his own part of the farm work. She longed to be hugged, to be held and to be told that she was still loved and valued. She missed her husband though he was ever present in the house.

His spirit had left their marriage months ago. Grady wanted to be hugged and cuddled, too, but he was too shy to speak about his needs. They passed each other like ships in a dark night, each a stranger unto the other. The incessant hard work in pursuit of wealth drained their bodies, hearts, minds and souls of the experiences that made life worthwhile.

On Sundays the two of them dressed in their best clothes to go to Clyde and Jesse Pearl's church, not so much for the religion, but for a moment away from the farm and the sadness it had brought into their lives. They sat together in the middle pews.

Grady often fell asleep from exhaustion. Often he rested his head on Coleen's shoulder. She wept softly wanting so much more of his warmth and love. They did not join the shouting antics because that required energy they could not muster. When he woke up, Grady would go outside the church to stretch out on the green grass. He left an empty, gaping hole in the pew beside Coleen.

From his vantage point on the last pew, Elam watched the pair of them. Something stirred in his heart. He wanted dearly what Grady was throwing away. When Grady did not come back into the church, Elam got up from his pew and sat in the empty space beside Coleen. They spoke not a word. Neither did they look at each other. She could feel the dynamic energy emanating from his body as he felt the heat from hers. This could not end well.

Each Sunday thereafter, Elam waited outside until Grady and Coleen were seated. He went looking for a seat as close as possible to her. Church members slid further down the pew in order to make room for him. After a few months, church members automatically left a vacant place on the pew directly behind Coleen for they knew that Elam preferred this spot. Keen, nosy eyes focused on him, suspecting that worship was not his motive. It wasn't. At times Elam slipped his right foot forward under Coleen's seat gently nudging her shoe with his toe. She flushed red. Other times he made occasion to bump into her or to smoothly touch her shoulders. His passion grew. So did hers. Being more concerned with his fatigue and naps on the grass outside the church, Grady remained totally oblivious of them.

One night at church Grady went outside to nap. Knowing that he would not come back until service was finished, Elam promptly arose from his seat and occupied the space where Grady had sat. He and Coleen did not look at each other, rather they sensed each other. Coleen's chest heaved as she struggled for breath. Elam restrained a great impulse to place his arm around her shoulders. Taking a well-used wooden pencil from his shirt pocket, he wrote these words on a small piece of paper he tore from a church program, "meet me outside." Her heart fluttered with anticipation as Elam got up, went to the door and disappeared into the dark. Coleen waited, not wanting to be obvious. Putting her lace handkerchief over her mouth, she feigned a coughing spell. She coughed incessantly until she exited the building. Her heart filled with fear, she searched for the place where her husband was napping. Fortunately this night he was fast asleep in their car. She could not see Elam in the darkness until she heard a gentle whistle from around the corner of the church. As she approached the sound, a giant hand reached out and pulled her into a warm embrace. He pressed his lips against hers as they enjoyed their first passionate moment.

The congregation inside stood to sing the final hymn of the service.

"Sinners all are we," opined Clyde in a loud voice, "but salvation is available. Turn from your wicked ways." Coleen felt so guilty.

These last words stung her to her very soul. Pulling away from Elam, she fled back into the church hoping that personal salvation had not passed her by. Had her husband seen her? Elam disappeared into the night, warm and fulfilled inside.

Coleen stood at the kitchen sink washing dishes. When Grady came in from the fields, she approached him with a steaming cup of hot chocolate. She asked him to sit at the kitchen table because she had something on her mind.

"I've been thinking," she said sipping her own cup of hot chocolate. "We have discussed the possibility of hiring some help to do our farm work. There is a young man named Elam who attends church a lot. He is devout, devoted to God as shown by his never missing a service. Why don't you talk to him to see if he is looking for any extra work? Maybe he won't charge a high fee."

Realizing how tired he was, Grady gave her proposal serious consideration for the first time. What was the point of generating wealth if one were too tired to enjoy it?

"I'll give it consideration," he told her, finishing off his hot chocolate.

He went to his bedroom. She finished her kitchen work and retired to the heavy armchair in the living room. As she sank into the comfort of the armchair, she imagined that its arms were those of Elam embracing her, warming her heart.

Grady and Elam agreed that he would help out on the farm on Tuesdays and Thursdays. He would receive ten dollars total for both days plus home cooked meals while he was there. On his first day at work, the two men planted wheat in the main fields not too distant from the farmhouse. Coleen watched them from the kitchen window as they moved about the fields, their bodies silhouetted against the horizon. They both hoped for a chance to get together, but it did not happen this day.

One night Coleen came to church alone. Grady was ill and decided to rest in bed. She sat in her regular place and Elam sat directly behind her. As if on schedule, Elam arose, leaving the church quickly. She took her cue, following him. They met on the incline of the hill where Eli parked his Model-T ford. He embraced her, both leaning against Eli's car not knowing that I was sleeping inside it. They did not know that I was defying my mother. He kissed her passionately. They could not wait one moment to consummate their desires. He lifted her on to the spare tire of my bed chamber. Model-T fords carried spare tires in full view directly below the back window.

I heard strange sounds and the car began to shake. Thinking someone was trying to push the car off the hill, I climbed up on the back seat, let fly the window shade over the back window. I had pulled it down at dark so no buggers could peek in at me. It rolled up with a loud clacking sound. I placed my hands and face against the cold glass and looked directly into Elam's eyes.

He screamed. I screamed. She screamed. Coleen darted away holding her dress tail above her thighs. Elam waddled behind her, his pants down around his ankles. I fell back on the seat afraid, not understanding what had just happened. I asked my mother why Elam pulled down his pants behind our car.

Ottie did not explain anything to me. She wanted no competition from other women where valley men were concerned. She took umbrage at Coleen's actions for she had her eye on Elam too. Not having been with Elam yet, she decided to eliminate any competition. She went to Grady and told him what I had seen that night. She sealed everyone's fate.

The time for spring plowing came. The two men fired up the old tractor, attached the harrow to it with the intent of leveling out the soil for planting the yearly cotton crop, and went to work. Grady drove the tractor as Elam balanced himself on a metal piece covering the huge tractor tires. They navigated an incline that led to the cotton field. Suddenly the tractor wheels began to spin as the harrow lodged on the incline. As Elam leaned back to access the situation, Grady pushed him. He fell from his perch on the tractor on top of the hard metal parts of the harrow. The fall stunned his senses. Grady floored the gas on the tractor causing it to spin its wheels forcefully. The harrow rolled full force over Elam's unconscious body. Grady drove the tractor and harrow around the field and ran over Elam a second time.

"Morning time is a good time to kill wife stealers," he thought to himself.

Meanwhile, Grady whirled the tractor for a third pass over Elam, who had enough consciousness to know that he was about to die. With all his strength, Elam rolled into a ditch and picked up a large stick that had fallen from a tree. As Grady made his third pass, Elam rose striking him a fatal blow across his face. He fell down under the tractor tires. Elam pulled himself up on the tractor and drove it and the harrow twice over Grady's body.

Elam was covered in deep cuts. Blood soaked his clothes and ran down his legs. When night fell with neither man coming home,

Coleen went to the field where she found both men lying under the harrow. Only Elam still breathed.

Elam described for the sheriff how the accident transpired. There were no witnesses.

"I was driving the tractor when Grady fell off behind and got run over," he explained.

Since Elam was a steady churchgoer, the sheriff took his word implicitly. Afterward, Elam and Coleen spent three nights together each week fulfilling each other's needs but soon he became restless, bored, disinterested. Then one night at church she saw him sitting next to Ottie, holding her hand. It was more than she could bear.

Coleen stood up yelling in front of the crowd, "I'm going to kill him in the morning time."

Every person in the church heard her threat. A rigid calm fell over her. Her face froze in a mystical gaze. Some of the women consoled her and walked her back to her car. Ottie kissed Elam on the cheek, squeezed his hand harder, and looked at Coleen with disdain.

The following Sunday the congregation was already seated in the small church when Coleen entered. She wore the same stoic face as before. Her eyes were narrow slits as if she were staring directly into the sun. Numbly she took her seat in the pew behind Elam and Ottie. The choir struck up the song "There is Power in the Blood" with Clyde inviting the congregation to sing along. A shot rang out. Elam slumped on the hardwood floor. Coleen sat with a smoking pistol in her hand. Then she turned her pistol toward her own aching heart and sent a bullet through it. Her body collapsed across the pew in front of her. Her right hand fell across Elam's blond hair as if she were caressing it. Ottie fled. Outside, the sun shone warmly on this bright Sunday morning. It was morning time. And it was a time for mourning.

DON'T EVER TAKE A CHANCE
ON AN INDIAN BLANKET

The large metal prison door clanged loudly as it swung shut behind Eli. He wore a new suit of clothes with a fresh, crisp twenty dollar bill in the pocket. The suit and money were standard issues from the federal government to the state of Ohio given to help an inmate start a new life. He stood alone in front of the prison doors. He clutched an envelope with his release papers. Now that he was free, no police, guards, or officials bothered with him. Having served three and one-half years instead of five, (he got out of the pen early for good behavior), for getting caught making moonshine.

The nearest town was a mile away from the prison so he started walking toward it. Looking over his shoulder, Eli saw the gray prison walls covered with razor wire along the top. He remembered the loneliness and boredom of his stay. An exuberant feeling of freedom rose within him. He began to run in the direction of the town lest some prison official summon him back.

Reaching the town, he went to a bus station where he purchased a one-way ticket to Forest City, North Carolina, for seven dollars. He paid with the twenty dollar bill and placed the remaining thirteen dollars in his pocket.

He breathed a sigh of relief as the Greyhound bus crossed the Ohio River into Kentucky. It took the bus some three hours to cross the state, because it stopped in every little town and village along the way. Eventually it pulled into Knoxville.

There Eli changed to another bus headed eastward to his North Carolina home. He noticed the schedule took him through Cherokee. Just the name itself conjured images of First Nation people, teepees, and the west. Having been locked up so long, he could use some diversion. He intended to spend a little time in First Nation country.

What a disappointment. The store where they stopped was filled with fake merchandise. Every item was stamped "made in Japan." The real Cherokee Nation lay among the laurel and valleys hidden from view of the tourists. Its power and beauty would awaken in the next twenty years and drive out those who had tarnished its image. No teepees, no wild west, very few real First Nation people, just a ratty old man in a headdress charging tourists fifty cents to stand next to him for a photo.

That was an unfortunate image the dumb tourists wanted.

Eli walked through a store laden with junk gifts purported to be "real" Native American. He reacted with disdain at all this useless merchandise until he saw a stack of blankets marked as genuine and made in Cherokee. Eli felt anger when he saw a tag attached to the blanket which read "made in Japan."

He thumbed through them pulling out a brown one with a green frieze on both ends. In the center was a giant starburst of colors. The blanket was five feet long and three feet wide. He paid the cashier, a fat, dumpy white woman dressed in buckskins wearing a headband with a feather sticking up. Sticking the blanket in a brown paper bag, he boarded the bus thinking he might give his wife Lily the blanket as a peace offering for being gone so long.

Three hours later he stepped off the bus in Forest City to a new life.

He was free, but he was not yet home. Home lay twenty miles to the east. No buses went that way. No family members came to meet him. He would have been glad to ride in a sled at this point. He just started walking.

He reached the little town of Bostic seven miles into his journey. Bostic had one road running through it. There was a railroad track crossing the road. Near the tracks stood a small diner formed from a cast-off railway car. Above the door flashed a neon sign announcing "Eats." Eli walked up the four steps into the warmth of the diner. The sweet smell of freshly-brewed coffee wafted through the air along with that of apple pie and doughnuts. Eli had hardly eaten since his release in Ohio and now he was famished. He sat down on one of the round stools and swung his feet underneath the counter. He ordered meatloaf, mashed potatoes, cornbread, fresh coffee, and a large piece of homemade apple pie. He ate like a pig at a trough. No food in the whole state of Ohio could match this little diner. He gulped down the fresh coffee and asked for more. Having finished eating, he leaned back on his stool, savoring every bite of the apple pie. He took a moment to consider his life. Would he get his job back with the state highway crew? Would his family and friends have him back? What about Ottie? She let him get caught. Did she do that intentionally? His freedom did not imply an easy road forward. He had to rebuild his life with a reputation as an ex-con.

As Eli sat thinking, drinking his hot coffee, the door to the diner opened and through it walked a tall, burly, rough-hewn man in his fifties. He had a death head tattoo emblazoned on his left arm and a dagger printed on the underside of his right arm. He looked around the diner with suspicious eyes trusting no one he saw. He sat down at the counter leaving an empty space between him and Eli. He ordered coffee and a doughnut. As he ate, he turned his eyes on Eli, staring with great interest at his new clothes and the white skin.

"Where'd you get the new clothes," he asked impersonally.

Eli was caught off guard and did not know how to reply. How would people react to an ex-con? His face flushed a crimson red. He looked down into his coffee cup not responding at all

"I had a new suit of clothes once," the stranger continued. "I got them from the correction officers at Central Prison in Raleigh."

Eli then understood that the man, like him, was an ex-con.

"Chillicothe, Ohio," Eli mumbled softly under his breath.

As the stranger stood to pay for his food, he tapped Eli on the shoulder saying, "Come on, partner, I'll drive you home, wherever home is."

The two men rode in silence in the man's pickup truck toward the valley. Each was deep in memory of his own incarceration. Both knew prison life well. Each was in his own enormous flashback. The stranger lit and smoked a cigarette as Eli chewed on his fingernails.

As they reached the crossroads at Miss Lucy's school, the stranger spoke "I'll let you out here. I judge you not. May life bless you and bring you your heart's desire."

Inside Eli felt as if God had just given him a lift along the highway. Another former convict, like him, was not defeated by his experience. He still had enough love in his heart to reach out to Eli.

"How much do I owe you?" Eli asked.

"Nothing," the man replied. "We've both already paid our debts in full."

Eli stood watching the red tail lights of the truck until they disappeared into the darkness. He went to a copse of trees on the roadside, unfurled the pseudo Indian blanket, and went to sleep. He dreamed of his first son, Pet, who had died of sickness at the age of twenty-one. Emotions flooded over him. Eli began to weep convulsively, tears washing down his cheeks like a cleansing balm. No one could replace Pet in his secret heart of love, not even another son. It was just a dream.

"Please, God," he silently prayed, "Don't send me another son to finish breaking what heart I have left."

When he awakened, he folded the blanket, put it under his arm, wiped his tears, and walked the rest of the way home.

Ottie was working in the south field hoeing corn when she saw a lone figure top the hill and walk the road to the white farmhouse. Her heart fluttered as she recognized Eli. She wanted to run to him, to embrace him, to tell him they had another daughter born while he was in prison. However, the honor of welcoming him belonged to his legal wife.

She watched him closely, each step, each movement. He saw her, too, but he dared not acknowledge her. Eli's anger rose toward Ottie for having left him to the revenuers at the moonshine still. He knew he would get his enjoyment from her anyway. Eli decided not to give the blanket to his wife Lily. He hid it near the well.

A week later, Eli went to Ottie's house and knocked on the door. When she opened it, he handed her the blanket brought from Cherokee. She took the blanket and wrapped it around her shoulders. The two of embraced each other warmly, pushing him out the door through the yard to the woods on the other side. She spread the blanket neatly on the ground, laid down on it, pulled Eli down on top of her. They made up for a three-year absence. When they finished, Eli lay sobbing once again.

It was August 23, 1942. I was conceived that day on that pseudo blanket. Nine months later on May 23rd, 1943, I made my appearance in the valley. Forever after, as my mother looked at me when she got angry, (me-looking exactly like Eli), she would trumpet to anyone present,

"He's my consolation prize for taking a chance on that damn cheap Indian blanket."

WATCH THEM JUGS A-FILLIN'

Her dark pair of overalls stretched to their breaking point as Ottie squeezed fat buttocks into them. If she had squeezed any deeper, her pants would have split wide open down the seams. She fastened her suspenders over both shoulders tucking in her dark, man's shirt. She slipped both feet into a pair of rough plough shoes, then covered her head with a straw hat dyed solid black.

Ottie wasn't dressing for church or a date. She had serious business deep in the woods and needed to blend with the trees and bushes. She took down her shotgun from its rack above the mantel and tucked it under her left arm. She stuck several shotgun shells in her shirt pocket and strode out the kitchen door to the horse stables in the barn. Two wooden buckets of corn awaited her.

She pressed the shotgun heavily under her left armpit, picked up the buckets of corn, and set out in the direction of Griff's Old House. Turning left, she aimed directly for Devil's Creek Fork and the milk spring. She certainly wasn't bringing milk this day. Passing the milk spring, she strained to climb the ridge above.

Reaching the summit of the ridge, she sat down to rest. Her breath came hard and fast.

After a short respite, Ottie picked up her buckets and went down the hill on the other side into the laurel thickets back of the waterfalls on Devil's Creek. Hidden among the laurels was a medium-sized moonshine still. It sat on a solid foundation of river rocks piled three levels high, each stacked perfectly without mortar. On these rocks rested the main reservoir for mash and water.

Beside it sat several wooden barrels where mash fermented. A large copper coil snaked from the metal reservoir into a smaller container where the condensed moon shine flowed. As well-hidden as the moonshine still was, Ottie had two problems. She had to light a fire to cook the mash. It was impossible to hide the smell of cooking corn. She did not even try.

Ottie was clever. Like Brer Rabbit, she lived in the briar patch. The woods were her home. Long ago she helped to create the evil, scary reputation of Devil's Creek Fork. She told everyone up and down the valley that a wild man lived up there, that robbers hid out from time to time. You risk your safety, even your life, if you hang around the Devil's ground she told people. She terrified all of us children with her tales.

The fear carried over into our adult lives so we just avoided the area. She had to prevent strangers from coming up Devil's Creek lest they smell fire or the cooking mash. That way they would not accidentally stumble on her moonshine still.

She spoke often of the wild man called Knobby telling people how he had tried to break into our kitchen one night and Curtis had shot him through the door. Then one day she had a very clever idea.

She cut two huge feet, eighteen inches long, out of a piece of plywood and nailed straps across the top so she could slip them over her feet. She walked up and down the soft sand bars in the creek bed making it look as if the wild man were taking a walk there. She tossed chicken and pig bones from her cooking pot all over the area giving the impression someone had been killed and eaten up the Fork.

If Ottie saw any person go up the Fork, she quickly moved ahead of him hiding in the bushes and making growling noises. Then she threw rocks out of the thicket at them. Very few people were brave enough to face such an assault. Fear drove them back down the valley leaving Ottie's still safe. Thus did she perpetuate and enhance the evil reputation of Devil's Creek Fork.

Beulah kept a vigilant eye out for lawbreakers and sinners. Ottie ranked high on her list of sinners, if not in first place. In early spring Beulah decided to go out looking for ramps and young polk salat. Though she loved to eat greens, collecting them was not her real intention. She wanted to find Ottie's still. She noticed Ottie going down the main highway frequently, sometimes in cars, more often on foot. Something was going on in the Devil's Fork woods and Beulah was going to find out what. Tying on her flat, straw hat, she picked up a hand-woven basket to gather whatever the woods offered this time of year, and set out on the path toward our house. She walked past the Ida Place and took the path to the main road. She picked a few bloodroot or coon root plants as she called them. Their white blossoms spread across the forest floor making them easy to find. Her finger plucked some wild ginger, two galax leaves, and one ginger plant and deftly dropped them into her basket. At the next branch flowing across the road, she gathered several ramps. It was necessary to handle them carefully as their odor is so pungent.

As she walked, Beulah kept a keen eye out for anything out of the ordinary. She saw car tracks and Ottie's tracks where she walked. Then, by accident, she found the Mother Lode. In plain view there lay a broken moonshine jar on the road, its contents smelling strongly. She picked up the broken glass and put it in the basket with her plants.

Ottie saw Beulah as she topped the hill overlooking the road to our farm. Beulah saw Ottie, too. Both women pretended not to notice each other. Beulah continued along the road toward Griff's Old House as Ottie peeked around the corner of our farmhouse. She had to act quickly. Ottie raced the route by the barn across the creek past where June Jr. stole Dahlaree's prized chickens and up the Fork ahead of Beulah.

Beulah stopped at the entrance to Devil's Creek Fork. She stuck her canine nose high in the air sniffing in all directions. She smelled a hint of burning wood mingled with cooking corn.

"I've got you now you little heathen," Beulah thought to herself. She headed up Devil's Creek.

Meanwhile, Ottie snuck to her still and put on the eighteen inch plywood shoes she had made. Running back down to the Fork road, there she stamped several large prints where Beulah could see them. She then hid behind a clump of laurel and waited. Beulah hesitated when she saw the huge footprints. At that moment Ottie began to howl at the top of her lungs in the laurel. It was a high pitched OOOOOOOO. Picking up a piece of wood, she smacked it against a tree three times as Sasquatch do. Picking up some small river rock, she hurled them in Beulah's direction. Not at all afraid, Beulah picked up the rocks and threw them back in Ottie's direction. Ottie shook the bushes even harder, screamed a notch higher, and struck the stick against the tree with more force.

"Cut it out, Ottie," Beulah yelled. "I know it's you in the bushes. I'm going to find your still and bust it up for good."

Ottie said nothing. Her answer was another barrage of river rocks over Beulah's head.

Suddenly Beulah let out a blood-curling scream. She stopped dead in her tracks, threw her basket into the air, and ran at top speed back down Devil's Creek toward her own house. Ottie hid herself more deeply in the underbrush. She wondered why Beulah had given up the encounter so easily. Then she smelled a foul odor, a cross between wet dog and dirty human. Along with the odor there came a thumping of bipedal feet down the ridge above her. She saw a nine foot ape-like creature walking by. Covered entirely in long dark hair, its arms reached well below its knees. Its mouth was covered with Ottie's fresh corn mash. It had helped itself to a free meal. For over fifty years people had claimed a Bigfoot lived in these woods. Bigfoot was known to communicate through moans, tree pounding, shaking bushes and throwing rocks. Ottie mimicked Bigfoot; therefore she caught its attention and it came to investigate. Beulah had thought Ottie was the culprit until she had seen the Bigfoot on the ridge.

Ottie did not tolerate interference in her personal matters, especially her moonshine still. She got even with Beulah. The next Sunday, Beulah was strolling to the white church on the hill near Bertha's house. The sides of the road were lined thickly with kudzu vines. Ottie hid in the kudzu and let fly a barrage of rocks. She growled under her breath. Not knowing if she were dealing with Ottie or a Bigfoot, Beulah fled. Her fear prevented her looking back to see what was chasing her. It was Ottie, her face covered with a cloth. She wore the huge plywood Bigfoot feet too. Ottie ran Beulah down and beat her to a pulp. As a final act of victory, as animals in the wild urinate on their victims, Ottie poured a fresh quart of moonshine all over Beulah's clothes. When church members found Beulah, they saw a paper note pinned to her coat which read,

"Please help me. I'm a hopeless drunk."

The sourwood trees on the hillsides cackled with laughter.

THE PATH

There is something about a path that refuses to go away or die. Roads from long ago civilizations are still used today. The imprints of some early roads in America are still visible. Once established, paths carry people from a beginning to their destinations, from a definite point to an uncertain end. Life is a path that leads from birth to death and transition. Paths come into being as shortcuts, as a means of making a journey easier. That is why my brothers and sisters and I made our own path that refuses to die.

Our path on the farm came into being without any certain plan or idea. It was a natural outcome of a desire for easier, cleaner walking for we did not care for the thick mud that formed in the ruts of the regular road. The road to our house formed too many turns and switchbacks as it led from the state highway. The path formed wherever we children decided to walk.

There was a roadway with two ruts leading from the front porch to the road going toward Griff's house on one side and toward where Gentry stayed on the other. It was not an official part of the path. However, the real path started up a small embankment. Our feet dug steps out of the embankment over time. The path went through trees where the land was covered with soft pine needles, coming back to the main road through a large patch of honey-suckle vines at the Wright Old House. For about a third of a mile it was a part of the main road again because there was no mud here; it then veered left down a long hill emerging into a thick stand of beech trees at a fresh spring of water. The path struck out from there on level ground through hazelnut bushes and laurel until it connected again with the main road at the Ida Place. Next, the path skirted several cotton fields and crossed a log over a deep ravine and stream. It wound around two more fields, emerging at the state road at Effie's house.

This path was our superhighway to the outside world---to school, to church, to town, to country stores. Twice a day we walked the path to school and back. On Sundays, we walked it to church ser-vice. Ottie walked it to visit our neighbors and to get away from the drudgery of the farm. People walked it to see me and my sisters when we were born. Others tramped sadly along it when Eli's first wife died. Effie came along the path to bring us a grape pie when we all had the whooping cough. Lela carried her opened umbrella to protect her delicate white skin when she traveled the path to bring Griff some food. He occasionally ploughed a garden at the old house near Devil's Fork but only if one of us children stayed with him. Griff was uneasy with Devil's Creek Fork too. A group of neighbors made the trip along the path when it was our turn to host preaching service at our house. The truant officer followed the path when he nabbed June Jr. and so did the sheriff when he came to arrest him for stealing a car. Knobby probably used the path as well.

The path was alive. It carried all of the memories, all our daily emotions. It knew us well. It led us, directed us and consoled us as we moved through the days of our lives. It connected us to unseen worlds.

My sister Carrie was not yet in school when she first saw them. On the return walk from church on a sunny day in May, as we reached the location of the Wright Old House, I heard her carry on a one-way conversation with someone in a patch of wisteria. Purple chunks of wisteria in bloom with its sweet fragrance hung over the pathway. Its vines had run wild from the Wright Old House where someone had lovingly planted it years ago. Now they created a virtual forest of purple blooms cascading around the path. Carrie said some little people lived in the wisteria patch. They wanted to be friends with us and come out to play.

After lunch that Sunday, Carrie begged me to walk back out the path with her and play with the little people. She was five years old and I was seven. The wisteria vines were not far away for an adult, but much too far for us to be alone. Her pleading won me over, so the two of us returned by ourselves to the Wright Old House. I just wanted to know who she was talking to.

We sat down in the wisteria vines and fell asleep in the warm afternoon sun. I awakened to the sound of child laughter. I woke Carrie up.

"Did you hear someone laughing?" I asked her.

"No."

We got up to go back home. Then I saw a tiny man about three feet tall wearing a shirt, leotard pants, and a wrinkled stove pipe hat. It was an elf or a fairy. My mother often told us stories from the Cherokee Indians about little people they used to encounter in the lost valleys and coves of the Smokey Mountains. Indian children played with these little people who always ran away when adults showed up. A stove pipe hat stuck out of the honeysuckles as two beady eyes peeked through sizing us up.

"Come out and play," Carrie said.

The little fellow came into full view. He danced around in the vines, and then climbed up a piece of wisteria into a tree where he disappeared. My sister continued to talk to him. I could only hear her side of the conversation. Each time the two of us walked the path by this spot, she stopped to visit with the little people who seemed to want only her friendship. As we grew older, the little people went away.

Sixty-two years later I went back to the valley and found the path. Its imprint was still strongly visible there. I was able to walk every step of the way to the farm. Everything was grown and changed except the path. It seemed to sing out to me, "I have not yet gone away. I will hold your love and memories of childhood here for you forever."

YOU GAVE ME A MOUNTAIN
TO CLIMB

Gertie was a pillar of strength among the children of our family. Ottie's first baby girl had died of pneumonia in the first year of life. She put the second girl up for adoption, but the child ran away from the orphanage. Her third female child, Gertie, (Eli's first child with Ottie) became a surrogate mother for the rest of us children.

It is dreadfully unfair to put adult responsibilities on the shoulders of a child. Ottie found it impossible to care for all her children and take care of the farm and moonshine business. It was only natural for her to abrogate some of her responsibilities to the available daughter.

Our valley people took a medieval attitude toward children. They treated us as little adults and considered us grown up at the age of twelve. From the day he could walk, a valley child did work and had daily chores. They fed animals, gathered eggs and vegetables, carried water and wood, swept, washed dishes. They could not have an idle moment to play until all work was done. Such was the nature of our survival. If you did not work, you did not eat. If you did not finish your work, you did not go to school or church. There was no time to get into trouble and, if we did, retribution was swift and sure.

Gertie had no childhood and never learned to play. At first, Ottie used her as a step-and-fetch-it child. Whatever job she did not want to do, she sent Gertie to do it.

Ottie needed meal and flour to bake cornbread and biscuits. She filled a sack with a half bushel of shelled corn and told Gertie to take it to the grist mill over a mile away. The sack was too heavy to carry. Gertie dragged it along the dirt road with both hands gripping the top. She crossed the same creek twice, once at the ford and again at Gentry's place where large rocks impeded her progress.

When she arrived at the grist mill, small holes had formed in the sack and, like Hansel and Gretel, she left a return trail of corn kernels up the road. Harry, the miller, felt sorry for her and re-placed the lost corn from his own stock. He poured the kernels of corn down a chute into the jaws of the gristmill, and then he lifted a latch from the water spout that fed the gigantic waterwheel.

A deafening roar came from the grinders as the waterwheel turned under the weight of the water. Smooth, dusty corn meal poured out the lower spout into the sack Harry had put at its end. When all the corn was pulverized, Harry replaced the block in the spout to bring the operation to a close. He dipped out three cups full as payment for his work. Then he traded half the corn meal for ground wheat flour so Gertie got what she came after.

Harry put the cornmeal and flour in separate sacks, double bagging them. It still weighed the same. It was still too heavy for Gertie to carry. She put the bag of flour under her left arm and dragged the cornmeal along the ground behind her. When she reached the rocks in the creek at Gentry's, she slipped on the rocks and fell into the creek. She sacrificed her body for the safety of the flour by holding it above the waterline as her arms, legs, and back sustained cuts and bruises. Gertie began to cry from her hurt and the fear of a physical beating if she lost the flour and meal. When corn was not available for grinding, Ottie sent Gertie to Beulah to beg for flour.

At other times, Gertie had to ask the bus driver to stop at Stan's store so she could pick up grocery items for Ottie. Being too shy to ask, Gertie had one of the older girls to ask the driver to stop. Gertie got the items, telling Stan to put their cost on Eli's bill. Children stared at her from the bus windows with pity in their eyes, being thankful they were not her. Gertie hung her head in shame silently weeping at her situation. Ottie did not care one whit about feelings for she had no pride. Poor Gertie suffered in silence. Her heart became a fortress of steel. Her gentleness strangled inside her like kudzu warping an unsuspecting tree.

Gertie told me that when I was five years old, time came for me to be inoculated for smallpox and diphtheria. My mother sent me with Gertie on the school bus to Miss Lucy's school where the vampire nurses waited to vaccinate us. Gertie had to take care of me all day as well as do her own school lessons. I made no trouble for her because I partly understood her plight. Had Ottie brought me, we would have had to walk there and back. Eli was at work, so the car was not available. The school bus was our only means of transportation.

Gertie failed the first grade. She did not attend Miss Lucy's school then. Her brothers would not get up to go to school with her. Neither June Sr. nor Ottie bothered to get up early enough to see the children off to school. They did not value education for neither of them had been to school. Making moonshine mattered to them and hanging out with Eli mattered to Ottie. This early failure lit a fire under Gertie.

When the family returned to live in the valley, she went to Miss Lucy's school. Her youngest sister Justine was old enough now to go with her. Gertie never missed a day of school from then until she graduated from high school. She made sure we didn't either.

My mother stayed in bed and slept mornings while Gertie got my two sisters and me out of bed, washed and dressed us, fixed some breakfast, made sure we had our homework, and led us down the path to Beulah's house where we met the school bus. She insisted that we be on time. We had no clock. Gertie watched the position of the sun as it rose above Grassy Knob. The sun rose farther south in the winter months. She read the sun positions correctly for we were never late to school. She washed clothes on the weekend and ironed them with old-fashioned irons heated on a hot wood stove. She walked with us to carry milk to the spring on Devil's Fork.

At school Doris, one of her friends, gave her a rattail comb for Christmas. It was a light blue comb with a long handle to allow a person to comb her hair without touching the head. She was proud of this comb and gave all us siblings a directive not to use or play with it. When she was away for a week at Ridgecrest on a retreat, I decided to undo the kinks in my youngest sister's hair. I found Gertie's rattail comb and dug into Carrie's hair, pulling it forcefully across the knots. The comb was made of cheap Japanese plastic so it snapped in two pieces in my hand. I put the comb pieces back where I had found them. Upon discovering the broken pieces of comb, Gertie wailed and moaned, "You broke my rattail comb." The comb was still usable; it just didn't have a tail. Without warning, Gertie slapped my sister and me across the head several times, then pulled our hair yelling, "I'll show you how to get knots out and I'll put some knots in your heads." She threw the pieces of comb in the trash. I felt bad about the comb for years.

When Ottie went away with Eli to sell moonshine or to visit the Boneyard, which was the local flea market, she gave all responsibility and care of the children to Gertie. She told her that whenever she got back, she wanted the kitchen floor to be clean, cows milked, wood and water brought in, and supper on the table. It would have challenged Ottie to do all this work in the amount of time allowed. To clean the kitchen floor, Gertie carried buckets of white dirt from a bank near the road. She spread the white dirt on the floor then swept it up. The dirt absorbed oil, water, and debris. We went with Gertie to milk the cows, helped carry wood and water. She was unable to finish supper.

Upon returning, Ottie was irate when food was not there prepared for her. She probably felt as angry as we did when she had let us go to school hungry. Going to the orchard, Ottie selected a small limb of a peach tree and beat Gertie until whelps appeared on her legs. Gertie ran for refuge to the well house weeping and whimpering. Her legs were bloody and stinging and Ottie had opened a hole in her heart that could never be repaired. She would not come back into the house. It was cold and rainy outside. She sat shivering from the trauma of the beating and from the cold. I coaxed her back into the warm kitchen promising to protect her. I, myself, went to the peach orchard and broke a small switch with the intention of giving Ottie a similar beating if she threatened Gertie again.

"I'll turn her legs red like yours if she hits you again," I cried out with childish courage.

At times Ottie could be violent and cruel. It wasn't Gertie who had failed. It was our mother Ottie. She was mad at Eli. Gertie looked exactly like Eli. He wasn't there to hit, so she beat Gertie.

Gertie taught me to write my name by kerosene lamp and let me read stories out loud from my school books. I laboriously formed the "f" and "r" with black charcoal from the fireplace. Then I swirled the letters in cursive on the hearth: "Fred." To this very day, my cursive writing is identical to Gertie's. She always signed my report cards and made sure that I did my homework. Ottie was in charge, but Gertie was the real mother.

When we left the valley because June Jr. stole a car, Gertie helped load the truck, then walked barefoot with me to the main road. She held my hand as the two of us looked back at our abandoned farmhouse, at the cows, pigs, and dogs left behind.

Then Gertie stooped to wash her feet in a small cold stream. The frigid water caught the impacted mud on her feet and washed it down the hillside, eastward toward the rising sun. The two of us were heading for a new life in a new place. She symbolically washed away the old one. I was still new at fighting the hardness of life. I had not yet finished the third grade.

"We'll make it," she reassured me. "Someone gave us this mountain to climb. We'll make it to the top."

And so we did. Gertie and I worked together years later as professional teachers in a large high school. If I looked discouraged when she passed me in the hallway, Gertie would pat me on the back, smile and whisper, "We've always had it rough. No one in this school can possibly imagine what we've been through. Keep up your spirit. You and I have not only climbed life's mountains, we've made it to the top."

A CHRISTMAS GIFT FOR ME

My older brother Curtis was a gentle soul who felt compassion toward all his brothers and sisters. When his father June Sr. left the family, Curtis quit school in the fifth grade in order to find work to help feed the family. He worked with Gentry at his sawmill for fifteen dollars a week, a decent salary in 1950. Once Ottie needed money badly so she sent Curtis to try to find his father, June Sr. He was now staying at his girlfriend Caldonia's house. Curtis walked the fifteen miles one way in the pouring rain and found June Sr. He begged him for some money just for himself and his brothers, not for Eli's four children. Upon Caldonia's advice, June Sr. refused him, sent him back empty-handed in the rain. Caldonia's car sat in the garage, but June Sr. let his son endure the emotional refusal and hard walk back home. Curtis had nothing more to do with his father for the rest of his life. From then on, he tried to be a father to the rest of us children.

Forest City was our metropolis, although it was only four regular city blocks long. In the early 1950's it had two signal lights, a small movie theater, a cafe, Mr. Tom T. Tuttle's Clothier, many

small variety shops, and, of course, the Boneyard. My mother and
Eli occasionally took all of us to this town, but we never really got
to see much. We rode through it in a car on the way to their destinations. In his own kind way, after he was on his own, Curtis
wanted to treat my sisters and me, (Eli's children), to a larger world
experience. The effort and expense from his own pocket attested
to his genuine care for us. He took the oldest sister Gertie to town
at Easter; he took Justine at Halloween; he took Callie, the youngest, during the summer; and he took me with him at Christmas.
The first two sisters returned filled with excitement and joy with
stories to last a lifetime. When it came my turn, Christmas bells
were ringing.

My oldest sister dressed me warmly in a shirt and bib overalls,
socks, jacket and hat. We left early in the morning since we had
miles to walk to our destination. In the modern world it is so
easy and quick to travel thirty-nine miles, but in our valley in the
1950's, it was a struggle. We had no car. There were no local buses
or taxis to ride. A Greyhound bus went along Highway 64 from
Morganton to Forest City once a day. A person could flag down
the driver, pay for the trip, and get a ride to the city. We were not
even sure what time the bus would pass near Bolding's Gap, so we
had to leave early.

It was a misty, cool morning a week before Christmas in the
year of our Lord, 1950. I was seven years old, tiny, frail, blond-
headed. Today was one of the most exciting days of my life. I had
always wondered what lay beyond the hills and hollows of my valley. I had longed to soar like an eagle just to look down across the
earth to see. It was happening today. I was going a distance away.

Curtis and I took the path to the main state road, turned right,
walked past Mrs. Lindendahl's cabin, past Lake McCall and climbed
the curvy, gravel hill across Bolding's Gap. Midway through the
mountains, we stopped to drink some water where some enterpris-
ing individual had placed a metal pipe into a crevice in a bank

from which crystal clear water flowed. They had even provided a drinking gourd. We learned later that Eli and his road gang had set up the waterspout because they needed water to make their concrete as they worked on pipes and bridges.

It was amusing to consider that my real father's work helped quench my thirst on this most auspicious day. It is he that should have been taking me for a Christmas experience. He could not accept me for he grieved still for a son lost long ago. I was a greater gift to him than his first son, but he would never live long enough to see it.

We drank some of the refreshing water and continued our journey down the opposite side of Bolding's Gap to the Highway 64---a paved road. It was the first paved road I had ever seen. I examined the asphalt, touched it, and walked up and down on it. The broken white lines, looking like sewing machine stitches in cloth, ran away into the long morning. I climbed on a red-clay bank getting my shoes dirty. Curtis told me to stop playing in dirt because we should not look like hillbillies when we got on the bus. I calmed down and waited.

I saw Curtis raise his right hand in a waving motion as a huge bus approached us from the east. On its side was the image of a Greyhound dog extended in full flight. I smelled burned gas and heard the roar of the bus engine as the monster vehicle rolled to a stop. Curtis lifted me over the steps because I was too small to get in myself. He paid the driver, and then we went slowly down the aisle looking for a seat. There were none. Long distance passengers had claimed all the seats. We stood all the way to Forest City.

From that experience of having to stand all the way, for the rest of my life, wherever I have traveled, I have never let a woman or child stand. I have always gotten up and given them my seat. I'm sure the good people who rode the bus with us that day did not realize that their actions made life difficult for a little boy. In this long-away time now, I thank them for showing me that I could be a better friend to my fellow man than they had been.

The bus bumped its way along the pavement, shaking us, first against one seat, then another. Curtis placed me firmly between his two feet to keep me from falling. We accidentally bumped a passenger who scowled at us. One overbearing lady passenger wearing too much rouge and lipstick blurted out, "These hillbillies should not be allowed to ride the Greyhound bus." I was glad we were not carrying pigs or chickens. There, we finally heard the word "hillbilly" applied to us.

"What's a hillbilly?" I asked Curtis.

"It's a woman who wears too much rouge and lipstick and can't keep her stupid mouth shut," he replied.

The lady flushed red and buried her nose in a magazine. I'm sure she saw herself as on the way to Heaven where there would surely be no "hillbillies."

The bus driver let us off at the edge of town at a service station that served as the bus depot. Once again we had to walk. I am sure in my life I have walked the distance to the moon and back.

The spirit of the holiday season seemed to animate shoppers who walked by us, for their faces were focused on something ahead of them. They walked as if in a trance with sugar plums already dancing in their heads. Above our heads, colorful decorations hung from the trees and lampposts making the sidewalks festive. We had no electricity at home so the streetlights and Christmas lights swept me away to a dream world where I thought myself one of them. I moved in rhythm with their blinking and glowing pouring my own beauty out with that of the town. I became one with the decorative bells, angels, and stars.

My face beamed when I looked at decorated Christmas trees in shop windows. One window had an animated display depicting a boy and girl trying to elope. With a ladder on his shoulder, the boy circled the house until he came to the girl's bedroom window.

As he started up the ladder, her father opened the front door and scared him away. Christmas carols accompanied this display. Curtis and I watched this scene for a long time, then came back later and watched it some more.

We bought some gifts from shops overflowing with beautiful merchandise, much of it new to me. He took me to the "Little Choo-Choo Diner" next to the Boneyard. This cafe once had been a railroad car. It served food, now, instead of ferrying passengers up and down the mountains. We sat down on circular stools and swung our knees underneath the counter. I ate a wondrous hotdog with mustard, chili, and slaw. It left residue on my mouth, nose, and fingers. Curtis bought me a moon pie and stuffed it into my pocket.

"Merry Christmas," he joked, "that's your Christmas gift."

Then I had the greatest experience of my life. We went to the movie theater and saw the western, "Red Rider" starring Gene Autry. Curtis treated me to a box of popcorn. On the farm where I lived, we dealt with animals and plants and hard work. It felt like I was sinning to be at this place, at this time, watching a movie, eating popcorn and drinking an R.C. I was having too much of a good time. I am not supposed to have this much fun. These thoughts were vestiges of my religious background. It was luxury. It was Christmas time. It was my special journey. A warm glow came over me. I felt happy. I felt accepted. I felt loved.

Curtis and I strolled out of the theater into the dark of night. The December sun had set early leaving us in a cold, winter land of multicolored lights. We circled once more around the town to see the spectacular show of lights, and then Curtis got a taxi to take us as far as Miss Lucy's school.

As we rode to Bostic and Sunshine and points eastward, I pressed my face against the taxi window staring into the night. We sped past cornfields now barren, their broken cornstalks standing like sharp swords in the furrowed rows. Bare tree limbs moved slowly in the wind as a full moon rose like an exploding star above some distant hills. Here and there a lit-up Christmas tree pierced the darkness with its red, yellow, and green lights. Houses swished by in the dark, showing only their silhouettes against the sky. Our car lights shone on the asphalt in front of us, illuminating the broken white line dividing the highway. The white, dotted lines made me think that someone had preceded us with a giant piece of chalk, marking our way homeward. It was an exhilarating ride for me, like the rocking of a cradle in a mighty wind.

Curtis and I walked home from Miss Lucy's school through the cold, winter night clutching our precious purchases close to our breasts. I still had part of my moon pie and some popcorn stuffed in my pockets. My shoes got wet crossing the murky creek at Gentry's place, so Curtis hoisted me on his shoulders and I rode the rest of the way home on his back. I rode like a hero of old, lifted high on the backs of conquering soldiers. It was my victory parade.

Oh, I have lived through some seventy Christmases since then, with gifts and treats aplenty, and today Christmas holds no more magic for me. Curtis is gone forever. But his gift of the trip to Forest City so many years ago was the greatest Christmas gift of my life. If I forgot to say "thank you, Curtis," for your kindness, then I do so now. This story is my Christmas gift back to you.

When it is my turn to slip away from life and cross over into eternity, I will probably take a Greyhound bus. And if I do, I hope the ride there will be as wonderful and sweet as the one I took with Curtis on that magic Christmas long ago.

REMEMBER ME

His large hands were calloused from heavy plowing. On his feet he wore work shoes, the kind made from thick shoe leather and worn for difficult farm work. He rolled the cuffs of his overalls into circles, like hemp is rolled between one's palms in order to braid rope. He had wavy, brown hair that was natural. His red, cotton shirt fit tightly around his shoulders showing sweat stains under both arms. When he removed the red shirt to let the open sun brown his body, scars from the horse reins tied around his neck showed dark red and purple on his skin. He looked as if someone had beaten him with a whip. He was physically strong from years of demanding farm work and wood cutting. This was Willard Worth, my half-brother, second oldest son to June Sr. and Ottie.

Few believed that June Sr. was his daddy, for they did not favor and were quite different in personality. He left school after the fifth grade to take on full responsibility for working the farm we leased from Eli. Worth was quiet, shy, withdrawn. He did not like being in crowds of people, nor did he speak much when he could not escape it. It was as if he sat like a painted flower on the living room wallpaper, seeing and listening to the world going by, yet choosing not to be a part of it.

Nine years my elder, he took responsibility for me, treating me as his adopted child. He brought me pretty rocks from the plowed fields. He left shiny buckeyes in my coat pocket and a pen knife on the kitchen table with my nickname carved on it.

He called me "Clods" because I walked in front of his horse and plow trying to remove all the clods of dirt which impeded the movement of the plow. If he were to trip on one of the clods and slip under the plow, it might sever one of his feet. My little legs and feet tired quickly, so Worth sat me up on the cross plank of the plow. I rode in front of him, watching the plow turn the earth upward. I sat directly behind the rump of the horse. At times the horse passed gas or dropped clods of manure down on the freshly ploughed ground. The horse manure mixed with the soil. White mist clung in the air from the warm manure. It smelled bad.

"Hey, Clods, you sure you don't want to pick up that manure so I can move more smoothly?" he teased me.

"I'm not touching warm horse padookies," I replied, "Not even for you."

"What is the matter, Clods, don't you like me?" he asked. "Won't you even remember me when I am gone?"

"I'm not touching horse shit, hot or cold, even for the Queen of England," I said emphatically. "I'll remember the horse manure longer than I will you," I teased him back.

He jerked on the horse reins bringing the animal to an abrupt stop, tossing me off the crossbar into the midst of the still-warm muck. We both lay down on the ground laughing hysterically. He picked me up lovingly under his right arm and dumped me into the cold creek.

Throwing some big clods of dirt behind me he yelled merrily, "Let the smell of horse wash away to the sea. You'll remember this day."

Willard Worth owned a prized sweater he had ordered from a mail-order catalogue. It was white with red letters printed on the front that spelled out "Hi-Ho Silver." A red ribbon swirled under the words as if to outline them. Whenever he wore the sweater, he always returned it carefully to its original box. One time he let me wear his sweater. I knew then that Willard Worth was trying to be a father to me, for he had certainly not had one in his life.

Eli was never pleased with any work that Willard Worth did on the farm. It was as if he disliked him intensely and expressed the dislike through criticism of his work.

"You plowed the rows too deep or too shallow. You didn't lay by the rows properly. The horse is not washed and curried right. The corn has too many weeds left in it. Can't you do anything right?" Eli chastised him unmercifully.

Willard Worth usually took the berating in silence but this particular time he bristled.

"Come do it yourself," he said looking Eli directly in his eyes. "You don't pay me for doing your farm work anyway," he blurted out.

"No I don't, but your work pays the rent for you, your family, and your mother to live on my land," Eli argued.

"And what does my mother's bedding down with you every week pay for?" Willard Worth hurled the words at him. "Is that dessert, a tip, or taxes?"

"I'm going to stomp your little smart-aleck ass," Eli yelled, lunging forward in an attempt to strike him.

"You're not my father. You don't pay me, support me, or love me. You don't screw me like you do my mama. You come to the farm and bitch about what I do. You take what we raise on the place and sell it at the Boneyard. We never see a penny from it. Then you hop on my mother like a fat, rutting hog until you are satisfied. We don't see you again until you are ready for seconds. Lay a hand on me and I intend to shoot you dead in a gutter. No one will know who killed you nor will they care. From now on when you set foot around this house, know I'm sitting in the woods somewhere with my rifle aimed at your damned head. I'll decide on the spur of the moment whether to pull the trigger."

Willard Worth was a deep, introspective man who did not boast. He meant every word that he said.

The next day after the argument, Willard Worth asked me to walk with him to the Ida Spring. It was a natural spring of water bubbling up from the ground. Someone long ago had cleaned it out and placed rocks to pond up the water. It was good, cold, drinking water. The spring was surrounded by huge birch trees with gnarly roots sticking above the dirt and leaves like engorged veins. Ferns grew in the perpetual dampness as did several kinds of moss. The drain water from the spring created a short stream that emptied into a faster-flowing branch.

Willard Worth chipped some flakes of bark off the birch tree and handed it to me to chew. It was our beechnut chewing gum, for that is how it tasted. We sat down at the base of these gigantic trees to rest and talk.

"I don't belong here," he began to talk in a pensive way. "I'm a stranger in a strange land. I don't feel a bond to my mother Ottie, and June Sr. is not someone I could even like, much less love. So, I guess you're it, Clods. I think the world of you. Were it not for you, I would have killed Eli long ago and gone to prison or been shot by the sheriff. I could lose them all, but the prospect of losing you has been too much. It has kept me in check."

He began to cry. His huge shoulders accustomed to carrying rocks, sacks of grain, and fodder shocks shook under the weight of his emotional sorrow and I felt shame and hurt in my own heart for him. He was an overgrown kid, lost and alone on his pilgrim's pathway of life.

Not knowing what else to do to comfort him, I reached out my hand and laid it on his mid-back, where the back heart chakra is located. He cried some more.

"What is it that you are looking for?" I asked him in a plaintive, child voice.

"I want someone to remember me. I want it to matter that I lived here in this time and this place. I want someone to care."

"I care," I said, my kid's eyes looking up at him as if to a hero.

"Yes, I know, Clods, but I want an adult, a grown-up person to care," he explained.

"Like Ottie," I said knowingly.

He choked on the lump forming in his throat and more tears wet his cheeks. Then, like a sudden summer storm which has ebbed and fades with distant thunder, he ceased talking. He said nothing more to me that day, as if he were ashamed that he had revealed so much of what he felt and thought.

"Let's carve a giant heart in the tree and put your name in it," I suggested. "It will then be there forever for people to see and remember you by."

We spent a long time carving the heart with his name inside. We cut deeply into the bark so our tree tattoo would be permanent. Willard Worth went on carving after we finished his name. When I looked up again, the words "Remember me, Worth" stood etched on the tree bark. He stood back proudly accessing his work. He seemed happy. I felt that the trees of the forest were smiling for they were proud to remember kind souls like Willard Worth. The cool winds murmured through the branches as if to say, "I approve." The tree on which we carved our message made a mental note to itself to live to a ripe old age so time could not erase the memory.

Not long thereafter, Eli came back to the farm because Willard Worth had lost control of our old horse Buck. The wagon had hit a deep rut in the field and the wagon flipped breaking the wagon tongue. That cost Eli plenty. He cursed Willard Worth, railing at his stupidity, and then he struck him a hard blow across his right cheek. Eli left him on the ground and walked on to the barn to check on the damaged wagon. Willard Worth rose slowly from the ground rubbing the pain from his eye socket and a trickle of blood from his nose. He went to the mantle and took down his rifle.

I ran to him crying, "No, Worth, no," but in vain.

He pushed me roughly aside and headed for the huge rocks on the side of Oaky Knob. Eli huffed and puffed around the barnyard. He did not know that at that moment his life rested in the hands of a sixteen-year old boy who was scared and angry. All he had wanted was for someone to remember him. Killing Eli would ensure that everyone would remember.

Among the rocks high up on Oaky Knob, Willard Worth sat with the sights of his rifle set directly on Eli's head. Were he to squeeze the trigger, Eli's head would explode like a pumpkin. Willard Worth was a crack shot, a talent honed by many years of hunting small game in the woods. He dropped the rifle's aim down to Eli's left shoulder and squeezed the trigger.

Hearing the shot, Ottie ran screaming toward the barn, for she knew the antipathy between the two men.

Not knowing if he had killed Eli, Worth hid the rifle among the rocks where he sat.

"I must go," he said out loud to himself.

It was dark when he made his way to his Uncle Tom's house in Casar. He wanted to know how to get to Mary Lovada's house in St. Louis, Missouri. Tom wrote down the directions and gave him a twenty dollar bill. He set out on foot. A stranger gave him a ride to Fontana Dam and another one took him to Knoxville. With

Uncle Tom's money, he bought himself a Greyhound bus ticket to St. Louis.

In the ensuing years, Willard Worth transformed himself. He dropped Worth from his name and only used Willard. He married and had three children, one girl and two boys. One son drowned in a bathtub at age eight months; the other died at thirty-one. Willard always thought God took his sons in retribution for his shooting Eli. It was unfair, for Eli did not die. Willard got his high school diploma and became manager of a shoe plant. He became a wealthy man.

"I make shoes to bless feet," he explained to everyone as he remembered the poverty of his youth.

Unfortunately, he did not stay in touch with me.

I experienced his profound loss. My rudder and anchor washed away on life's ocean in a fit of rage and a rifle. I saw him maybe three times during the rest of our lives.

His son-in-law called one September to tell me that Willard was dying, and my brother wanted me to come to see him. St. Louis was far away and I decided not to go. He was no longer in my life and I felt that he had abandoned me. I chose not to remember him and that was the very thing he feared at the Ida Spring long ago. My memory of him had dimmed through the years. At times, I could not even remember what he looked like. If I were to pass him on the street, I would not recognize him.

"Willie is dead," read the next message.

The many years apart had taken away our closeness. Besides I had known a person called Willard Worth, not Willard or Willie. On the day they buried him in St. Louis, I suffered a great guilt. I found my way back to the mountains to the old birch tree where we had carved the heart on the day before he shot Eli. The tree groaned in the wind seeming to say, "What kept you so long?"

"Life, and stubbornness, and stupidity," I shouted out loud. I found the big heart carved on the tree. It was brown and gnarled now with some moss growing on its edges. His message was still legible:

"Remember Me, Worth."

The words cut at my heart like a sword. I began to weep. I wept for his lost youth, for the sadness of his life, for my terrible loss when he had fled westward and for my own refusal to go visit him. I hated Eli for causing us this pain. I hugged the birch tree as if hugging my brother in abstencia. I spoke softly out loud, addressing him as if he were present:

"These trees remember you, Willard Worth, and so do the streams and mountains that nurtured us. These very rocks and this blue sky remember you. As long as there is breath in me, for as long as my heart can feel, I will remember you. If ever I had a true friend in all this earth, I had a friend you."

PUT IT ON ELI'S BILL

S tan's Country Store where Rufus gave me the peppermint candy was two miles away from our house. It seemed much farther because our road twisted and turned through the woods and across streams. An adult could walk there in less than an hour, but for my sister and me, who were five and seven years old, it was a formidable trip. When my mother needed supplies from this store, she sent whoever was available.

During the school year, she had my sister Gertie ask the school bus driver to stop the bus at the store so she could get groceries. This practice may seem strange today, but in the 1940s when few people owned cars and there was no other transportation in the valley, it was the norm. The driver always stopped. It was a time in history when people worked together, when people looked after one another. The driver knew he was in violation of somebody's rule somewhere, but he did not care. He knew that Ottie sent her small kids through the woods and along this public highway to buy items for her at the store, usually snuff and coffee. He chanced censure or loss of his job rather than have a child risk his safety along the road. This driver also let adults ride the bus in the morning and evening to get to work or to go somewhere in the valley. They only had to wait by the roadside and lift their right index finger into the air to signal him to stop. When school ended in May, we all walked wherever we went.

One day my mother needed moon pies, sliced bread, as well as her usual snuff and coffee. She fixed lunches for my brothers who now worked at the saw mill. She usually did not pack a lunch for us kids to go to school for we did not bring any money into the house. She called my sister Callie and me to the kitchen and wrote on a piece of paper the items she wanted.

"Tell Stan to put it on Eli's bill," she informed us.

Most people had an open account with Stan. They put what they bought on the account and then paid him in full at the end of the month. That system was an early forerunner of today's credit card system. Any violators got banished from the account list and could charge nothing more. Eli paid his account in full each month.

Callie was the last of Ottie and Eli's children. The mother was forty-five when the last child was conceived. It was the end of World War II and in the waning years of the Great Depression. Ottie was not in the best of health and the hard farm work did not help the pregnancy. Callie was born premature. She was so tiny that the midwife held her in two hands and breathed oxygen into her tiny lungs. Callie survived.

Young as we were the trip to the store was quite a journey, but we were unafraid. No adults would cause us harm and animals of the wild seem to respect human children.

Callie and I left the farmhouse at eight o'clock in the morning and took the river road toward Gentry's place. It was full spring. The trees formed a high canopy above while a myriad of wild flowers lined each side of the road. We had walked a short distance when we saw a small, grassy field beside the roadway. Thousands of purple violets covered the field. We gathered several bouquets not caring about time. At the ford where we crossed, the water was somewhat high. The water rushed swiftly by and there was no bridge or plank to help us cross over. The water could easily sweep us down the rushing stream. I had Carrie hold on to a stick I found along the roadside in case she stumbled as we waded across the stream. We emerged on the other side with wet shoes and socks.

The road wound forward through pleasant sourwood trees not yet in bloom. It wound down a hillside toward Gentry's house. In front of his house the stream flowed over flat rocks forming a small waterfall. Along the water someone long ago had planted Rose Colombier which now thrust their purple blossoms upward on gray stems. There were hundreds of them in a patch. Callie and I picked some of them to add to our bouquet of violets. The road rambled on past Mr. McFarland's grist mill and connected with the state road. It was a gravel road where we had to be careful for cars came by at times.

The two little adventurers turned southward on the dusty road past where the Potters lived, past the church parsonage for the white church on the hill to where Mr. Johnson had his hay fields. To the left there stood a very high embankment cut out by the bulldozers of the CCC crew. The dirt was soft and pliable. My sense of adventure overcame my common sense. I told my sister to keep on walking. Step by heavy step I climbed up the bank leaving my footprints in the dirt. I succeeded in reaching the top of the bank. A slight movement in the trees on top of the bank caught my attention. I thought I saw a big cat lurking in the bushes. It amazed me because on our farm all the cats were small and cuddly. You could hold them in your arms. This cat was as big as a mule. I rejoined my sister and we continued our journey.

Callie and I were happy when Stan's store came into view. The sweet smell of moon pies, RCs, tobacco and coffee greeted our entry. Stan was busy making baloney sandwiches for customers as we went in. Men in the back of the store talked loudly among their group. I waited until Stan saw me.

"What can I do for you little fellow?"

Stan recognized who we were. He knew we were Eli's illegitimate children.

"My mother wants what's on this paper," I said. "Add to it two RCs and two moon pies."

I saw no reason why we should walk all this distance to the store without a reward. Eli had to pay for it anyway. He never brought us moon pies.

"Put it on Eli's bill," I smirked.

Stan gave us our moon pies and RCs. He did not add them to the bill. He said nothing because they were his gifts to us. We drank from the fizzing bottles as Stan packed our items into a brown paper bag.

"Be safe," Stan said as we left the store and began the long trek back home.

Reaching the embankment where I had climbed on the way to the store, I saw large cat tracks alongside my tracks. It puzzled me. Callie and I paused at the crossing at Gentry's place thinking we heard something following us in the bushes. There were huge cat tracks among the flowers along the creek bank. Fear took hold of us as we walked down the road near the violet field. Suddenly in the road ahead, there appeared that mule- sized cat. It was an off-yellow with black lines over the eyes and huge paws. It sat watching us as it flicked its tail back and forth slowly.

"Here kitty, kitty," I said out loud, thinking I was saying hello to one of our farm cats.

The big cat jaunted off into a pine field. When we reached home, I asked our mother why we didn't have any big cats like the one we saw in the road. She told us not to make up stories. She thought it was imaginary child tales.

When our older brothers and sisters came home from swimming at Lake McCall, they told Ottie about seeing large cat tracks in the soft dirt on the road. They had heard something following them in the bushes. They laughed, thinking someone was trying to scare them. Ottie took them more seriously. When she went to feed the farm animals next day, she found one of the pigs with its guts ripped open. It was covered with fang and claw marks. She sent for Gentry.

His eyes narrowed as he surveyed the situation.

"We have a serious problem here. It's a mountain cougar. It can kill a human. Keep the kids inside and be careful yourself," he warned Ottie.

Word spread down the valley that a cougar was loose. Neighbors locked their doors and worried eyes peeped through closed window curtains. Men carried shotguns wherever they went.

As Ottie was cooking supper, she saw the cougar come down from Grassy Knob, cross the stream, and head once again toward her hog pen. She grabbed her shotgun and went to meet him. He would kill no more of her farm animals nor would he harm her children. As the cougar crept around the barn, she fired directly at him. The animal let out a yell and retreated toward the forest. Ottie fired the gun again to further frighten the animal. The cougar did not come back. Ottie carried her gun with her for several weeks. It was only when I reached adulthood that I realized what danger Callie and I had been in when we were coming back from Stan's store. The cougar could have killed both of us.

Had that happened, my mother would surely have snorted, "Put them on Eli's bill."

UP DEVIL'S CREEK FORK

My family's farm lay nestled in a small valley flanked by two imposing mountains. Grassy Knob lay to the east. It was covered in trees and vegetation with an occasional blank spot referred to as a knob. Summer rains swept from the east across Grassy Knob sending my mother and sisters scurrying to pull freshly washed clothes from the clotheslines. My first sight of a jet plane was above Old Grassy. The jet swept upward across the mountain leaving a twisted vapor trail in the sky. The craft looked like a silver ball resting on a white string being flung haphazardly across the sky. This mountain seemed always to herald new, exciting events.

On the south side Oaky Knob stood in stark contrast. It was a bold mountain covered in forest and huge boulders that challenged the summer storms and lightning. There were ancient oak trees upon it, gnarled and twisted, flinging their limbs breathlessly against the sky. Wild, sweet fox grapes ripened in October. Their fragrance pulled my brothers and me to its slopes to pick them in the cold autumn wind. Rain seemed afraid to cross this mountain, preferring rather to climb the gentler Grassy Knob.

To the north of Grassy Knob and Oaky Knob was a place called Devil's Creek Fork. It was not a mountain though it had some elevation. It was more of a deep forest with pine, fir, balsam, and spruce trees. These trees made the area dark even at midday. A tall, cascading waterfall flowed across isinglass rocks and descended to the valley floor with a roar that could be heard a half mile away. Old folks referred to the sound as the Devil's voice cursing his wife. (I never knew the Devil had a wife). I also never knew why the old folks called this place Devil's Fork either. They certainly had their reasons.

Few people chose to wander up this fork. A medium-sized creek formed from the waterfall meandered down the rocks and disappeared in a distant meadow. At one spot it formed a pond deep enough for swimming. Boulders piled around in the stream by eons of flood waters made perfect diving boards for us kids when we swam there in the summer. That is as far up the fork as we would go and only if there were several people in a group.

Ottie, my mother, made Devil's Creek Fork her personal abode. She carried heavy rocks up the steep hillsides and piled them smoothly on top of one another to form the foundation for her copper tanks that made up her moonshine still. She carried fifty pound sacks of sugar and corn for mash up the same hillsides. Her heavy work made her a physically strong and powerful woman. Only five feet tall, she could beat up stronger men who crossed her. One time one of her slick city moonshine customers cheated her out of ten dollars on a liquor deal. She returned to his house and proceeded to beat him severely with a large stick.

Ottie tolerated no interference in her moonshine business for that is how she survived and supported her eight children. Because she located her moonshine still in the laurel bushes above the Devil's Creek waterfalls, she wanted everyone to think that it was a fearsome place.

She spread rumors about a wild, ape-like creature that lived there. She told everyone that the place was haunted and that she had seen the "haints" themselves. No valley people wandered far up the fork and we children took no chances. Devil's Creek Fork was off limits.

At the entrance to the fork, the stream flowed past an old cabin called Griff's Old House long abandoned and forlorn. This house marked the usual limits where we kids would go alone near the fork. People told tales of something living up there. No one ever said what it was, yet no one wanted to go up there and find out. It just so happened that in the depth of the fork, near the waterfall, there was an ice-cold natural spring of water running out of a crevice in a rock. Even in the heat of summer this spring remained very cold. Green moss and ferns flourished around it and spring lizards scurried back and forth in its crystal clear water. Periwinkles dotted the rocks in the stream bed like polka dot aprons. It was an air conditioned spot where breezes swirled around cooling everything.

It was a curse for me that my mother discovered this spot. The natural spring became a refrigerator for her milk and butter. After the morning milking, she cleaned the milk, put it into gallon glass jars, sealed it with wax paper, and put it into the cold spring water up Devil's Creek Fork. My mother was a strong woman, not afraid of the Devil, and certainly not a place called Devil's Creek Fork. She cared nothing for our fears either. It did not bother her to send the milk with my sisters and me to be left all day in the spring. As long as two or three of us could go together, we did not mind taking the milk.

The walk was fun until we reached Griff's Old House. Something then came over us. Laughter ceased. Our steps became reluctant.

Our hearts beat faster. We were about to enter the Devil's territory. We stopped talking. We walked slowly in silence along the path and stream. All eyes looked straight ahead for fear we might see the Devil in our peripheral vision. We quickly placed the milk into the frigid water and beat a hasty retreat. We could not catch our breaths until the path emerged at Griff's Old House. We children made that trek up the fork daily; feeling that in numbers there is protection. The winds blew, the water roared, and that old Devil man stayed on.

A fateful day fell upon me. It was a day of all days. It was a life-changing day. It was a day when I was forced to face my worst fear. It was a day of no return. It was D-Day. It was milk day. My sisters left early that summer morning to go to town to buy cloth for new dresses. I remained at the house to keep my mother company and help out with small chores. The morning went well. I carried some sticks of wood for the stove, fed the chickens, and curried the horse. Little did I know that my tranquil world was about to end. Suddenly my mother's shrill voice broke the stillness of the summer day:

"Fred, come take the milk to the spring."

I froze in mortal fear. I had always had numbers when we carried milk to the spring. Not today. The Devil had me for sure.

"Mom, I don't want to go," I whined.

"Don't you whine at me," my mother said. "Come get this milk or I will give you something to whine about."

One was wise not to contradict my mother.

"Take the milk to the spring and don't drop or break it."

My muscles grew weak. My stomach churned. I felt sick all over. My arm circled around the glass milk jar but there was little strength to lift it. My mother placed the jar firmly in my arms and turned my body toward Devil's Creek Fork.

I looked back at the farmhouse where she stood in the kitchen doorway, arms placed defiantly on her hips. I supposed that would be my last sight of her, considering the fact that the Devil would surely get me up the fork. My life flashed in front of me. Each episode of my short life floated before my eyes. I placed one foot in front of the other all the while repeating, "Don't let it get me. Go away Devil man. I don't want to go to Hell."

I knew people had a reason to call it Devil's Fork. What was up there? What had someone seen? Was something up there someone did not want people to see? A still? Money? What did this Devil look like? What would it do to me? Why couldn't my mother walk with me? Why did she never take the milk to the spring? Alas, she would never see me again.

I trudged past Griff's Old House and started up the path into the fork. Every sound was magnified. The wind threatened, shaking the trees and my insides. It whirled around the rocks like the cry of a banshee. The day turned darker as clouds closed over the fork. The milk jar got heavier and heavier. Each step drew me closer to my doom and into the arms of the Devil.

In the distance I saw the spring. The water roared over the falls, ferns tossed in the wind, spring lizards scrambled across the rocks. I set the milk jar into the cold water quickly making sure that the water covered it thoroughly. Then I froze in terror.

Something was moving in the bushes above the spring. The leaves and branches shook as the "something" was quite huge. I began to cry. My breath was short and my chest heaved from the excessive beating of my heart. My vision was blurred from my crying. Suddenly my feet caught fire and I began to run. Down the path I flew. Trees and foliage blurred as I pushed through them. I heard my own footsteps crashing on the path, and worse still, I heard heavy footsteps running behind me. I tried to scream but no sound came. Something grabbed me from behind. I fainted.

As I awakened, my eyes began to focus on my surroundings. I felt two huge hands holding my shoulders. The Devil had me for sure and could do as he will. I began to pray and confess all the sins I could possibly think up. As my vision cleared, I saw a face that resembled the Devil and my mother. Were they one in the same? Was my mother the Devil????

"Wake up, Fred," the voice commanded. "Did you put the milk in the spring?"

"Where did you come from?" I asked.

"I knew how afraid you were of the walk to the spring in the fork; I followed you to make sure you would be fine. It was me in the bushes above the spring. I intended to walk back with you, and that's why I ran after you down the path. Anyway, this afternoon you can walk back to the spring and get the milk for supper."

I shuddered at the thought, but said nothing.

I lived in Ottie's world where she reigned supreme. If she ordered me to go back to get the milk from the spring, then I darn well better go. I would prefer to face the Devil than to endure her wrath. Ottie's world had me.

This episode fired off in me a life-long hatred of Ottie. It also set me on a life-long road to self-forgiveness.

HUSTLEBUTT AND GUMTOOTH

Nature does not make all people physically beautiful. Men do not take being ugly as seriously as women do. There seems to be a compensation system at work in nature for what she leaves out or takes away, she returns in some other form. Ugly people can be smarter or richer or more talented. They compensate for a perceived loss with deeper, more compassionate hearts and souls. They can be treasures wrapped in a less attractive package. There are some people on earth, however, that are ugly in body and soul. This is the story of two such people.

Hustlebutt had a short, truncated body that rested on two skinny legs like an elephant suspended on deer legs. Two pendulous breasts hung down toward her navel. She had huge buttocks that gyrated, jiggling left and right as she walked, enormous ham hocks that gave her the name, Hustlebutt. Her face held two beady eyes set on the sides of a hooked, Roman nose. There was a short cleft in her upper lip, not quite a hair lip that forced her smile inward.

Her black hair hung in ringlets. She had big feet that splayed to left and right from her body. She smelled bad.

Gumtooth had only one of thirty-two teeth left in her mouth. It was an incisor on the left side. She gummed and garbled her speech unable to say 's' or 't.' When she smiled, she looked like an upside down vampire. She was tall, overweight and frumpy. She was exceptionally strong, having worked hard on a farm as she grew up. She beat up men on a regular basis, rarely losing a fight. She loved being pugnacious. Inside, Gumtooth was warm, kind, and friendly. When angry, however, she was mean as a striped snake. These two women ruled over a place called the Boneyard. At times they were rivals.

People came from far and wide to buy, sell, or trade items at the Boneyard. It was a wide, open block of land in the city located behind the main row of buildings downtown. The buildings blocked it from view because it was such an eyesore. The area was dirty like the people who frequented it.

Paper, cans, debris of all sorts lay strewn about where vendors and customers alike failed to clean up after themselves at the end of the day. Years ago people placed dead animal carcasses in this place to rot, leaving a pile of bones. That's how it came to be called the Boneyard.

Once a week, now, people came to the market to make a little money. They socialized a lot, catching up on gossip and news. Excessively poor people who do not fit anywhere else patronized the Boneyard. It was a world unto itself.

Hustlebutt and Gumtooth took up residence here controlling the ebb and flow of business on the weekends. Hustlebutt built herself a primitive hut out of cast-off planks from which she sold contraband goods. Thieves from everywhere brought their stolen goods for her to sell or trade. They paid her a stipend. In the back of the plank hut, she set up a small cot with a mattress stuffed with dry straw and leaves. She slept there at night. She brought men for a nominal fee of five dollars to her hut to take care of their needs. She shared the space with Gumtooth. When the cot was occupied, they placed an empty milk jug outside the door implying business deal in session. Do not enter. This arrangement worked well. Business flourished.

All was happy at the Boneyard until the day Ottie decided to show up to sell her moonshine. It was the hot, sultry dog days of August when life moves in slow motion and people are generally in a foul mood, when Eli drove Ottie to the Boneyard. He backed the Model-T into an empty space directly opposite Hustlebutt's hut. Gumtooth was not far away. Ottie set out a basket of tomatoes, some ears of corn, and some peaches in a bowl. These were cover items to mask the fact that she was selling moonshine. She poured a glass half full of moonshine for tasting purposes, but left the cases of moonshine concealed in the car.

Vendors on the Boneyard perked up from their lethargy as Ottie began to do a brisk business. Men who regularly did business with Hustlebutt and Gumtooth now gravitated to Ottie. Anger and jealousy began to grow in the two women. Men buying the moonshine drank it openly becoming inebriated in short order. Some began to disappear into the back seat with Ottie. The car shook and gyrated for a moment or two. Then Ottie emerged to sell more moonshine. Gumtooth and Hustlebutt did not take in much money that day. Ottie became the talk of the Boneyard. Men flocked from all over the county to buy her wares. Dark, thunderhead clouds of anger hovered over the Boneyard. There was a storm coming.

A man dressed in ironed slacks and buttoned-up shirt walked onto the grounds of the Boneyard. He was forty-five, rather good looking. People fell silent for they recognized Buford the county sheriff. He strutted around the lot studying the merchandise on each table. He paid little attention to Hustlebutt because he knew her stuff was illegal. She paid him a weekly bribe not to arrest her.

He did not bother Gumtooth because he went often with her to the plank shack. He was here today to collect from a new vendor. He sauntered up to Ottie's car sniffing the air. He knew the smell of moonshine. He engaged her in whispered conversation while all the Boneyard vendors looked on with keen interest. Both got into the back seat of the Model-T. There came a shaking and rocking. Gumtooth fumed with anger and Hustlebutt began to slam items down on her table. The shaking ended. Buford pulled up his now-wrinkled pants and made his exit through the fence at the back part of the Boneyard. Ottie paid her dues and would often do so in order to operate her business in peace.

Gumtooth scratched her one tooth with her index finger as if polishing her one fang for battle. She fumed. She saw a direct threat to her power and control of the Boneyard. Hustlebutt's anger turned to a desire for some action. She jumped up from her chair hastening directly to Ottie.

"You're leaving this market right this minute," she barked at Ottie.

She grabbed the basket of tomatoes and some ears of corn throwing them back into the Model-T to force Ottie to leave. Ottie pulled them right back out setting them back on her table. As Hustlebutt reached for them again, Ottie slapped her violently across her left face leaving a ringing in her ears. Hustlebutt had second thoughts about striking Ottie. She returned to her chair, a trickle of blood running out of her left nostril.

Gumtooth watched the action with profound interest. She hastened over to talk in private with Hustlebutt. They planned a two-pronged attack against Ottie. Both together, they could take her down for sure. For a brief moment, peace reigned at the market. Without warning, though, Hustlebutt ran at Ottie shoving her forcefully against the front of the Model-T. With one powerful blow, Ottie knocked her out cold on the ground. Gumtooth attacked Ottie with a rage. She landed a blow to Ottie's chin sending her reeling backward over the table. Gumtooth was on her, grabbing her in a headlock. Barely able to breathe, Ottie grabbed one of Gumtooth's bulbous breasts in her right hand, tearing at it as if it were a sack of corn. Gumtooth let go as Ottie rolled free. Standing now, the two furies circled each other looking for an advantage. Gumtooth had already whipped all the women and most of the men at the Boneyard. She was a bully. She was used to victory in fights. Up until now, she had never encountered an adversary like Ottie.

Ottie stamped her feet, pulled at her hair, snorted like an enraged bull. Any person who attacked her or threatened her moonshine business would rue the day. She lunged for Gumtooth's legs throwing her on her back. Grabbing her by the hair, she pulled her toward her knee, smashing it into Gumtooth's only tooth. The tooth fell loosely upon the ground. Ottie pulled her to her feet then punched a left, right, left blow to each side of the face. Gumtooth fell and did not get up.

Ottie stomped away shaking handfuls of hair from her fingers. As she rearranged her vegetables on the table, she looked back across the Boneyard lot only to see Eli bending over Gumtooth, tending to her wounds. Overcome with grief and anger at a perceived betrayal, Ottie kneed Eli in the groin. He rolled on his side moaning. The sheriff came to drive Ottie back home.

When Eli's second wife died later that year, he did not come to marry Ottie. He drove to the Boneyard, got Gumtooth, and married her.

THE FIGHT

Ottie fed Eli his platter of crow. He ate deeply of the bitter dish. What he did not eat was the box of moon pies she presented him at his release. He did not even see the humor in the event. The year in the slammer gave him time for thought. He was not treating Ottie well, for sure. She outsmarted him. Twice, the law caught him at the same moonshine spot, but she always escaped. He began to see that she was a valuable ally and business partner. He decided to give her more of his time in an effort to rebuild a working relationship.

Ottie was also pragmatic. She needed Eli's resources. Now that she had her own small farm with animals and an acre of land, she was less dependent on the men around her. She buried the hatchet with Eli but not with Gumtooth and Hustlebutt. Eli kept them at bay. Eli and Ottie resumed their moonshine business. As long as they included Sheriff Buford in the payoffs, they were relatively safe.

Eli would not go back to the location of the moonshine still on Devil's Creek Fork. It did not ever serve him well. They came up with a new plan. Using hand shovels, they expanded a cellar under Eli's house large enough to set up the moonshine still there. Eli drove a horse sled up the Fork to the ridge behind the Devil's Creek waterfalls. They loaded the big reservoir and copper coils on the sled and brought them down to the farmhouse.

Underneath the house, Eli built a flue from river rock. He connected it to the regular house chimney that emptied smoke from the upstairs fireplace. The barrels fit easily in the expanded cellar. Now they could build a fire under the cooker and cook the mash without concern for the smell of wood smoke and cooking corn mash. At times a double amount of smoke poured out of the chimney. It curled upward on the wind. Anyone passing by assumed the family ate a lot of corn.

Eli and Ottie often told outsiders that they made hominy to sell at the Boneyard. It was pure deception and it protected the moonshine business. There was an entrance to the cellar from upstairs. It opened from behind the wood cook stove on to a set of five stairs descending to ground level. There was an exit tunnel from inside the cellar leading to the chicken houses outside. A trap door opened on the apple orchard so neither Ottie nor Eli could be trapped inside by revenuers.

They felt secure in their new operation. Ottie never went upstairs because Gumtooth lived there. She used the entrance at the chicken houses. Business flourished. Ottie's sales at the Boneyard doubled. They were travelling the high road. It seems, however, that there is always a stupid person that appears on every occasion to throw a monkey wrench into other people's success.

Of course the stupid person was June Sr. Ottie married him, not out of love, but because she needed someone to help her raise her childen. The fact that she had two babies out of wedlock did not help her chances at finding a suitable mate. She married beneath herself.

June Sr. was a dull, uneducated man who did sawmill work and odd jobs for people in the community. He was 5'6", had black hair, and a prominent Hapsburg lip that looked as if someone had struck him in the mouth with a hammer. He brought very little money into the household. He was repulsive. He blew his nose with his fingers and did not bathe often. It is amazing that he and Ottie had three boys, for she did not want to sleep with him.

Ottie had four children with Eli. That made eight children that June Sr. was expected to feed, to care for, to support with his meager salary. Ottie contributed her share by farming and selling moonshine. But June Sr. watched her affairs with Eli knowing that the four blond, blue-eyed children were not his. He endured the situation for several years until the birth of Ottie's last child. She was a premature girl, so small that the midwife doubted she could survive. Unfortunately for the marriage, she did. Only three of this large family belonged to June Sr.

He was caring for the group one day while Ottie made liquor at the still in Eli's cellar. Anger began to stir in his feeble brain. He looked around at all the kids he had to care for. He looked at the paltry amount of money in his pockets. He did not want to live like this. He would no longer share his wife with Eli. Because Ottie did not keep her wedding vows, he would not keep his vows to her.

He walked to the farmhouse and entered the cellar through the chicken house entrance. Ottie looked like a wizard as she moved among the bubbling cauldrons of hot steam that rose to the ceiling, looking for an exit. June Sr. stood in the entrance way, focusing his beady eyes on Ottie. His anger boiled over into action. He walked up to her and struck her a hard blow across the head. She fell backwards knocking over a case of moonshine. The glass jars cracked into pieces and the precious liquid seeped out on the cellar floor. Ottie pulled herself to her knees. Realizing what was about to happen, she decided not to be whipped by this troll. She lunged forward, hitting June Sr. in the solar plexus, knocking him against one of the barrels of mash. He grabbed a long birch stick used for stirring the mash in both his hands then swung it wildly at her head. She ducked, letting the copper coils absorb the dangerous blows. She managed to grab this troll around his neck in an arm lock. She pulled him across the cellar, smashing his skull into the wall.

Upstairs Eli and Gumtooth heard the commotion. Eli lifted the trapdoor behind the stove and ran down the five steps into the cellar. He saw a partially wrecked moonshine still and splotches of blood on the floor. Ottie let go of June Sr. who was on the verge of passing out, for her headlock had cut off the circulation to his troll brain. Eli helped Ottie to a small wooden stool.

When June Sr. came back to consciousness, he yelled at Eli, "You expect me to take care of the bastard children you sired with my wife, do you?" he huffed. "I intend to geld you like a goat and fix you so you can't sire another baby with any woman."

He whipped out a rusty switchblade knife and struck for Eli's groin. Eli had spent time in prison so he knew how to fight. He kicked the knife away with his right foot and then struck the troll a hard blow across his Hapsburg lip. June Sr. howled in pain.

He yelled at Ottie, "What kind of woman are you? You have no morals. You birth one kid after another not caring who the father is. You whore around with this man in front of my eyes and he has a wife sitting upstairs."

"I am a woman who knows love," she answered him, "something you will never know. I define what morality is for me, you don't tell me what it is. The kids I had with Eli are a product of the love I have for him. Yours are a product of disgusting lust. I would rather be married to one of the cattle in the field as you, you nasty little son-of-a-bitch."

The troll fight continued. June Sr. whacked Eli on the side of his head with both fists leaving a nasty bump. He fell against the reservoir filled with mash knocking it off its foundations. Ottie leaped on June Sr.'s back beating him with her fists.

Disengaging from her, he stumbled toward the exit. The troll had had enough. "I'm leaving you,: he yelled at Ottie. "You take care of your own bastards."

"I left you long ago, you misfit," she responded. "My bastards will grow up to put you to shame. I'm glad they have none of your disgusting blood and ignorance in them. A time will come when they will stand proudly as Ottie's children. We don't need you to survive."

Gumtooth feared that someone might get killed. She had already had a fight with Ottie and knew her strength. She ran out on the porch yelling for my sister and me to go get Sheriff Dawson. Ottie was trying to kill her husband

Sheriff Dawson came.

The sheriff's car passed June Sr. walking in the direction of the main road. He carried a burlap sack on his shoulders. He did not look at the sheriff. That is the last time I ever saw him.

Eli saw the sheriff's car approaching his house.

"I'm not going to prison a third time."

He knocked over the fire on to the spilled moonshine and set it on fire. Ottie ran out the tunnel entrance as flames leapt over the contents of the cellar. Eli pulled Gumtooth out of danger. Sheriff Dawson saw the entire house burst into flames and he could not stop it. The moonshine still popped and gurgled as the flames consumed it. The business went up in a fiery storm.

The ignorant troll was gone and so was their livelihood.

"Is everyone out of the house?" Dawson asked.

"Yes," Eli answered.

From our vantage point on our porch, we watched the house collapse into a heap of ashes. Sheriff Dawson stopped by our house to make sure we were fine. He cared about children.

Eli did not go back to prison but his price for freedom was the loss of his house. Gumtooth went to live with Hustlebutt and Eli went to live with his brother Roy and his aging father Julius.

June Sr. made his way on foot up the curving road above Lake McCall and headed for his girlfriend Caldonia's place ten miles away. Ottie came home and washed her wounds. The whole family sat down in the Little Old House crying, wondering what would become of us.

RESURRECTION

Tragedy struck the valley in the form of a fire. Eli lost his home and possessions. Ottie and her children lost June Sr. and her livelihood. It does not matter how the house burned. Individual suffering matters more than the why of an event. Communities draw together in time of need to support a suffering family and so the valley people rallied around Eli. It did not matter that he made moonshine or that he was an ex-con. Nor did his womanizing enter their minds. He was hurting and he was one of them.

Gentry and his crew volunteered to come to work on their day off to cut planks for Eli's new house. While they were sawing logs into planks, another group of people gathered at the burned-out house place. They rescued what items they could. Very little of the house remained. All of them suspected what caused the fire, yet no one judged him. There but for the grace of God they understood. They were there to build him a new house, to help him start life anew.

Sheriff Grayson helped remove the debris. He knew the story of Eli, but he judged him not. He was first and foremost his neighbor. Not much else counted. By the time Gentry had sawed enough planks, the men and women had cleaned the foundation spot. It was ready for the new house.

Women brought food for everyone. They worked in unison, nailing, sawing, and painting. Women joined their men with hammers nailing joints and beams. This outpouring of love came from valley people who did not attend church. They believed in no religious dogma. They were good without God. They did not shout in the aisle of a church. They did not pray in public like the Pharisees and Publicans. They followed the dictates of their own hearts which were driven by deep compassion for fellow humans in need.

Clyde and Jesse Pearl did not come to help. There was no money in it for them. Beulah did not come to help because she considered them all sinners and beneath her. Bertha, Mrs. Palmer, Mrs. Lindenhardt, the missionaries who were in the valley to tell people about God, did not come. They were too busy judging Eli and Ottie's morals.

Miss Lucy and Mr. Rawlins would not dirty their hands with this group. Tom T. Tuttle, who gave clothes to poor children in order to aggrandize himself, refused to help. There was no one here he could humiliate. Kindness did not become him. Hustlebutt and Gumtooth were there carrying fresh buckets of water to quench people's thirsts. Ottie baked baskets of sweet potatoes to feed hungry stomachs.

The scene was biblical, reminiscent of the feeding of five thousand with five loaves and three fishes. The three women laid aside their hostilities for a greater purpose. One does not kick another when he is on the ground. Had the valley people never heard of God or religion, they would have done the same. If goodness is not innately in one's heart, religion cannot put it there. There was a powerful energy of unconditional love flowing, embracing Ottie and Eli, putting them back on their feet. This is all of God they needed to know.

Eli felt the love of this community deep in his soul. He sat down on a rock, head resting in his hands, feeling the power of non-judgment. It was he who judged himself, not they. The full weight of missing the mark fell on his shoulders. Mistreatment of women, his exile in prison, his not caring for his own children, all rode upon his mind in self-sorrow, bringing him to tears. He did his own life revue. It was his rejection of Ottie that drove his greatest feeling of regret. The past was over and done. He could not retrieve that arrow. His treatment of her constituted real sin for he had missed the mark. He was wasting his time on Gumtooth for she was a pathetically dumb creature. She lived at the level of the cattle. She had improved her station in life by marrying him. It was he that had gone to get her at the Boneyard for she had not pursued him. He intended to get even with Ottie, but he brought the pillars of the temple down on his own head.

Gentry saw Eli in his agony. He went to him, placing his arm around his shoulders, saying, "We all have our sorrows and regrets, Eli. Loving neighbors and friends help us to cleanse our souls. Let go your sorrows and drink in this joyful moment. If you are seeking God, look around you. These mountains stand proud and tall. So do these valley people. This place is a church, these people are the congregation. They are a denomination called humanity."

The sun broke across the trees over Grassy Knob and everyone paused from their work to gaze on a double rainbow stretching across the valley. The group love was so intense, they rebuilt Eli's house in record time.

Where the house had burned, Ottie walked around the ruins continuing her farm work. No animals suffered, no crop went neglected. She was alone now except for her children. Gumtooth and Hustlebutt were living elsewhere for the moment. A peace fell over the farm and fields. A peace fell over Ottie, too. June Sr. left her for this woman Caledonia and now he spent his meager income on her. None ever came back to her or his children. She sorely missed the income from the moonshine still. The other moonshine still belonged to Eli, not her. She wanted her own still because Eli always managed to get caught. She focused her mind on her goal. She knew somehow it would come.

Everything is mind. Spirit is life. Mind builds. The physical is the result. Everything in our physical world comes from somewhere else, from a world of thought. Ottie did not consciously know this principle. She just wished really hard. Thought enters an empty space, emotion kicks in and the physical of the thought forms in the empty space. There was a moonshine still taking form.

Gentry's truck moaned up the river road. It pulled a heavy load. Ottie watched from the field as it came into view. Gentry waved at her from a distance. She laid her hoe on the ground wiping perspiration from her forehead with the back of her left hand. She walked across the furrowed field toward him. Four of his work crew jumped down from the back of his truck and greeted her. She fixed them fresh coffee and then Gentry spoke.

"When my men and I first came to this valley, you welcomed us with a quart of moonshine. Your moonshine has quenched thirst and healed sick people for many years. You have never cheated anyone in selling your liquor. Your hard work in supporting your children is respected far and wide. The loss of the still in the fire was a severe loss to you. People in the valley do not want to lose their moonshine. Many of them contributed money for the purchase of this brand new cooker and coils we have loaded here on my truck. We want to help you to resurrect the moonshine business."

They climbed up Oaky Knob looking for a place of resurrection. It seemed as if they were climbing toward Heaven as they moved over rocks and dead trees. The blue sky soared above them and giant spruce trees stood sentinel as if to assure Ottie she would be safe here. We will protect you. The farm below looked tiny, miniscule in comparison to the stalwart mountain. Ottie found a fresh mountain stream and pure water that would guarantee outstanding whiskey. Here is the place. A stream, clean and cold, emerged from a cluster of rocks. Sunlight came in from the west only. A far view ensured no person could surprise her.

Ottie asked the men to leave her for a moment. She looked at the balsam trees with their long cones and dangling branches. She looked at the mountains and blue sky. She smelled the moss and fresh water. She touched the branches of a dead oak tree. She felt dead inside like this oak that had already relinquished its spirit. She had lost both June Sr. and her true love Eli. She was alone now. The valley, through Gentry, hoped for her a new life, a new beginning, a resurrection. This sacred spot on the mountain held a new beginning for her, a hope to revitalize her heart and soul.

"I am not defeated," she thought to herself. "I will live for and through my children. They will lead me onward. I will no longer live in Eli's shadow. My heart is mine. My life is mine. I am my own person."

The winds rose sighing through the rocks and trees. Thunder rolled across the distant mountains.

ON STRIKE

Hustlebutt decided to pay a visit to her friend Gumtooth now that her buddy was married to Eli and lived in a nice house on the farm. She knew that Ottie lived next door to Eli and that she was going deep into enemy territory. Like Brecht's Mother Courage, she was a businesswoman who sold to all sides, who took contraband turning it into a profit for herself. She took items to sell from any source available. She stole merchandise from other vendors at the Boneyard. On garbage days when people set their cast-off items outside so trucks could take them to a trash pit, she collected lamps, furniture, clothing, dolls, whatever she thought would sell at the market. She pilfered farmhouses when no one was at home, taking whatever she could find to sell. If any person went to the Boneyard and saw his personal property for sale on her table, she denied their accusation saying that she had found everything in a trash pile. She intended to steal from Ottie on this trip.

Ottie saw Eli's Model -T come down the road by her house with Hustlebutt proudly occupying the front seat that once had been hers. Hustlebutt's fat ham hocks spread out across the front seat filling it like jello pudding. She smoked a cheroot cigar and blew puffs of blue smoke out the passenger window. To Eli she was just another female occupant important to him only if he needed her services. This day, by her request, he brought her to see his new wife Gumtooth. Emotions ran high among the whole group.

The entire farm and everything on it belonged to Eli including the moonshine still. Ottie's hard work produced all the vegetables on the farm. She could claim no ownership. She received a pittance in return for her work. They reduced Ottie to the level of horses on the farm, stripped of all power, living like the serf she was. People petted the horses and farm animals, but no one petted Ottie. They took from her. Eli, Hustlebutt, and Gumtooth set about to take from Ottie the little she had left. Gumtooth did not have to work at the Boneyard very much now that she was married to Eli. Hustlebutt wanted her to come back as her partner. She was at the farm to steal items to sell. They all stretched their tiny minds to come up with ideas of what would sell.

Tiny minds indeed. Gumtooth had a brain the size of a dried pea resting on a slender Medulla Oblongata. She was incapable of thought. She reacted to life. The pea brain had a nerve connected to both arms so that when stimulated, she reacted by hitting. Hustlebutt had a large brain that was empty like a vacant house. Events echoed through her mind like a voice off canyon walls. She, too, reacted without thinking usually striking out at whatever stimulus was there. Eli was superior to both women. He had good intelligence but low morals. He was self-serving to a fault. Eli disrespected all women. They existed to serve his every need. They were on the level of cattle. These three brains formed a half brain that tried to plot against Ottie.

Eli gathered most of the mason jars of moonshine from the still and placed them in the back of his Model-T. Gumtooth took a basket of sweet potatoes belonging to Ottie from the cellar and stashed them in the car. Hustlebutt jiggled her fat buttocks through the hen houses gathering all the eggs in a basket to sell at the Boneyard. All three went to the beehives where they emptied most of the honey into sacks. While Ottie was working in the fields, Hustlesbutt entered her house and stole one of her kerosene lamps. The thieves packed their contraband in Eli's car in anticipation of a successful day of selling at the Boneyard.

They left early on Saturday morning for the Boneyard. Ottie saw them go. Gentry agreed to take Ottie there to sell her moonshine. When she arrived at the market, the three adversaries were already doing a brisk business selling the products of her labor. They were so mercenary that one of them put up a hand lettered sign reading, "All items on this table priced at fifty cents. Proceeds go to pay for my mother's funeral."

Ottie did not sell much moonshine that day. She saw one of her regular customers with a quart of shine already in his hand.

"Where did you get your moonshine, Gus?" she asked him.

"From Hustlebutt and Gumtooth," he replied. "They are selling it for six dollars a quart. You charge eight. Are you cheating us, Ottie?"

She was nonplussed. She had many faults, but cheating customers was not one of them. Ottie sauntered across the market pretending to shop until she came to the table where the two women sat selling their wares. She saw there on their table not only her moonshine, but also her sweet potatoes, eggs, honey, and one of her kerosene lamps. She did not acknowledge either of the two women for they were dire enemies. They looked away pretending to be busy. Eli glared at her knowing that she had caught him in the midst of a scheme. Ottie spat some snuff from her mouth on to the ground as an act of disgust. The brown liquid sprayed as it hit the ground, some of it splattering Eli's shoes. He wiped the spittle off with a piece of discarded newspaper. Ottie returned to her selling space and reduced the price of her moonshine to four dollars a quart. The three interlopers did not sell any more moonshine that day.

Ottie was mad and hurt; mad that they had successfully trumped her with their scheme, hurt that Eli no longer patronized her. A desire for revenge rose within Ottie. She fretted and fumed that her hard work had produced money for the pockets of Eli's harlot and her girlfriend. She went to sleep wondering what course of action to take.

The sun was shining brightly through her kitchen window as she arose from her bed the next day. She was in a good mood. She baked herself a pan of homemade biscuits letting them brown to a crisp. Making some extra strong black coffee, she poured herself a cup as she spread muscadine jelly on one of the biscuits. A guttural laugh escaped from deep in her throat and her shoulders heaved as a fit of laughter rolled over her. Her answer to the three enemies' actions came like a sunburst exploding in her head. She would go on strike.

It dawned on Ottie that she did all the work on the farm. Her tireless toil produced the corn, potatoes, and moonshine. She milked the cows, slopped the hogs, hoed and tended the crops. She risked her life in the woods making Eli's liquor. She fed the animals, did the washing, collected eggs from the hen houses. Starting this very day, she would do no more labor for them. Let those three do the work if they could. She leaned back in her chair enjoying the coffee and biscuit more than anything in her life, even a moon pie.

The cows stirred up a fuss. They were used to being milked twice a day. Their heavy, full udders hung heavily toward the ground. The horses neighed, kicking at the stable gates, wanting out to their fresh grass and water. The hens clucked demanding their scratch food. Pigs in the hog pen nudged the sides of their enclosure waiting for food. Dirty clothes piled high at the washing bench. No fires burned, no mash cooked inside the moonshine still. Cats and dogs remained unfed. The whole farm stagnated. Ottie watched the disintegration with glee. At this moment she was glad that everything in her sight belonged to Eli. Let these three cretins produce what they would sell. She would stay home and enjoy herself a good rest. Ottie was on vacation.

As Shakespeare would say, it was a comedy of errors. The two women knew little or nothing about Ottie's work. Gumtooth tried to slop the hogs but she left the door to the pen open. The hogs fled across the meadow into the woods. Hustlebutt took two buckets to the barn stalls in an effort to milk the cows. She raked and pulled on their teats but no milk came out. The cows kicked the buckets over swishing her with their long, wiry tails. She went back to the farmhouse in defeat, her shoes covered with cow manure, her face covered with whelps. Eli managed better with the horses and chickens but Gumtooth was too stupid to gather hen eggs. She broke half of them and traumatized the hens so that they did not lay eggs again for three days. The three searched the woods for days looking for the escaped hogs but they did not find them. As weeks passed, weeds and grass grew in the cotton and corn. No clean clothes were available to wear. It does not pay to cross Ottie.

Ottie enjoyed her warm breakfast every day. She even got up early enough to feed her children and pack a lunch box for them. She focused on her needs. She did not even work in her own house or for her own family. For the first time in years, she was not tired. She felt alive, vibrant. Eli and his women stopped going to the Boneyard. They had nothing to sell. It was a desperation time for them. Their only way out was to appease Ottie. They were getting ready to eat a heaping platter of crow.

Eli went into Stan's Country Store where he bought a case of chocolate moon pies, twelve in all, in a cardboard box. He tied a string around the box leaving it in the form of a bow. He knew he had to walk into the lion's den, but he would not go unarmed.

He stopped at Ottie's house and knocked loudly on the door. She took her own good time opening it. She did not greet him.

"I brought you some moon pies," he cooed.

"Are you the same man who would not buy me a moon pie at Tony's store?" He blushed.

"I want you to come back to work," he pleaded.

"I need a milk cow to provide milk and butter for my children," she said. "Then I will consider coming back."

Eli left. He knew now he would have to pay through the nose. He haltered one of his cows and led her back to Ottie's house. "Here is your cow," he said.

"I don't feel like working right now," she said. "I need a plough horse to farm for myself."

Eli went back to the barn, picked out a horse, and led it to Ottie.

Looking at him, she ordered, "I need pens to hold this cow and horse."

He spent three days building her animal pens. "Are you ready to work again," he inquired.

"I want a hog to butcher in the fall," she commanded.

He went to the Boneyard and bought her a pig and built a pen for it.

"I want a brood of hens of my own for eggs and dumplings," she informed him.

He divided his hens with her.

"I want the seventy-five cents refunded that I paid Gumtooth to get my own lamp back," she said. He gave her a dollar.

"I want an acre of bottom land to call my own," she stated.

He wrote her a promissory note for an acre of land. "Now will you go back to work on the farm and help me make moonshine again?" he requested.

"Back to work I will come," she said. "My moonshine days are over. It is too risky. Gumtooth and Hustlebutt will have to help you."

She returned to her farm work the next day.

Eli choked on his plate of crow which Ottie was glad to supersize.

When Sheriff Buford arrested Ottie for public drunkenness and inciting a riot at the "calling out," he took her to jail in Forest City. While there, she struck a deal to include him in her moonshine business. He got a kickback from each quart she sold. She also dated Buford making sure his needs were met. They became partners. He protected her. When she told him what Eli and Gumtooth were doing by undercutting their sales at the Boneyard, Buford took action. Ottie meant to take back her moonshine operation. Buford came to her house and waited until the three were busy at the still on Devil's Creek. Ottie led him to the location. Eli was hard at work stoking the fire, sweating now for he did all the work. Hustlebutt and Gumtooth sat in the leaves packing quart jars into boxes. Buford and Ottie walked in on them. Buford already had a profitable working relationship with Hustlebutt and Gumtooth at the Boneyard, so he did not bother them. He arrested Eli once again at the same moonshine still, in the same way. Eli met his fate again. The judge gave him a year in jail at Forest City. The two women went back to the Boneyard. Ottie took over the farm.

When Eli's year in jail was up, Ottie stood outside the jailhouse waiting on him with a case of chocolate moon pies.

"You've become a regular jailbird, haven't you?" she chided him.

She chuckled as she handed Eli the box of moon pies.

"You thought that you could buy my love and loyalty with a box of cookies, didn't you? When will you stop hanging around with white-trash women and ask me to marry you, Eli? Now, are you ready to come back to work and treat me decently? I hope so. You, yourself, have been on strike for over a year."

The moon pie she handed him melted in his hand and its chocolate covering fell on the floor. His plate of crow was melting.

THE RECKONING

E li was Ottie's love forever. Affairs of the heart do not follow any rules, any laws and any mores. Her heart chose him at the Peddler's Stump when she was fourteen and he was twenty-five. No earthly person or event could remove him from his exalted place in her heart. She knew Eli in all his evil ways and betrayals, yet her heart saw only his goodness. There was no room for judgment of him in her soul. He brought her pain. He brought her sorrow. He brought her great joy. He gave her four children without legal bonds of marriage. She married him in absentia in her mind. Only God had the power to judge that marriage as right or wrong. The deepest hurt he had inflicted on her heart was to marry twice without coming to her, without taking her feelings into consideration.

His choosing a woman like Gumtooth as his marriage partner was more than she could bear. Bringing her to live in the farmhouse next door to her plus giving her the status of overlord, piled humiliation on her. This daily thought of rejection rode her mind. How could he pass her over, choosing a riff-raff woman to occupy the place that was rightfully hers? This toothless scum now had the power to tell Ottie when to work, how long, and what she may not do on the farm. It filled Ottie's heart with bitterness. She did not talk to Eli now. She refused to acknowledge Gumtooth. She toiled in silence in the fields and returned at dusk by a long route to her house. She made and sold her moonshine alone, risking her safety at the prying eyes of nosy neighbors.

One day Eli came to tell her that she had to move out of the Little Old House. Gumtooth no longer wanted her there and he no longer wanted her family as tenant farmers. He would hire Negroes to do the farm work. This blow felled Ottie greater than any tragedy of her life. Where could she go? She had no money, no means and no position from which to negotiate. She felt like the children of Israel banished to wander forty years in a desert. She felt weary. She sat down on the porch steps looking upward to the rugged heights of Oaky Knob. I will lift up mine eyes unto the hills. I will get through this. The next day it rained. This time the storm rose over Oaky Knob and left a rainbow in the sky. No more rain, but the fire next time.

Salvation came unexpectedly. Curtis sent word that night that the saw mill was moving to Burke County. In order to keep his job, we had to move with them. Ottie's smile broke like a rainbow across her face. They could turn her out of the house, but they could not quell her spirit. She did not want to leave the valley. She did not want to leave Eli, her home, her moonshine still. However, one grows accustomed to the miseries of his life. Even though her unrequited love hung like a millstone around her heart, destiny intervened. June Jr. stole a car. They had to flee like thieves in the night.

Ottie would not forget nor forgive her trespassers.

Three years passed. Eli and Gumtooth had a baby girl they named Sweet Cakes. Now he had eleven children. Negroes in the valley refused to come and work for Gumtooth. She was too stupid

and overbearing and she did not pay them in full. She knew nothing about running a farm and less about how to handle people.
Eli's house and land began to fall into ruins. When he could bear
it no longer, he crossed the mountains to see if Ottie and her family would come back. He offered her the Little Old House rent free.
She could keep seventy-five per cent of the money from the sale of
moonshine. What she planted and harvested would belong to her
family. He never offered himself. He never expressed regret for
not returning to her when the sourwood was in bloom. He never
told her he loved her. He did not talk to her about marriage. He
did not agree to care for the four children that were theirs. He did
not consider her except for the times he was in need. He used her.
She pondered his offerings. He was offering all these promises
that emanated from his need, but he did not know he opened the
way for Ottie's revenge. In time he would see his error.

Ottie agreed to come back twice a week, on Tuesdays and
Thursdays. Gumtooth must stay away from her. He had to pay her
in cash each week. She took as much produce and items from the
farm to fill her needs and more. She harmed no one intentionally.
As a survivor, she responded in the moment to life's challenges, be
they good or bad. It is not possible to expunge long-time hurts in
the "Now time." Sins can be expunged a little at a time. Instant
salvation would kill a soul. Ottie drew within herself and focused
on her work.

Coming back from her moonshine still one day, Ottie carried a
case of filled mason jars on her shoulders. Gumtooth saw her take
the path from the barn to walk across the front yard of her house.
Gumtooth could not allow Ottie to trespass on her property. She
made the mistake of confronting Ottie.

"Get out of my damn yard," she yelled at Ottie from her front
porch.

"Sluts don't have the means to own a yard," Ottie replied.

"You are the only slut I know in this valley," Gumtooth retorted.

"I may be a slut," Ottie replied, "but I have all my teeth and I don't have to find my husband at a place like the Boneyard. I knocked out your last tooth and I won't hesitate to rip out your gums."

"I've been looking for an excuse to beat your ass since our fight at the Boneyard," she said. Now is as good a time as ever."

"When you feel Froggy, Gumtooth, jump."

Ottie laughed at her. She set the case of moonshine aside on the path. Gumtooth descended down the steps from the porch with fire in her eyes and stupidity in her brain. Ottie readied for the impending conflict. Gumtooth threw the first punch, but missed Ottie's face. Ottie glared into the face of her adversary with utter contempt. She saw those empty gums unable to say 's' or 't'. Her bulbous breasts that could suffocate a person shook from side to side. How could Eli take this misfit as his wife?

A riff-raff, white trash woman had taken away her life. Ottie grabbed a piece of stove wood lying at the edge of the yard and began beating Gumtooth with it. Blood spurted from her head, ribs cracked, screams pushed through gums devoid of teeth. In a frenzy, all reason left Ottie. She was a fury, a mother tiger defending her cubs. All the hate and anger and sorrow of her life welled up in this moment of rage. She struck Gumtooth with hands made more powerful by all the hurts of her life. Long before Ottie ceased the beating, Gumtooth lay dead in the ruts of the road. Ottie felt dead inside. In the distance on the porch of the farmhouse, Gumtooth and Eli's baby Sweetcakes cried for her mother. Ottie packed her belongings, took the road westward, and made her way over the mountains out of the valley. No one could have her Eli.

In the distance, a tenant's voice mourned in song the old Negro spiritual:

"God promised Noah a rainbow sign
No more rain, but the fire next time."

THE COUGAR IN THIS VALLEY WALKS ON TWO LEGS

I t never ceases to amaze me how funeral directors can make ugly people into pretty corpses. Gumtooth lay in her coffin surrounded by satin sheets, her head resting on a satin pillow. The undertaker rearranged her face taking care to give her a smile. It looked like a smirk. Since she had no teeth, he packed cotton gauze inside her mouth lifting the jaws and cheeks outward making each side of her face even. Red rouge lined her cheeks giving a show girl hue to her sallow skin. He crossed her arms on her chest and placed a small Bible and cross in her fingers. This gesture was humorous to all who knew her. Gumtooth had never attended church and would not have known Jesus from a hound dog. It was perhaps a warning to all sinners to repent their sins or end up like her. The message fell on fallow ground for few people had bothered to come to look at her corpse. Venders at the Boneyard did not care for her, besides they could not afford the gasoline to drive to the funeral home.

Eli kept lonely vigil by himself sitting in a straight-back chair beside her coffin. She was the third wife he sat beside in death. He did not know how to mourn. If it were his body in the coffin instead of hers, he could not have summoned a tear. Two baskets of white flowers rested on each side of the coffin. They smelled like plastic, but they were real. Not even the flowers respected Gumtooth.

Hustlebutt did come to look upon her friend's corpse. She entered the funeral home with hesitation as if she did not know what to do. Eli motioned her in pointing his finger in the direction of the coffin. She slowly approached the body of her friend. The spray of flowers on the casket oozed a sweet fragrance like lilacs which permeated the room. Upon viewing Gumtooth's serene face and false beauty created by the undertaker, Hustlebutt muttered out loud, "Ain't she looking so natural?" Beauty had not been one of Gumtooth's natural attributes. Hustlebutt did not touch the cold corpse. She wondered why there were a cross and Bible in her hand.

"Gumtooth is in Hell," she said to herself. "She always kept vigil with the Devil when she was alive."

She sat down on a cushioned bench opposite Eli's chair. She nervously fingered the handles of her black purse as her mind fell into deep thought.

"How did she die, Eli?" she asked softly as if the question must be posed in reverence.

Eli looked up at her perplexed. "The cougar," he said. "They think the cougar got her. That's what the sheriff wrote in his report."

After the fight that left Gumtooth dead, Eli came home from work on the CCC road to find her deceased. In despair, he rushed in the Model-T to bring the sheriff.

"The cougar killed Gumtooth," he told Sheriff Dawson. "It tore her up badly. She is hardly recognizable. There is blood everywhere."

The two men went to the death scene. Sheriff Dawson sent Beulah to Forest City for Sheriff Buford to help him in the investigation. Beulah sounded the alarm down the valley that the cougar everyone was seeing struck down Gumtooth.

"Lock your doors and load your guns for we are all in mortal danger," she screamed in fear.

Rumors ran along the valley like a cold, biting wind in autumn. Housewives barred their doors and men loaded their rifles and shotguns. Leaders organized patrols to go along the roadways, to skirt the edges of the fields and woods, looking for the denizen. They wished they had listened earlier when Ottie's children told of seeing a big cat on the river road.

Buford and Dawson studied Gumtooth's corpse for bites and claw marks. They found none. There were no cougar footprints anywhere around the death scene either. They pulled a couple of wood splinters from wounds on the side of Gumtooth's head.

"That's a very talented cougar," said Sheriff Buford, "It knows how to wield a piece of wood."

Buford and Dawson strolled a few steps away from everyone for a moment of private conversation.. Buford spoke first.

"You can't try a cougar for murder," he said. "The valley people are already in fear of this animal. It's the only story they want to believe."

Dawson replied, "This was done by a human cougar, but which one?"

"There are no witnesses, we have no proof. We can speculate and accuse but we will come up empty handed with any jury," said Buford.

"Where is Ottie?" Dawson asked. "I wonder if she saw or heard anything. She lives next door."

"She and her family moved to Burke County some time ago," replied Buford.

(Neither man knew of Eli's arrangement with her to come work the farm on Tuesdays and Thursdays.)

"We can end this case right now or make years of endless work for us both," Buford informed him.

Both men's sins were woven into valley life through bribes and playoffs. It would be very hard to extirpate themselves from them. Gumtooth meant nothing to them. So they cut her loose in death as she had lived in life, unconsidered, unimportant, no better than the cattle in the stables. Buford wrote on his official report where it asked for cause of death "Killed by a Cougar." The two men spoke their condolences to Eli, telling him they would send the undertaker for the body.

Hustlebutt heard the story of the cougar but something inside her remained unsettled about it. She did not understand how her friend could get killed by a cougar. They hunted at night. She died in broad daylight. When Ottie shot at the cougar, it ran away and had not been seen since. Why would it come back? This was a great loss for Hustlebutt. Like the deputy, her tiny brain would not pursue the matter further.

Only six people came the next day to attend the burial service for Gumtooth. Beulah, Eli, Hustlebutt, Sheriff Dawson, Sheriff Buford and a woman dressed in black from head to toe stood on the hillside where Wasnett Funeral Home erected a tent over the open grave space. Gumtooth's coffin rested on a dais stretched across the grave which was waiting to receive her. A soft breeze blew through the trees, rippling the scalloped edges of the covering tent. A heavy silence reigned on the hilltop. A distant, rumbling thunder, barely audible, sounded like a kettle drum announcing Gumtooth's arrival in Hell. Beulah's beady eyes locked on the lady in black. She wanted to rip off the veil and hat to expose her identity.

No self-respecting Christian minister would agree to bury Gumtooth or say any words of grace over her body. She had never attended their churches; they would not come to her departing.

Gumtooth was already in Hell as far as they were concerned. They judged her severely. (Many of them were probably headed there without knowing it.)

Sheriff Buford, a simple, uneducated man spoke over her corpse:

"From Alpha to Omega, from beginning to end, from dust to dust,

From birth to death, there is life in between all of these.

It is this brief stay in life that defines us as human.

We come in clouds of glory; we depart in veils of sadness.

Grief this day belongs to Eli. We are here for him.

All of his tomorrows will come with an empty place beside him.

If we weep, we weep for him. We wish

Gumtooth's soul a pleasant journey to its final destination.

I cannot speak of God because I don't know if there is one.

I can speak with compassion to Eli's loss. It is good that Gumtooth was here, that she was a part of the simplicity of these Appalachian hills.

We return her now to the dust from which she came and

Send her spirit back to the goodness that made her."

Everyone at the grave site felt the power of Buford's words. Eli thanked him in his heart.

Sheriffs Dawson and Buford departed. Beulah left reluctantly because she wanted to know who the lady in black was. Time would tell. The two figures, Eli and the lady in black, stood silhouetted against the hillside, her flowing black dress moving gently in the breeze.

After a few minutes, a sweet, soft voice spoke from behind the gossamer veil covering the lady's face.

It said softly, "The hardest love is the love of goodbye, Eli. I have drunk deeply of goodbyes. All those whom I have ever loved left me. Some said goodbye; some did not. My heart aches for you in your sorrow, Eli. You feel today how others felt when you inflicted sorrow on them. In all of your tomorrows, I hope you search for and find redemption."

A gentle wind rustled the blades of grass on the hill. The figure in black glided down the hillside and disappeared into the trees. People in the valley spoke of seeing a lone figure, dressed in mourning clothes, walking ghostlike along the gravel road toward Lake McCall. Some heard a loud, wailing cry up the hollows. It was ghostlike, deep and painful as if someone's very soul were sitting in God's judgment seat.

THE JUDGMENT SEAT

Ottie sat down on an ancient boulder containing a seat that had been scooped out by thousands of years of sand erosion. A clear stream of water flowed beside it gushing over pebbles and sand. Honeysuckle vines climbed up the hillsides pouring their sweet fragrance over the spot. Sunshine broke through the branches of a buckeye tree. It shone on the rock seat with its renewing warmth. Birds whistled in the treetop canopy above. This was a magical spot.

Ottie removed the broad-brimmed black hat with the thin veil and laid them beside her on the rock. She was tired from the emotion of the morning, from the wailing and crying she shouted in the hollows, and from the hard, physical walk to this spot near the lake. She had twenty weary miles ahead of her to walk unless she could get Gentry to take her home. She wiped dust and grime off her dress. She had picked up this dirt from the walk on the long and dusty road. Her mind and emotions needed a rest as much as her physical body. Now that Gumtooth was buried, Ottie had to come to terms with herself, her deeds and her own life.

"Thou shalt not kill," was the commandment that weighed on her mind at the moment. The religion she followed, the church she attended, the people she lived around quoted this commandment and judged harshly those who broke it.

Her bible taught, "As you do unto others, it is done unto you." "If you live by the sword, you die by the sword." "If you lead into captivity, you go into captivity." "Whatever you do unto others comes back to you tenfold."

It was only on this day of self-atonement, in this situation that her mind seriously considered the meaning of the sayings. In her anger, she had violated the most important commandment. Now upon this ancient rock, she must sit in her own judgment seat. She could not understand that all these commandments, set up by universal law, were merely effects of what she was doing. The churchgoers in the valley did not understand their meanings either. They were only capable of shouting and mumbling something about a Heaven and a Hell.

She had not meant to kill Gumtooth. The act had not been premeditated. The toothless one's trespasses against Ottie had been legion, and, in turn Ottie blamed most of the misery of her life on Gumtooth and Eli. The truth is that Ottie brought on the misery through wrong choices she had made. She did not understand the law of cause and effect.

Clyde and Jesse Pearl were unaware of the law of cause and effect as evidenced by their conduct. The missionaries did not know it either. No one in her life could tell her or show her.

Ottie studied in her mind the pros and cons of her murderous act. Gumtooth was an enemy. We have the right to protect ourselves against enemies, those who threaten us. It is permissible to make a preemptive strike against those who would destroy us. Gumtooth had committed many destructive acts against Ottie, the greatest being to marry the man Ottie loved. It is permissible to kill in self-defense. On the day of the killing Ottie had been minding her own business. She had not been the original aggressor not even in the fight at the Boneyard. Gumtooth had opened the aggression by verbally assaulting her and threatening her. Ottie had defended herself and the act had ended in murder.

One can destroy weeds in a garden or kill wild animals with rabies because they are a threat to the common good. One can't allow wild animals to destroy a person's corn crop. Gumtooth had been a destructive force in Ottie's life.

Is revenge permissible? Her church taught that, "Vengeance is mine saith the Lord, I will repay." Why believe that? When and where would this payback come? Would Ottie live to see it? Was this a foolish idea implanted in people by religion to keep them from blood feuds and from killing one another? Ottie believed that she must even her own score. The belief system, otherwise, was undependable. Is a person insane when he takes another's life?

The rushing water beside her rock was musical and lulled her into a hypnotic spell. The rhythmical trickling of water on wet rocks eased her mind into a deep trance. In the trance there appeared the transformed figure of the dead Gumtooth. She and Ottie sat staring at each other's faces, mirror images of each other. Did Gumtooth now know the universal truth of the Hereafter? Ottie sat guessing.

"Can I not rid myself of you, even in death?" Ottie thought.

"It is your own guilt you can't rid yourself of, Ottie," Gumtooth replied. "It is your bad choices in life that haunt you, not I. You need no redemption from me, Ottie. You are your own true enemy. As to whether God exists, I will not tell you. You must learn to be good without God. Why do you need an enforcer? Why do you need a judge? You sit now in your own judgment seat and you are your own judge and jury. Convict yourself or acquit yourself. I am not able to affect anything in your life, Ottie. I rule only mine."

How dare this ignorant woman lecture her? Anger rose once again in Ottie's heart.

"If I could follow you into eternity, I would kill you again," she screamed at the phantom figure as it faded into the mist. Ottie unclenched her fists, released her heaving chest and slowly returned to a more settled state of mind. Had she been insane in that moment of the murder as she claimed to have been? She decided that she must have been in an altered state of reality when she had killed Gumtooth.

Ottie began to consider the idea of bad choices in her life. Heretofore she had viewed life as something fate had sent her, something over which she had no control, or as Christians put it, "God's will in their lives." Suppose she were the driver of life's car? All her bad choices had brought all the bad results of her life. Maybe she was baking her own cake. It was too much of a leap for her uneducated mind to make; besides she discounted any wisdom coming through the guise of Gumtooth, living or dead. "I'm innocent," she sputtered, but her individual conscious had not yet voted.

Ottie took notice once again of her physical surroundings. It was late afternoon and she needed to see Gentry for a ride home. She tossed her hat and veil into the bushes. As she strode toward Gentry's house, a profound thought entered her mind. It was there all along, but she just now realized the answer.

"Judge not lest ye be not judged." "That's it," she cried out. "It is a sin to judge my own acts."

"I will not judge myself," Ottie said out loud. "I will not condemn my own soul."

LOOK BACK IN SORROW

As Ottie made her way over the mountains into Burke County where she now lived, Gumtooth lay dead in the roadway of Eli's farmhouse. Their child, Sweetcakes, cried on the front porch from having seen the brutal fight and from the trauma of being alone. She climbed down the front porch steps to her mother's mangled body. Getting no response, she crawled to the edge of the yard into a clump of forsythia bushes. She fell asleep.

Ottie paused at the water spout on Bolding's Gap and washed the bloodstains from her arms and face. She was still filled with anger and rage from the fight. She did not think about consequences for herself should the sheriff determine that she had killed Gumtooth. It had been self-defense she reassured herself. They have to believe my story for there had been no witnesses.

As Ottie approached her house, she began to feel better. She was glad that she had eliminated the woman who had brought her daily pain and sorrow. Perhaps her act would not raise her status with Eli. She did not know. She made sure that this low-class woman could not have him forever.

Eli came home from working with the road gang to find Gumtooth lying dead in the roadway. Thinking the cougar seen earlier in the valley had killed her, Eli sent Beulah for the sheriff. Then he searched for their daughter Sweetcakes inside the house but did not find her.

In panic, he hurried to Beulah and told her to bring people from the valley to search for the child. Gentry and his crew came to help; so did the sheriff and Beulah. They fanned out searching the fields and farmhouse. They looked in the barn, corn crib, and horse and stables. Then Gentry heard a movement in the forsythia bushes. Pulling aside a branch, he saw Sweetcakes lying asleep in the bushes. He yelled across the farmyard, "I've got her."

They wondered how the cougar had gotten Gumtooth but had left Sweetcakes untouched. It was a puzzling situation. Beulah cared for Sweetcakes as the men helped Eli milk the cows, feed the animals, and arrange the farm implements.

The undertaker came for Gumtooth's body. Eli lit a kerosene lamp and sat quietly drinking a cup of coffee. His neighbors went back to their homes. Eli's agreement with Ottie stated that she would work on Tuesdays and Thursdays for him. In two days she would be back.

Meanwhile, Eli was alone. It was his first time without a wife since he had met Ottie.

Ottie sat at her house thinking. If she did not go back to work for Eli on Thursday, the neighbors might get suspicious. Besides, she now had the farm to herself if Eli still wanted her. Life had finally moved her way. What if he asked her to help care for Sweetcakes? Could she do it?

She wondered if Eli would elevate her to the status of overlord of the farm. He could not run the farm and work with the road gang as well. What about the moonshine business. There seemed to be too much work for the two of them. Eli might have to hire a farmhand to help out. Her best action, she decided, was to return to work as if nothing had happened.

When Thursday came Ottie got a ride to the foot of Bolding's Gap and walked the rest of the way to the farmhouse. Beulah had Sweetcakes and Eli was at work with the road crew on the CCC road. Ottie revisited the site where the fight had occurred. In her mind, she exonerated herself of murder. With her shoes, she raked dirt over the darkened bloodstains erasing the event and any guilt from her mind.

She worked hard all day for Eli neglected the farm. About midday, Ottie decided that she and Eli must talk. She must know where she now stood in his plans. What was he now thinking? What were his plans for the future? She was so tied to the farm and the moonshine business that, whatever he decided for himself, it would affect her profoundly. Whenever her work was finished for the day, she lingered at the farm. She sat on the swing on the front porch and waited for Eli to come home.

When he topped the hill in his Model-T, he saw Ottie from a distance sitting in a swing as if her body were set in stone. As his car drew nearer, her body seemed to grow larger in stature and she towered over him. For the first time in his life, Eli felt afraid of her. She sat like a crouched tiger long suffering from hunger. He was her prey. He recognized that it was only her love for him that had kept him safe these many years.

\He exited the car and went to sit beside her in the swing. She stared ahead without looking at him, without acknowledging him, as if her eyes were frozen in a direct gaze. The two of them swung back and forth for a long time with only the creak of the swing audible on the evening air. A sigh escaped Ottie's lips as her shoulders heaved.

"Well," is all she could say.

Whatever she meant with this word could only be discerned from its context. Did she imply that all is well? Was it an interjection to break the silence? Was it an invitation for him to speak? It left Eli perplexed. The silence continued.

Ottie broke the silence with the words, "I fell in love with you at the Peddler's Stump. You broke my heart when the sourwood was in bloom. You trampled my heart like a dance floor. You found yourself three wives and, each time, you left me standing broken hearted at the altar of my own love. What shall I do with you, Eli?"

He did not answer. He could not answer.

The swing continued to rock like a boat on a stormy sea. Eli stared at his shoes. Guilt and shame swept over him. Confronted by his past actions and choices, his mind froze. Love did not reside in his heart as it lived in Ottie's.

After the death of his son, Pet, Eli had locked his heart shut and thrown away the key. The notion of love was alien to him. He had married his wives for convenience and had lived to bury them all. Eli was incapable of loving. He could not invest emotion in anyone. Poor Ottie would have loved him to death had he given her a chance.

Finding his voice, he finally replied, "I have always feared your love, Ottie. I saw what power your love for me held. No matter what I did, it prevailed. I am powerless in the face of your love."

"You are selfish, Eli. Life is all about you. You can't love people because you think you own them. It is a moment's gratification you seek, for you are unable to invest in emotion for the long term," Ottie lectured him.

He responded, "I knew I had you in my back pocket, Ottie. I could have my cake and eat it too."

They lapsed again into silence. Crickets began to chirp for night had fallen. A red-tinted moon rose over Oaky Knob casting ghostly shadows across the porch and well house. Ottie had dreamed for so many years to be with Eli in a romantic night like this one. But bitter memories denied her feelings and blocked the beauty of the night.

Out of the blue, Eli popped the question, "Will you marry me, Ottie?"

Oh, how she had spent so many years waiting, hoping to hear him say these words. They now rang hollow in her brain and heart. She knew Eli well. He sought to assuage his own sorrow and to hedge his bet for another wife whom he would not love.

Ottie thought deeply about this sudden proposal. All power in their relationship had now come to her. The pain and heartache from having waited for his return at the Peddler's Stump and having waited for years for the slightest consideration of marriage was too great.

"No," she said to him, "I will not marry you."

There, she had the courage to say it.

"We have four children together. You have never cared for nor supported any of them. There is nothing more you have to give me, Eli. Furthermore, there is nothing more I want from you, especially not another child."

She rose from the swing and descended the steps of the porch. He watched her silhouette disappear into the moonlight. Her footsteps sounded on the gravel long after her form was no longer visible. Eli sat back in the swing with his head in his hands. He looked back at his life in sorrow.

GOODBYE MY VALLEY

It was October and the fields lay golden with grain. Dry corn ears bent low on their cornstalks as if paying homage to the ground. Plump, orange sweet potatoes lay curing in the warm autumn sun. Green fall cabbage lined the fields ready for harvest and the making of sauerkraut to feed hungry stomachs during the winter. Apple trees in the orchard dripped with red and yellow fruit, their ripening fragrance pulling flocks of birds in to feed. The cattle were fat, the pigs were fat, and the geese could hardly fly. The whole world was ready for harvesting.

Eli walked among his rich, productive fields on the farm. Autumn was a time of celebration and it was a time of sadness. Autumn winds blew down from the hills bringing a sense of completion. There was a longing in Eli's heart, though, that he did not understand. He felt a sense of incompletion. He had left something important undone. This wealth of harvest was Ottie's handiwork for her daily toil had produced it all. He felt sad that he had not married her. He regretted the many lost years they could have spent together. Eli walked around the edge of a cornfield then down one of the rows of dying corn. His footsteps crackled on the dead stalks and leaves which were as dry as his life had become. He shucked one of the ears pulling back the husk to reveal golden kernels of corn.

"It's a bumper crop," he thought to himself.

He crossed a clear stream and pulled himself up an embankment to the field where freshly-dug peanuts lay on the ground. He filled a wheelbarrow with brown-shelled peanuts and rolled it into the stream so that he could wash them. He poured handfuls of water over them until all were submerged. The water turned a dingy red as the red- clay dirt disengaged from the peanuts. He left them in the wheelbarrow in the creek to dry.

Eli climbed up Grassy Knob and found himself a place to sit that overlooked the entire farm. The white-washed farmhouse sat in the midst of green and brown fields. The majestic mountains, now covered with colored leaves, cradled the farm. Eli could make out the barn and stables, the pig pen, the well house and rock chimney holding to the north side of the house. He looked at the roadway leading to the Little Old House. His eyes followed the dirt road crawling and curving like a brown snake away from the farm and into the woods. He gazed upward at the magnificence of Oaky Knob and he could pick out the wild fox grape vines now laden with heavy, purple bunches of sweet grapes.

Hawks circled high above the rocky hillsides, their wings floating effortlessly on the thermal currents like gliders of old. Their sharp hunting-cry whistles pierced the air striking small echoes from the mountain top. White, fluffy clouds punched up over the mountain's summit casting a momentary cool shadow over Eli and his fields.

Eli was an integral part of the memory of this place. He had been born here. His father Julius and his mother Elizabeth had built this farm and farmhouse with the sweat of their backs. They had raised eight children (Eli being one of them), then left the farm in perpetuity to him and his descendants. His first wife, Ossie, and his son, Pet, had died here. All his daughters had been born here. All his life with Ottie had been on this land. Eli thought about Ottie and her refusal to marry him. Now that he needed her desperately, she did not want him. Eli had used up all his emotional coupons with Ottie. He was getting old now for he was sixty-six. He would never have another wife. There would be none to see him to his grave. He had squandered the love of four women by looking for fresher pastures. Women existed to serve his needs, his wants. It never dawned on him that they wanted reciprocity, that they wanted him to love them, too. He had sired fourteen children and barely knew any of them.

A mild rumble of thunder rolled far away over the summit of Oaky Knob. Bird whistles blew on the wind and a restful quiet, a hush fell over this peaceful scene. Eli felt a sudden sickness come over his stomach and he felt a little faint.

"I've over-exerted myself on this walk," he thought.

As he rose, a slight, sharp pain moved from his stomach and shot down his left arm ending in the fingers. At Griff's Old House, he bent over and washed his face in the cool water of the creek. He walked down by the cherry trees and through the apple orchard where he plucked a yellow, golden delicious apple and bit into it. Maybe the apple could settle the pain in his stomach. He sat down on the front porch and folded his arms over his hurting stomach. He sat in a self- embrace, waiting for his body to return to normal.

Ottie was in her own reverie on the opposite side of the farm. She was cutting ripe sugarcane making it ready for the press so they could squeeze the juice to make molasses for the winter. She paid little attention to the hard work because her thoughts were elsewhere. Her mind wandered back to the Peddler's Stump when she had been just fourteen and met Eli. His charm had filled the empty place in her life. Their lives had moved parallel with his marriages in a type of marriage of their own, one not sanctioned by license or clergy. They had had four children as if they were legally wed. No shame. All the wives knew. All the people in the valley knew of her transgressions, but Ottie had maintained her presence there as if nothing unusual existed in her relationship with Eli. Everyone knew Ottie, most liked her, but no one wanted her as a friend. Married women saw her as a threat to take their husbands. Those few who stepped forward to help Ottie recoiled at her fierce independence and limited understanding of life.

She remembered the sourwood and redbud trees with a warm feeling in her heart. She looked at the Little Old House where some of her children had been born. "Birth and death lock a person to a place, a memory, a life," she mused.

Ottie broke from her reverie and sauntered back across the field to the porch of the farmhouse where Eli sat. As she drew near the porch, she noticed that he was slumped over, his body bent so that his head rested in his lap. She lifted him into a seated position and saw that his lips were blue. His eyes were locked motionless in his head. His breathing was shallow. She cradled his head in her arms as he made an effort to speak, but for naught. His tongue was now silenced forever.

Eli could still see Ottie's face through his dimming eyes. He saw her black hair and eyes, her strong, solid face, her lips saying words he could no longer understand. She hovered over him like a protecting angel. Eli could now only form thoughts in his head. He yelled out the words from his heart, words that she would never hear.

"I have wronged you greatly, Ottie. In losing life, I now see and understand who and what you are to me. I have wounded my own soul and denied my own love by not accepting yours. Oh, forgive, please forgive me."

The words froze in his mind and heart for no outside force existed to forgive him.

Ottie looked deeply into his departing eyes and whispered, "Wherever you are at this time, Eli, forgive yourself. Do not part this life with the heavy anchors of grief and guilt tied around your soul. I love you."

In the power of her love for him, she passed this blessed message to his understanding. A reply came in the form of a smile that appeared on his lips. It froze there. Eli's gaze lifted from her face to the mountains, to the sourwood trees lining the hilltops, to the infinite blue skies. He departed the valley for the beautiful, infinite Forever. From Ottie's eyes there fell the tears of two.

THE REDBUD TREE

S pring came in a burst of color to the hills and hollows of our part of Appalachia, painting our valley in pink, white, and yellow. White bloodroot blossoms dotted the forest floor as trailing arbutus clung to the hillsides. Ramps looked like pinwheels twirling their leaves through rocks and dead debris. Clumps of flowers dangled from the limbs of bell trees. Redbuds opened their tiny flowers painting the mountainsides lavender. Wild Sarvis looked like weeping ladies with their white strings of blossoms spreading downward toward the forest floor. The mountains were awash with color. The streams were ripe and swollen with water from the winter's melting snow. Birds sang in the greening willows as alder trees unfolded their yellow strings of flowers. It was a time of joy and renewal.

Halfway to the summit of Grassy Knob, in this magnificent valley, there stood an ancient redbud tree known to the valley people as the Forget-Me-Not tree. No one knew its age. The oldest inhabitants recalled the tree being there in their youth. It stood proud and tall through storm and strife and bore serenely its scars from strikes of lightning. In spring it thrust its pink blossoms against a deep blue sky making it visible at a great distance. In all seasons people made hikes up the mountain to admire the tree. Sweethearts and lovers carved their initials in its bark. Those with troubled hearts and minds came to ponder their fates under its branches and to stare into the far distant skyline. It was customary to write wishes, prayers, and remembrances on small pieces of paper and pin them to the branches of the redbud tree. It came to be called the Forget-Me-Not tree.

The tree and I were namesakes. I felt as if my mother had forgotten me. She was not affectionate toward us children and I suspect that no one in her family had shown any affection for her when she had been a child. Hers was a life-long search to love and be loved, but she could not give what she never knew herself. The giant redbud tree brought people together. It helped them to deal with grief, guilt, sorrow, broken relationships and unrequited love. It spread its limbs outward in a universal embrace of suffering mankind. One day it spoke its message to my heart.

On a sunny Sunday in the month of March, after returning from church, my mother felt the power and beauty of the day. She packed a basket of food for us children and led us up the road past Griff's Old House, across Devil's Fork Creek, past Gentry's sawmill, up the muscadine ridge toward the land of Forget-Me-Not. I took off my shoes and walked barefoot along the dusty road stepping lightly on the sharp stones. My sisters picked wild flowers and chased butterflies. My mother seemed light hearted as she hummed a pleasant tune under her breath. The smell of rotting leaves in warm sunlight danced across the breeze. It was a rare moment among us when all was at peace; all was well. It was perhaps what love felt like.

The family felt exuberant as the mountains pulled us higher. White clouds jutted high above Old Grassy, making me think of cotton candy at a county fair. A soft breeze carried the spirit of spring across the mountains. I looked up where the road led into a clearing to see the ancient redbud arched against the blue sky, its pink blossoms sitting like a painting.

My mother spread our picnic on a cloth on the ground under the tree and we ate when we wished. This was a rare moment for us children because my mother was spending uninterrupted time with us and on this day she was free of the fields, the moonshine still, and the hard farm work, of Eli, Gentry, Mr. Stoutman and all the others. The day belonged to her and she claimed it fully. After eating a ham biscuit and sweet potato, I lay back on the grass crossing my arms beneath my head. The blue sky shone through the redbud branches with its pink blossoms looking like a beautiful, oriental tapestry. I contemplated the gnarled trunk with dozens of names carved on it and wondered about the people who had left their names there. What had been their destiny? Did the tree remember them? Had their wishes, prayers, and supplications been granted? Were they all still alive? I was in a magical place in a magical moment of time.

The soft breeze dislodged a piece of paper someone had left pinned to the tree and it fell down on my chest. The words written there were beyond my second grade reading level so I asked my mother what was written on the paper. She wondered if we should intrude on someone's private petition to the tree. I told her that the tree broke the paper loose and sent it down to me, so it probably had a message for me. She unfolded the paper and read these words "Send me your love, O redbud tree, when I am far away and lonely." For some unknown reason these words spoke to me, so I wrote them in my mind and on my heart.

"Who do you think wrote this message?" I asked my mother.

"It could be a man or woman. Perhaps someone, a soldier maybe, went far across the sea and missed his home and people. Someone lost a love."

These last words left her in deep thought. Hers was a life of broken loves, a tale of betrayals. If anyone in the valley needed the

Forget-Me-Not tree today, it was Ottie. She took a small piece of paper out of her pocket and wrote her own private message on it. She laid the paper against the tree trunk pinning it there with a small stone. To whom did she address the note? For whom did she weep? Whose tears were in her eyes with her? She rose from her place on the ground, packed up the basket, and signaled to us that it was time to go. I stood rooted to my spot, gazing at the blooms on the redbud tree. I did not want this magical time to end.

"You can take some of the magic with you," she said to me.

She reached above her head and broke a small branch of the redbud tree and placed into my hand.

"Forget-me-not," she said in a soft, sweet lilting voice.

This was one moment in my life when I felt that she loved me. I held the branch tightly as we marched homeward. I placed it in a glass of water until the flowers died leaving crisp, brown dead petals on a gray stem. The memory of this day warmed my heart for my entire life.

It did not come as a surprise when my mother died. She left me with many unresolved feelings of anger and regret. I blamed her for much of my own unhappiness. I refused to accept responsibility for my own bad choices. I saw her from a distance, not as a real person. My pain and sorrow hung like an albatross around my heart.

One day a tiny redbud tree began to grow beside the steps leading up to my front porch. I left it there. Throughout the years, it bloomed. Did some bird bring the seed to drop it where it grew? I nurtured the tree until it grew almost as big as the one in the valley.

I sat on my porch one sunny day in silence remembering my mother. I was angry. I was miserable. The redbud tree was in full bloom. As I stared at its blossoms, answers crept slowly into my knowing. I remembered the visit long ago to the Forget-Me-Not tree. I remembered my mother breaking a sprig of the tree to take with me. I felt that day that she loved me. Perhaps it was she that sent the bird to plant the redbud as a reminder to me. It was her gift across the years so that I would remember. I began to weep. I went into the house for a piece of paper and wrote upon it these words, "I forgive myself for blaming my mother Ottie."

I folded the paper and gently laid it in the branches of the red-bud tree.

The golden energy light that formed my soul glowed warmly as the original sweet words from God echoed in my spirit, "You can do it. Go for love. Go for self-forgiveness. The experience will bring you eternal peace."

THE LEGACY

The most difficult moments of one's life are often those that beckon to a higher challenge. Moments of transition pull one from childhood and hurl him, struggling, into the more certain realities of adulthood. Such a transitional event happened in my life. In the sadness of a single moment, I discovered the courage to aspire, to rise above my situation, to succeed against seemingly impossible odds. Sadly my mother had already died and now Paw-Paw, Ottie's father, was saying goodbye.

For as long as I can remember, my grandfather was a strong influence in my life. It was he that loomed larger than life against my childhood perception of the world. He always appeared on Saturday mornings, dressed in overalls and a straw hat, ready to go fishing with my brother and me. With our can of freshly dug worms dangling from our left hands and makeshift fishing poles slung over our shoulders, we marched with dignified gait to the small stream which bordered our farm. There we passed the best hours of the day sitting on the creek bank, hats over our faces, dangling our hooks in the water, pretending to fish.

Occasionally, we pulled in the line to see if some fish had been dumb enough to get hooked on our string. If nothing were there, "Paw-Paw," as we called my grandfather, would spit his tobacco juice into the stream, pat us on the head and say, "Well, boys, we can't do any more today." My brother and I would grin really big and spit into the water too. We longed to be like him. Catching fish on Saturday was not really the important thing. Being there with "Paw-Paw" is what really mattered.

My grandfather had retired from farming and made his living now by cutting winter firewood and selling it around the neighborhood. He trusted me to let me help him.

"Cut them just right, boy," he would say. "We don't sell people any second-class wood."

We worked until nightfall when he would say, "Better break off now. With the night around us, we can't get much more done."

He often had long talks with me about my plans for the future. He urged me to go to school somewhere, to make something of my life. He was sure I could find a way.

"Don't settle for my type of life. You were not meant to cut wood. Learn all you can. You have a good mind. Help others. Make your community better than the way you found it. Don't look for a hand-out. What you do not have today, you can have tomorrow. There is a school in Kentucky called Berea College. I want you to promise me you will fill out application to go there. You are smart enough and poor enough that they will accept you."

I loved him. He was my example.

I followed Paw-Paw's advice. I filled out the applications for Berea.

One morning a week before Christmas, my brother ran to get me from English class. Someone came to the school asking that we come home because "Paw-Paw" was sick. When we got home, he had already died of a massive heart attack. He would never know that Berea had accepted me for the freshman class of 1961.

The following day and Christmas holidays were the worst times of my life. I was in despair. I immediately put a change of clothes in a bag and hitchhiked to Spartanburg. My grief blinded my reason. After some thought, I realized that I needed to be present at his funeral. I got a Greyhound bus back to Stan's store and walked back home.

Everyone was preparing for the funeral. I dressed in a clean shirt and coat and rode in silence to the cemetery. When the service was over, I lingered sitting at "Paw-Paw's" grave. I closed my eyes listening to the wind. It blew cold against my cheeks. I looked back over my life with grandfather reliving some events. What would I do now without his guidance? My best friend was gone. His spirit followed that of my mother, Ottie. They left, quiet like, softly as feathers rising as prayers on the wind. In the quietness of the hillside, I remembered his words:

"This is not the end, my boy; it is a new beginning. I went home in order to set you free, so you could live life your own way. Do not feel sorry for yourself and do not weep for me. All your tomorrows beckon. I expect you to seize each moment and rise to prominence. Find a way, or make one. And do remember, you've got to love life to live life. Love it and live it."

My old life was over and a spirit of rebirth took hold of me. Ottie's World had finally coughed up some goodness. "Paw-Paw" had gifted me a small amount of money. He had obviously worked and saved it for my education.

I used the money to go to Berea College in Kentucky. I later received a Master's Degree from a university not far from the valley.

Even in death Paw-Paw would not allow me to falter. So I will honor his legacy to the end of my days and I shall rise to make my valley proud.

EPILOGUE

Go for Love. Go for Self-Forgiveness

Each and every inhabitant of our valley and those strewn over the highlands pondered at times their purpose for living on planet earth. They were all well-versed in what the churches taught and what ministers told them, yet an empty longing weighed on their souls. Something of utmost importance was missing.

It was as if a nugget of gold were theirs and all searched desperately, but no one could find it. An accumulation of bad attitudes and wrong choices had built up from the moment they were born. By the time they died, they all carried their burdens like ships' anchors around their souls. The key to the whole problem was forgiveness. Everyone was searching for forgiveness.

I do not speak of a belief where some deity forgives us. If someone else did the forgiving for us, where, then, would our responsibility lie? What would we learn in the process? Such a belief causes people to be lazy because no effort on their part is required. If parents do homework for their child, what does the child learn? I have had enough of this idea that something else forgives us. Forgiveness of self by self is the missing gold nugget.

An individual accomplishes freedom from pain through his own efforts. It is a path of self-correction. We are our own judge and jury. When we awaken to this aspect of living, we are then ready to live. Whatever happens after death is what it is. We should be focused on the present, making an effort to cleanse ourselves daily. We should focus all our efforts on learning how to forgive ourselves our own trespasses.

Ephraim was looking for forgiveness and did not know how to find it. He committed suicide. Fred needed to forgive Ottie for the experience at the milk spring at Devil's Creek Fork. He needed to forgive the way he felt toward her and Eli, her neglects, her poverty, her refusal to let Bertha and Mrs. Palmer give him a better life.

Ottie's life would improve immensely were she able to forgive herself for foolishly loving a man like Eli. He was an emotionally broken man. Were he able to forgive the death of his son, Pet, he could begin to love others and treat them better. Could Raymond have forgiven his feelings toward his father, he would not have died on the bench in the snow in Charlotte.

In self-forgiveness, Coleen would not have felt a need to kill Elam and herself. Ottie should have chosen self-forgiveness instead of murdering Gumtooth. Bertha and Mrs. Palmer, missionaries themselves, did not understand this concept of self-forgiveness. They taught that some omnipotent god out there had the unique power to forgive.

Gentry and his men, as good as they were, needed to forgive their betrayal of their families with Ottie.

June Jr. sought Ottie's love when neither was prepared to love. Without self-forgiveness, neither would ever accomplish his desire. Clyde, Jesse Pearl, and all their church goers were off base and could have improved their lives had they been aware and practiced self-forgiveness. Rufus was the only one who exhibited self-forgiveness. He forgave his feelings about being a black man and, in so doing, lifted an entire community to a higher manner of treatment. In the process, he erased his own hatred. Phyllis and her family saw themselves as victims. Only when she trusted her daughter to my care and acknowledged our friendship in the valley, did we both forgive and heal. Carole could go to Oregon only after forgiving her own feelings toward her mother and her forgiveness paved the way for Old Swayback to save her life. Ottie spoke forgiveness for herself and the crowd at the "calling out."

I had to forgive my own feelings when I misperceived the intentions of adults when they gave me the free clothing. My forgiveness of the misperception I held was the "something of value" for which I searched.

Harold Cody understood forgiveness more than most and so did Little Eva. It was not their tormentors that forgave, it was they. The ex-con who gave Eli a ride home when the former moonshiner was released from prison, had forgiven everyone long ago, opening the way for him to help Eli without judgment. Eli had an opportunity for self-forgiveness then, but did not take it.

Ottie went on strike against those who were mistreating her. That was the closest moment of her life to self-forgiveness. The act of saying "no more," is an act of self-forgiveness. Sheriff Buford demonstrated self-forgiveness when he spoke Gumtooth's eulogy when Christian ministers refused to do so. I wonder what their omnipotent God thought of that action.

Ottie forgave herself when she sat in the judgment seat. "He sees within mine eyes the tears of two" (Elizabeth Barrett Browning) spoken at the redbud tree is the ultimate in love and self-forgiveness. Gomer, a simple man, had nothing to forgive for he lived life in the moment. Therefore, no blockages stood in the way of great wealth for him. He already had great wealth inside himself. It simply flowed outward.

Through murder and intended future murder, Barbara is actually forgiving herself for allowing superiors to abuse her. Grandma forgave herself for eighty years of anger and resentment for the devastation of the Civil War. Abe Lincoln no longer holds hero status in my life. I forgive myself for believing the lies told about him.

Ottie cleared her own slate when the power to marry Eli lay within her grasp and she said "no." Not feeling sorry for myself at my grandpa's funeral set me free to accomplish the seemingly impossible in my life.

This book is about the need and desire for self-forgiveness. It is an active force. No one is going to do it for us. It cannot and should not be left to another. Self-forgiveness is a project on which we must work daily. The rewards will take care of themselves. The people of the valley intuited this truth and worked toward it in their own way.

I love these valley people. In creating them, I make us all proud. I am proud to tell their stories. Their issues are my issues, for these people came from the depths of my brain, my heart, my life experience.

They exist only in my mind. Even though I call them my family, my brothers, my sisters, none of them are truly real people. They are composites of those I met and admired along the way.

But self-forgiveness is very real. Through writing about these characters, I have grown to be a better person.

I forgive myself everything in this life.

Now, dear reader, you take these stories wherever you wish them to go in your life. I sincerely hope that you will use them to heal your own hurts and resentments from childhood. All humanity deserves the joy that self-forgiveness can bring.

Now, as for me, I'm going down to Stan's Country Store and treat myself to an R.C., a moon pie, and fifteen cents worth of that long baloney. Bye.

55873853R00222

Made in the USA
Columbia, SC
20 April 2019